SYRACUSE UNIVERSITY

VOLUME I. - THE PIONEER DAYS

<u>The Syracuse University</u>
<u>Incorporation</u>

Be it known that we the undersigned Citizens of
the United States and of the State of New York to wit;
Jesse T. Peck, Francis H. Root, Albert D. Wilbur,
James N. Scatchers, James E Latimer, David
Decker, Ezra Jones, Dallas D. Love, Anzu J Phelps,
Joseph F. Crawford, Spencer D. Fuller, George F.
Comstock, Charles Andrews, Thomas B. Fitch,
Wilfred H. Porter, Ebenezer Arnold, with our
associates do intend to establish and organize
and we do hereby establish a corporation under
and pursuant to the act of the Legislature of the
State of New York, for the incorporation of benevolent,
charitable, scientific and missionary societies
passed April 12 th 1848 and the various acts amen-
-ding the same and for such purpose we do declare
as follows.—

I. The name of such corporation shall be "The Syracuse University"

II. The object of such Corporation shall be the diffusion of knowledge among men & for that purpose to found establish and maintain in or near the City of Syracuse, in the County of Onondaga & State of NewYork an institution which shall be known by the name of "the Syracuse University" and in which Christian learning, Literature and Science in their various departments, and the Knowledge of the learned professions shall be taught.

It being the design and purpose of this act of incorporation that such Institution shall be under the Control and general patronage of the Methodist Episcopal in the State of NewYork.

III. The number of Trustees of said Corporation shall be forty one, subject to the right of the Board of Trustees by its ordinances and By laws to reduce the number not below twenty five and the following persons shall be trustees for the first year & until their successors shall be chosen in the manner to be provided in the by-laws or ordinances of the Corporation — that is to say, Ex officio, the Governor, Lieutenant-Governor, Chief Judge of the Court of Appeals and Superintendent of Public Instruction of the State of New York, and the President of the Faculty of the University: Thomas Carlton, Francis N. Root, James N. Scatcherd, Albert D. Wilbor, James E. Latimer, David Decker, Darius A. Ogden, Ezra Jones, Dallas D. Love, Arza J. Phelps, Benom I. Ives, Joseph F. Crawford, Eliphalet Remington, Isaac L. Bingham, Spencer R. Fuller, Williard Ives, Horatio R. Clarke, Horace G. Prindle, Daniel W. Bristol, Jesse T. Peck, Joseph E. King, Henry Wilson, Morris D. C. Crawford, Alonzo Flack, Philip Phillips, George Lansing Taylor, John Stephenson, John H. Ockershausen, George F. Comstock, Charles Andrews, Thomas B. Fitch, Wilford W. Porter, Ebenezer Arnold, Edmund S. Janes, Reuben E. Fenton, John Crouse.

In witness thereof we have hereunto set our hands this _24th Day of March_ in the year of our Lord One Thousand Eight Hundred & Seventy.

Jesse T. Peck   George F. Comstock,
Dallas D. Love   Charles Andrews,
Ebenezer Arnold   Wilford W. Porter.

James N. Scatcherd
Ezra Jones
J. F. Crawford
James E. Latimer
Albert D. Wilbor
Spencer R. Fuller.

Francis H. Root.
Arza J Phelps.
Thomas B. Fitch.
David Decker.

State of New York
Onondaga County
} SS.

On this 24th Day of March A.D. 1870
before me personally came, Jesse T. Peck. Dallas D. Low,
Ebenezer Arnold. James N. Scatcherd Ezra Jones,
Joseph F. Crawford, James E. Latimer, George J Comstock
Charles Andrews, Wilford W. Porter, Francis H Root,
Arza J Phelps, Thomas B. Fitch, David Decker,
Albert D. Wilbor, and Spencer R. Fuller, to me Known
to be the persons who executed the foregoing instrument
and acknowledged that they executed the same
severally.

W. Gilbert
Commissioner of Deeds
Syracuse, New York.

SYRACUSE & UNIVERSITY

VOLUME ONE

The Pioneer Days

W. FREEMAN GALPIN

Professor of History, Syracuse University

1952

SYRACUSE UNIVERSITY PRESS

First Edition 1952
25 26 27 28 29 30   6 5 4 3 2 1

For a listing of books published and distributed by Syracuse University Press,
visit https://press.syr.edu.

ISBN: 978-0-8156-2010-5 (hardcover)

Library of Congress Cataloging in
Publication Control Number: 52002118

The authorized representative in the EU for product safety and compliance is
Mare Nostrum Group B.V.
Mauritskade 21D, 1091 GC Amsterdam, The Netherlands
gpsr@mare-nostrum.co.uk

Preface

America's contributions to man's spiritual and physical well-being have stemmed, to a marked degree, from an educational system of magnitude and significance. To have done less would have been unworthy of a people whose mode of life has ever exalted the freedom and personal integrity of man. Thanks to a free public school system American ideals and aspirations, written so conspicuously and fearlessly in our Federal and State Constitutions and dear to all who value the commonweal of the nation, have been mightily advanced. And crowning the achievements of these schools stand our institutions of higher learning. Indeed were it not for the humanistic spirit of free inquiry, thought, and expression, so essential to sound learning and the good life, present in this nation's colleges and universities, our historical heritage would have been stinted and sadly impoverished.

Broad and lasting foundations in these attitudes and concepts characterize higher education during the Colonial and Middle periods of American history. From a modern perspective, however, there was an over emphasis upon classical learning and the mathematical disciplines. Relatively few went to college in those decades whose interest did not gravitate toward the ministry, teaching, and the legal profession. The significance and meaning of education for all and not for a chosen few was neither fully understood nor appreciated. Certainly there were some hardy souls who were contrary minded though it was not until the 1830's that the promise of a brighter tomorrow became evident. Spearheaded by a glorious company of men and women who believed in equal rights and opportunities for all there emerged the forces of feminism and abolition. The impact of these vibrating movements was speedily felt and in 1833 Oberlin College opened its classes to women and negroes. Antioch College declared for coeducation in 1853, a step that was followed by the University of Iowa in 1858. Meanwhile in 1832 Genesee Wesleyan Seminary at Lima, New York, matriculated its first woman student. Later, in 1849, the Trustees of the Seminary established Genesee College dedicated to the task of training men and women for service in the Methodist Church. And it was from Genesee that Syracuse inherited its spiritual and intellectual birthright. Equally distinctive in the annals of Syracuse is the fact that its Medical College had had its roots in the Geneva Medical Department of Geneva College, Geneva, New York. For it was there that Elizabeth Blackwell in 1849 gained a doctor's degree—the first degree in medicine to be granted to a woman.

Remarkable as these departures from an old order were their significance was nothing in comparison with the strides made in higher education during the 1860's and 1870's. "It would seem," so wrote an American scholar a few years ago, "that from this source [higher education] Americans expected to draw the inspiration and the information that would confound the critics of democracy and make of the United States a kind of Utopia. Even the uneducated masses showed a touching faith in the power of learning. Education, especially higher education, they tended to regard as an unfailing panacea for all the ills that beset both the nation as a whole and the individuals that composed it."[1] Leaders in the new education included men like Andrew D. White of Cornell, Frederick A. P. Barnard of Columbia, Charles W. Eliot of Harvard, Rev. Dr. Cummings of Wesleyan, and Dr. E. O. Haven of Northwestern. Of these President White, one time resident of Syracuse, frequently and wisely counselled the Fathers of Syracuse University, while Erastus O. Haven became Syra-

1. Quoted with permission of Houghton Mifflin Company from *A Short History of American Democracy,* by Dr. J. D. Hicks.

cuse's second chancellor. The incident of these contacts and associations most certainly had their effect upon the early life of the new institution. No pretentious claim is advanced. Most assuredly Syracuse did not immediately plunge into its great adventure unmindful of the considered and helpful experiences to be gleaned from the past. But it is equally true that the Trustees and Faculty of Syracuse lent more than willing ear and eye to the trends in education of the 1870's and 1880's. Syracuse, fashioned by older academic standards, was shaped and molded with a view to the future.

In one respect Syracuse did not enjoy the good fortune that befell many older institutions or newer ones for that matter. It possessed no financial heritage as did Harvard, Yale, or Pennsylvania, and it had no patron like Ezra Cornell, Johns Hopkins or Cornelius Vanderbilt. What financial support and backing Syracuse received was to come initially from the pockets of humble men and women who believed in the future of a great Methodist University. Small wonder, therefore, the Panic of 1873 all but destroyed the infant institution. Self sacrifice, patience, and loyalty, however, counted more heavily than money in those dark hours and the University emerged stronger from the crisis because of the trying problems it had met and partially solved. It is easy for the uninformed to dismiss these references of love and devotion, to speak of them as clichés, and to regard them as evidences of a nostalgic temperament. Conclusions of this type quickly disappear as one rises from a study of the sources upon which this volume rests for its historical validity.

Syracuse University did not sink amid the doldrums of the 1870's. Rather did it witness a modest but steady growth. New buildings were erected, the campus improved and landscaped, student enrollment increased, graduate, engineering and athletic departments were established, capital investments rose slightly, and a loyal band of alumni became conscious of their debt to Alma Mater. Typical of the feeling and sentiment that permeated the University early in the 1890's was a statement made by Chancellor Day in one of his inimitable chapel talks: "I see in my mind's eye a great University on the Hill. Instead of three colleges, I see a dozen colleges. Instead of several buildings, I see a score of buildings. Instead of a student body of 800, I see a student body of 8,000 and this University as the center of the educational system of the State of New York."[2] Chancellor Day had

2. Richard H. Templeton, '89, to Chancellor Wm. P. Tolley, April 22, 1950.

a vision and during his long administration, which is to furnish the core of a subsequent volume, much of that dream came true.

In one sense it was a dream that had its inception in the establishment of Genesee College at Lima, New York, in 1849. It is therefore, meet and right that a history of Syracuse University should contain more than a passing reference to the educational venture initiated by the old Genesee Conference of the Methodist Church. Antecedents, always unique in meaning to historians, are important, especially when in the case of Syracuse they tempered much of the thought and action of its earlier days. Much the same may be said of the Geneva Medical Department.

In the preparation of this volume, which covers the formative and pioneer days of the University, some difficulty was encountered in locating pertinent sources. The official records, such as the minute books of the Board of Trustees, the Executive Committee, and of the Faculties of the Colleges of Liberal Arts and Medicine fortunately have been preserved. Nothing of significance has been discovered relating to the College of Fine Arts and there is no body of correspondence extant reflecting the day by day, or even year by year, activities of the Chancellor's office. Much the same may be mentioned in respect to Genesee College whose chief sources are to be found in Syracuse University Library which also houses a fragmentary record of its own history. The vital antecedents of the Medical College are located in the offices of Hobart College, Geneva, New York. Supplementing these records are the newspapers of Syracuse, Rochester, Auburn, Geneva, and Geneseo, and the memorabilia preserved in the University Library and Alumni Association building. More significant than the latter is the extensive collection of letters and papers of Dr. Alexander Winchell, Syracuse University's first chancellor, which constitute a prized possession of the University of Michigan. It was through the personal kindness of Dr. Edward H. Krause, Dean of the College of Literature, Science, and the Arts of the University of Michigan and a loyal alumnus of Syracuse, that I was introduced to this important source.

Every institution of higher learning has a distinguished roll of devoted alumni. Few, however, have shared the good fortune Syracuse has enjoyed in a person like Dr. Frank Smalley, '74. A graduate of the College of Liberal Arts, Dr. Smalley served his Alma Mater in varied and important ways throughout his life. To the author of this volume,

Dr. Smalley's *The Golden Jubilee, Alumni Record,* and other publications have been of the greatest value. Without them much of the
University's history could not be told. Many other thoughtful and
kind alumni and friends have furnished helpful aid and counsel and
to these I wish to extend my warmest thanks. More particularly am I
indebted to Dr. Vernon C. Mackay, former member of the History
Department of Syracuse University for his kindness in providing the
chapter relating to the University Library. Dr. Mackay was at work
on a history of the library but on hearing of this study, most generously accepted the opportunity of incorporating his findings in this volume. I am also obligated to Professor Theodore Webster, Swimming
Coach at the University, for permission to use his most interesting
manuscript on the athletic contests at Syracuse, to Director Wharton
Miller and his capable staff of the Library for innumerable benefits
and services, and Miss J. Winifred Hughes, Executive Director of
the Syracuse University Alumni Association, whose helping hand
smoothed many a problem.

I wish also to express my thanks to Bishop Charles W. Flint, former
Chancellor of the University, whose deep knowledge of the institution's life assisted me on several occasions. Dr. William Pratt Graham
whose life on the Hill began in 1893 when he matriculated as a freshman in the College of Liberal Arts and who upon graduation joined
the faculty only in time to be elevated to greater responsibilities cul-
minating in the chancellorship during a most critical period in the
history of the University, has been a source of strength and inspiration.
It was through an understanding of his successful life and his abiding
love and loyalty to Syracuse that a vivid impression was obtained of
earlier years at Syracuse. Another son of the University who has
cheerfully given of his time and energy to the promotion of this study
is Chancellor William P. Tolley. Those who know Dr. Tolley will
readily understand how much his enthusiastic support has meant to
the author. Chancellor Tolley has a genuine interest in history and in
particular the history of his Alma Mater and in this effort he envisages
a quickening and awakening of spirit on the part of the alumni
toward the University.

Finally I desire to express my deepest personal gratitude to a life
long friend and colleague, Vice-Chancellor Finla G. Crawford.
Trained in the historical seminars of the University of Wisconsin and
for several years an active member of the history department at

Syracuse, Dr. Crawford most enthusiastically endorsed the idea of a university history long before actual work on the project was begun. And when a commission was received to undertake this volume, he immediately placed at my disposal all that any individual might desire. Though not a graduate of Syracuse, his loyalty and devotion to the University have been unbounded and in this volume and those to follow I trust the reader will ever see and appreciate Dr. Crawford's love for a great institution which he faithfully serves and to him I give unstinted praise and thanks.

Syracuse University
Syracuse, New York

Contents

The Genesee Story

1 Syracuse University was chartered March 30, 1870, in accordance with an act of the New York State Legislature which authorized, on the basis of a law passed in 1848, the incorporation of educational institutions. The Act of 1870 was general and not specific in nature; it did not so much as mention Syracuse. All of which was and is quite patent. What is not clear, at least to the historian, was the contradiction implied in this measure between fact and fiction. Tradition testifies, as does an inscription over the main entrance to the University Library, to an earlier foundation. Syracuse, so the story runs, had its inception in 1849 with the chartering of Genesee College at Lima, New York; later, in 1870, Genesee College was moved to Syracuse and given its present name. But nowhere in the tradition is there any explanation as to why it acquired the name of Syracuse University if it was Genesee College that had been moved. Had removal of a chartered institution taken place, would there have been any need for the incorporation of Syracuse University? But granted that it had been moved, would not a change in title have necessitated some form of legal action? These and other questions quickly raised a presumption that what had been accepted as an established fact of history and repeatedly stated in various University

publications, was nothing but fiction. Probing and searching for light, truth finally emerged: Genesee College was never moved to Syracuse. Legally, no continuity can exist between the two institutions, and Syracuse University must be content to date its birth as of March 30, 1870. On the other hand, it can most assuredly claim to have had its inspiration, spiritual, and intellectual foundations at Lima.

The antecedents of Genesee College may be traced to the 1829 meeting of the old Genesee Conference of the Methodist Church of New York. At this gathering a committee was appointed to investigate the possibility of establishing either a literary institution (a college) or a seminary within the geographic limits of the Conference. Recommendations favoring a seminary were presented and adopted at the next annual session. Whereupon the delegates from Perry, Brockport, Le Roy, Henrietta, and Lima vied with one another for the location of the projected school. Lima pledged $10,808 plus seventy-four choice village lots and received the award. On May 1, 1832, the Genesee Wesleyan Seminary opened its doors, the student body numbering five, one of whom was a young lady. Two years later the Seminary was chartered. Both promoters and faculty were exceedingly proud of their institution and when, in 1842, the Seminary buildings were totally destroyed by fire, the citizens of Lima rallied in a splendid manner and contributed close to $8,000 for the erection of a new building. Meanwhile, friends of the Seminary kept pointing to its high academic standards, some going so far as to claim parity with several older and well known Eastern colleges.

Six years of continued growth followed by which time voices were raised favoring the establishment of a collegiate department. The Trustees promptly endorsed the suggestion as did the powerful Genesee and East Genesee Conferences. Enthusiasm ran high especially after it was rumored the Trustees favored the founding of a college rather than a mere department. Stout hearts dug deep into pockets to make the dream, somewhat reminiscent of the Conference meeting of 1829, a reality. Foremost among the backers were the Reverends John Copeland and Daniel C. Houghton, whose service to Methodism is honored in Western New York to this day and who, as Trustees of the Seminary, were entrusted with the task of drafting a proposed charter. Before this task had been completed, the Trustees had enlarged their vision and now were talking of a university. This decision was predicated upon a fear that the founding of a college might mean the end of the Seminary. The Seminary, it should be stated, was little more than a preparatory school, but low as it was in a scale of educational institutions, its utility and value had been tested time after time. Nothing, it was argued, must arise to endanger the life of the Seminary and this a mere college might do. Precisely why a university might not threaten the existence of the Seminary is not stated in any of the sources. Possibly the Trustees thought a college, in which there would be a highly concentrated core of academic life, more dangerous than a university in which there would be a greater spread. The entire picture, however, is too blurred and confusing to warrant any interpretation. Accordingly, confining ourselves to what is known, the drive was steered into the new channel and Mr. Copeland was commissioned to visit Albany.

On reaching the State Capital, Copeland encountered unexpected opposition. The Chairman of the Legislative Committee on Colleges was strongly against a "university" charter though he was more than willing to sponsor one for a college. Why, is not known. Copeland accepted the situation, understanding that such a charter would not jeopardize the life of the Seminary. Thus the way was cleared for action and on February 27, 1849, a bill providing for the chartering of Genesee College passed the State Legislature. Genesee College, it was stated, was to be an educational institution, the object of which was the cultivation and advancement of literature, science, and the fine arts. The interests of the patronizing bodies, the Genesee and East Genesee Conferences, were recognized and protected, and the Trustees were granted the usual rights of receiving bequests, gifts, and contributions. Finally, the College authorities were authorized to acquire any property, real and personal, belonging to the Seminary—a provision that was crowded with meaning for the future.

The Board of Trustees of Genesee College met for the first time at Lima, July 9, 1849, Mr. John Lowber being elected President of the Board. Encouraged by the report of the Seminary's Committee on College Endowment, which showed pledges amounting to more than $50,000, the Trustees voted to set the drive at $100,000 and appointed a committee to present the claims of the College before the Oneida Conference. A summary of these activities together with a statement of courses to be offered at the opening of classes in September, 1850, appeared in a *Catalog* issued sometime during the summer of that year.

In the meantime, the Trustees were busily engaged in setting the young institution on its feet. Realizing the imperative need for buildings, the State was asked to aid in the undertaking. Albany, however, turned a deaf ear to the request. Unable to tap endowment funds, which were marked for instructional costs, the Trustees proceeded to invite the citizens of Lima and vicinity to contribute additional sums for the proposed college buildings. The response was none too satisfactory. Whereupon Lima was informed that unless immediate support was forthcoming, the Trustees might be forced to seek a site "on the line of the rail-road." A more telling argument could not have been presented for if there was one thing the citizens of Lima did not enjoy being reminded of, it was the fact that the recently constructed railroad between Syracuse and Buffalo had by-passed their village. Galvanized into action by this adroit threat, the people of Lima hastened to subscribe $7,000. It is significant to note that each and every pledge was predicated upon two conditions expressly stipulated on the subscription form. In the first place, one half of the sum promised would be paid upon the laying of the foundations of the buildings; the remainder being due upon the completion of the buildings. In the second place, it was stated that Genesee College was to be located at Lima. Shortly thereafter, a contract was let for a college hall and in August, 1852, appropriate dedicatory exercises were held. No other building was ever erected.

During the course of these activities, the Trustees of the College and Seminary arranged for the transfer of one-half of the latter's property, real and personal, to the College. In addition, joint use of all property was agreed upon. In return for these concessions, the College authorities quite willingly promised to pay "now and forever" all Seminary expenses, assume all debts, and "henceforth and forever keep and maintain and support a College, under their act of incorporation, upon the premises hereby granted." Legal recognition of this contract was evidenced by an indenture, dated August 25, 1852, a copy of which is preserved at the Livingston County Court House. The arrangement outlined in this document also provided for the administration of the major affairs of both institutions by the Trustees of Genesee College. At a later date, this contract was to be the subject of much criticism though in 1852 it was viewed in a far more favorable light. Indeed, it may well be questioned as to whether the College could have ever operated had such an adjustment not been made.

The original faculty, as selected by the Trustees in January, 1850, included Reverends Stephen Olin, President of the College; Daniel C. Houghton, Professor of Greek; James L. Alverson, Professor of Mathematics and Civil Engineering; George C. Whitlock, Professor of Chemistry and Natural History; James Douglass, Professor of Latin and Modern Literature; George Loomis, Professor of Natural Philosophy and Astronomy; and the Honorable Frederick Whitllesey, Professor of Law. All of these, with the exception of Dr. Olin, appear to have assumed their duties on the opening of the college. Why Dr. Olin declined his appointment is not known. In his place was named Rev. Benjamin F. Tefft, who at a later date became United States Consul at Stockholm and Acting Minister to Sweden. Rev. Benjamin Tefft assumed the headship of Genesee College in 1851, and proceeded to guide the young institution for the following two years. On his retirement, Rev. Joseph Cummings became President, a position he continued to hold until 1858; later in life, Dr. Cummings was elected President of Northwestern University. His successor at Lima was Rev. John M. Reid. Dr. Reid remained at Genesee until 1864, after which he served for a time as editor of the *Western Christian Advocate*. Syracusans remember him for his benefactions to Syracuse University during the administration of Dr. Sims. Rev. John W. Lindsay followed Dr. Reid at Lima and remained in charge of Genesee until 1868; a few years later he became Dean of the College of Liberal Arts of Boston University. Last among the executives of Genesee was Rev. Daniel Steele. Dr. Steele came to Lima in 1862 as Professor of Ancient Languages and Literature and upon Dr. Lindsay's resignation became Genesee's Acting President. Many changes also took place among the faculty among whom should be mentioned Rev. Wellesley P. Coddington, Professor of Modern Languages from 1865-1871, and Mr. John R. French, Professor of Mathematics from 1864-1871.

During the course of the first year, there were forty-eight students in attendance at Genesee College; the next year there were seventy-eight. For the following few years registration fluctuated, an all high being reached in 1862 when 142 students matriculated. From then on the enrollment declined though there is no evidence of the Civil War having had any appreciable effect. On the other hand, the continued development of the University of Rochester must have had an influence as did the agitation for Genesee's removal to Syracuse in the late 1860's. Again, it may be argued that had the Trustees been able to maintain higher academic standards, some students in up-state New York would not have gone elsewhere for their college training. It is of course impossible to determine the validity of the latter assumption though it should be noted that opinion in 1870 held it as a factor of considerable importance in accounting for the decline of Genesee. In that year there were but fifty-eight students on the rolls of the College. By this time Syracuse University was all but ready to open its doors and with the departure of some of these students and a portion of the Faculty to Syracuse, the Trustees of Genesee were more than uncertain as to the future. On July 13, 1871, the Trustees were informed only eight persons had registered for the new year. After considerable debate it was decided that no attempt would be made to replace the professorships vacated by the exodus to Syracuse though instruction would be continued for those who might matriculate. But the College year, 1871-1872, was a dismal failure. Genesee College to all intents had ceased to exist.

Most of the students who had registered at Genesee College came from New York, especially from the home county of Livingston and its neighbor, Monroe. At no time was the enrollment large and the total number of alumni in 1869 was only one hundred and ninety-five. Their loyalty to Genesee College was never and can not now be questioned as may be attested by their gifts to the institution. The spirited alumni gatherings at commencement indicate an attachment that could not be easily erased. Moreover, their oft repeated statement that Syracuse University was but a continuation of "Old Genesee" should not be forgotten. Nor may one read the speeches and toasts delivered at Syracuse Alumni meetings during the 1870's and avoid concluding that Genesee was uppermost in the minds of those present. Notable among the graduates of Genesee were Reverend Henry Fowler who in 1872 became President of Northwestern University, Mrs. Belva A. (McNall) Lockwood, one-time candidate for the Presidency of the United States on the Women's Suffrage ticket; and Dr. David S. Kellicott who from 1888 to 1898 was Professor of Zoology at Ohio State University.

Instruction at Genesee followed the approved patterns of that day. Obedient to the Grecian lines of its one college building, Genesee adhered to a program that was severely classical. Languages, Mathematics, Philosophy, History, Chemistry, and English were offered though in each case the approach was fundamentally classical. Plato, Herodotus, and Euclid reigned in undisputed authority nor was the peace of the classical world disturbed by courses in Civil Engineering, Law and Astronomy. With the exception of the latter, whose offering, enriched by a small telescope, was a hand maid to mathematics, these disciplines never effectively escaped from the curriculum as given in the college annual. Founded for the purpose of training men and women for service in the Methodist faith, Genesee College was also monastic in its outlook. Its location at Lima amply reflected a desire to be apart from the dangers of the market place. And, in pursuing the monastic ideals of the medieval age, attention was paid to agriculture. Interest in husbandry had been shown by the Seminary as early as 1848. The following year, the College Trustees petitioned the Legislators to establish a School of Agriculture at Lima on the ground that Western New York was sorely in need of such an institution. The request was denied.

Disappointed but not discouraged the Trustees never lost sight of this need and in 1863 voted to establish a chair of agriculture on the understanding an incumbent would be appointed after the necessary funds had been raised. Two years later, over strong protests of Lima, the State of New York harkened to a more vocal voice and established a College of Agriculture at Ithaca. Genesee College, however, was not slighted. In accordance with the act establishing Cornell University, provision was made for a Department of Agriculture at Lima; Mr. Ezra Cornell being required to furnish the sum of $25,000 for that purpose. Those interested in the details of this arrangement will profit from reading the volume, *The Founders of Cornell*, recently written by the late Dr. Carl Becker. Though brilliantly written—Dr. Becker never wrote otherwise—the story may be slightly marred by an unfortunate coloring of the Genesee episode.

The point need not be pressed; at least there is no sign of rancor towards its rival in the official records of Genesee College, which now showed its pleasure by advertising a battery of courses in agriculture. Students who completed the prescribed program received a Bachelor's degree. Similar degrees in Arts and Science had been given ever since the inception of the college. Higher degrees were conferred either as the result of professional experience gained in a special field following graduation, or in honorary recognition of one's service to the College, the Methodist Church, the State, or Nation.

Little need be said of student life at Lima; in general, it was the same as at those other institutions which had sought the solitude and peace of a rural village. Genesee, however, was coeducational, a fact necessitating a close if not rigorous supervision and control over student conduct. Violations of rules entailed severe punishment and the Faculty Minutes fairly echo at times with such matters. Visits to the local tavern or to one of the hotels in nearby Rochester were tabooed. Equally offensive were the "Mock Schemes" or fake graduation exercises staged by the undergraduates in the spring of the year. No matter how often or how loud the Faculty might protest against these burlesques, the citizens of Lima and visiting alumni thoroughly enjoyed these annual ribbings. Most of the students, however, seem to have obeyed the set rules of the College, paid sufficient attention to their studies to gain the coveted degrees, and found ample relaxation along approved lines.

Dating with the "coeds," though subject to what a later generation might view as petty and irksome restrictions, afforded considerable pleasure and entertainment. More significant were the literary societies whose public meetings attracted considerable attention. An examination of the records of these societies reveals that the members valued their associations and generally were punctual and faithful in the performance of all duties. In one or two cases these organizations were little more than Greek letter fraternities. The presence of such societies was strictly forbidden at Genesee but by clever subterfuge this prohibition was circumvented. Some of the earliest fraternities at Syracuse University had their inception at Lima. Finally, mention should be made of the absence of formalized athletics. Scrub teams played football and many students found relaxation and exercise by "walks" through the neighboring country.

Student expenses at Genesee were low. Nominal fees were charged for the use of the library and laboratories, and tuition amounted to $25.50 a year. Not every student paid tuition; those holding scholarships were relieved of this assessment. Nor did the college attempt to make any profit from the dormitory and dining rooms. During most of the life of the College the combined income from these sources was very small and in 1868 the Trustees, believing education should be free, abolished tuition. Denied any appreciable revenue from tuition, the Trustees from the first were dependent upon endowment, scholarships, collections, and state aid to keep the institution going.

State aid, though frequently sought, never amounted to much. A total of $11,300, spread over four separate grants, was all the State ever gave to Genesee. In respect to collections, the Trustees patiently waited upon the free will offerings of the patronizing conferences, but gifts from these quarters were never large. Other conferences and individual churches gave even less. As to scholarships, the amount received was much larger: by 1854 a total of $75,000 had been given to the College. Actually a scholarship was an endowment and usually consisted of a gift of one hundred dollars. Most of these grants, and between eight hundred and a thousand seem to have been made, were in the form of promissory notes which when paid entitled the donor to send one student a year to either the College or Seminary. The holder of a scholarship was not asked to pay tuition. The significance of these scholarships is revealed in part by the fact that most of the students matriculating at Genesee did so on the basis of one of these grants.

According to the financial statements of the College it seems likely that a number of the donors of these "perpetual" scholarships defaulted in whole or in part. Had all been paid, however, the total income arising from this source would have been barely enough to meet the expenses of the Seminary which, it will be recalled, was entirely dependent upon the College for its existence. The failure of the scholarship scheme to provide sufficient funds for Genesee College was a bitter disappointment to the Trustees who soon came to realize the necessity of relying more and more upon the endowment which originally had been set at $100,000. But even here misfortune dogged the heels of the Board. Subscriptions fell below that goal and some who promised never paid. Between 1850 and 1860, endowments ranged from thirty to thirty-seven thousand dollars which together with other funds, yielded a productive income of a little over seven thousand dollars a year. Small as it was, it did not equal annual expenses. Few individuals, beyond the select group of Trustees, were aware of these deficits which were well concealed in the yearly reports to the State Board of Regents. The Treasurer's books tell the true story. Here, annual deficits were balanced by the very questionable practice of drawing upon the permanent funds, each withdrawal lessening the amount of productive income.

It was this unhealthy condition that led the Trustees to initiate a determined drive for more endowment in 1860, the target being

$35,000. During the course of this campaign, which was pressed with much energy, a rumor freely circulated that the Trustees were seriously debating the removal of the College to Buffalo. The latter, so it was reported, had much more to commend it as the site of a greater Genesee than had the little village of Lima. It is difficult, on the basis of available evidence, to hold the Trustees responsible for this rumor though little if anything was done to counteract the impact of this unfounded tale. Maybe the Board saw the apparent advantages that might accrue to the campaign by not denying the story. Be that as it may, those who had an economic stake in retaining Genesee at Lima were visibly agitated. With a speed that must have astonished themselves, the people of the village quickly subscribed $10,000 to the endowment drive. Payment, however, was contingent upon the following conditions: first, the remaining $25,000 was to be raised within three years; second, all monies collected were to be placed in a special account and only the interest was to be used; third, of that interest the first charge was to be for a chair of chemistry and natural history; and fourth, each $100 subscriber, for the time being, was to enjoy all the privileges of a donor of a scholarship. Another condition, not stated on the subscription blank but which was verbally accepted by some of the canvassers was that in return for the $10,000 Genesee College was to stay at Lima *forever*.

The success of the drive was shown in the annual report of the treasurer for the year ending June, 1864. With the endowment fund standing at a paper valuation of more than $140,000, the future looked secure. Granted this sum included the estimated value of the college buildings and grounds plus some $20,000 which was classed as "contingent," the Trustees were tremendously satisfied. Expressed in terms of productive bonds, mortgages, notes and cash, Genesee's working endowment was close to $70,000. During the previous three years, the Board had been forced to tap the permanent funds for more than $7,000. But in 1864 there was a net profit of $131.40. In part, this favorable balance had been made possible by a rigorous policy of economy. Costs had been cut wherever possible though at no time was this done at the expense of the faculty whose combined salaries since the foundation of the college had averaged annually around $5,000.

Continued retrenchment followed during the next fiscal year. And it was well such a policy had been maintained because in June, 1865, the Treasurer reported a deficit of $1,786.44. This excess in expenses, occasioned by an unexpected drop in the value of certain productive investments, caused considerable concern. Later in the same year a turn for the better took place thanks to the timely gift of $10,000 from the Honorable Mr. Chamberlain of East Randolph, whose past donations had been of much help, and the receipt of $25,000 from Mr. Ezra Cornell for a chair of chemistry. The optimism of the Trustees knew no bounds and was well expressed by the Treasurer, Mr. Albert D. Wilbor, who in a public statement declared, "It may now be confidently affirmed that the crisis is past and the College and Seminary are destined to live and prosper in all time to come." A year later, the Trustees were forced to admit that where they had expected cream they had found skimmed milk. Needed repairs on the college buildings plus a belated increase in salaries for the faculty had produced a deficit of $2,529.98.

At this juncture fortune smiled upon Genesee College. The year 1866 was hailed through the entire country as a Centennial Year. One Hundred Years of Methodism within the United States had been completed. Everywhere Methodists glowed with deserved pride and satisfaction. The Church in America had had a noble history and like St. Paul of old, had fought the good fight. And in what better way, it was asked, could loyal Methodists show their eternal gratitude to God for his countless benefits than by undertaking the greatest drive in all history to continue the educational work of their beloved Church?

Each section of the country rallied to the attack and in Western New York Genesee College became the direct objective and beneficiary of the Centenary Drive. Appeals for help were made in the Black River, Oneida, and Wyoming Conferences, and promises of assistance were immediately forthcoming. By June, 1867, $21,000 of Centenary Funds had been raised. Truly, this was a good beginning and with additional help in sight and the Treasurer of Genesee College reporting a slight increase of income over expenses, the Trustees viewed the future with renewed confidence.

Lima Blocks Removal

2 Genesee College celebrated its sixteenth commencement July 11th, 1867. Ten students received their cherished diplomas. Charles Wesley Winchester, later to make a name for himself as a clergyman in the Methodist Church, delivered the valedictory oration, and Edward Gibbs Bickford, destined to win laurels as a missionary to Turkey, was the salutatorian. Both of these young men, if one may trust the *Rochester Democrat,* spoke exceptionally well and did much to make the day a happy one in the annals of their Alma Mater. Yes, sixteen years had gone by since classes first met at Genesee. Sixteen years of doubt and sorrow—years during which the Trustees often knew not where to turn, so hard had been the battle for survival. But through all this uncertainty, brave hearts had struggled on and now, in 1867, were witnessing the reward for past toil and privation. Methodism in Western and Central New York stood ready to shower their gifts and attention upon what alumni already were calling "Old Genesee."

But all was not as peaceful as it seemed. Here and there murmurs of dissent were heard. The Methodist Church, it was stated, never could or would have a college of national reputation so long as it thought and planned in terms of Lima. Genesee College had had a short but splendid history and its academic record was of the best, but its future was stinted by its location. Cold logic argued that if the Church really desired an alert and progressive institution—one that would honor the Centenary Year—Genesee College should and must be moved. Lima as an educational center had become an anachronism. Precisely when or where this hostile sentiment first showed itself is not known though it may have been at Syracuse during the month of January, 1866. For it was in that month Professor John R. French of Genesee College addressed a letter to the Rev. Arza J. Phelps of Syracuse soliciting financial aid for the Church's college at Lima. French's letter, it appears, was freely circulated among the local clergy of Syracuse who, after some deliberation, expressed their unwilling-ness to cooperate "on the ground that its [Genesee] location was quite uncentral and ineligible to meet the demands of our educational interests in the great Empire State." But having voiced a negative attitude the clergy hastened to urge upon Dr. French "the imperative necessity of a first class college under the patronage and supervision of the denomination in some more central position."

It is unfortunate there is no record of Dr. French's reactions to this communication. Truly, he may have reasoned, the Syracuse group had raised an important issue the solution of which might make or break Genesee College. In all probability, he must have discussed the problem with his colleagues, the local clergy, and college trustees. Finally, after continued deliberation he penned a reply of which neither the original nor a copy is available. According to Rev. Phelps, however, Professor French's answer was a complete acceptance of the Syracuse thesis and coupled with it was a promise to aid in the removal of Genesee. A more favorable answer could not have been received. There was no meanness or hardening of heart. Dear as Lima must have been to one who had come to love Genesee, Professor French realized the college's future was dependent upon a new lo-cation and to that end he now pledged himself. To what extent Dr. French represented Faculty sentiment or Trustee opinion is not known though it does coincide remarkably well with views expressed by both groups at a later date.

Encouraged by the turn of events, Rev. Phelps sought other con-verts. Possibly he communicated with his good friend, Dr. D. D. Lore of Auburn, editor of the powerful and influential *Northern Christian Advocate*. In any event, at a Centenary Meeting held at Buffalo on March 1st, Dr. Lore's voice was raised in favor of removal and that in the presence of President Lindsay of Genesee who had come to plead for financial aid. As to Genesee's past record and achievements, Lore sang a hymn of praise. But what of the future? Well, the Doctor had many misgivings—all because of the College's location at Lima. A more central site was needed, and when moved Genesee should have the unanimous and unstinted support of New York State Methodism; not a single member of the Church west of Albany should falter! Rochester, Syracuse, Buffalo, as well as Cherry Valley, Avon and Lima, must join this great undertaking so vital to the future well-being of the Church. And then, as though endowed with prophetic vision, Dr. Lore concluded with a note of warning as to what might happen should the local interests at Lima succeed in thwarting the wishes of the Church. Should such a mistake occur, Lima would have only itself to blame if the conferences to the east established institutions of their own. Lore's statement appeared in the *Northern Christian Advocate*, April 11, 1866 and immediately precipitated a torrent of comment.

Now it so happened that on the very next day personnel from the Genesee, East Genesee, Oneida, and Black River Conferences met informally at Syracuse to discuss the college problem. After a spirited discussion the gathering enthusiastically endorsed the suggestion of moving Genesee to a more advantageous location—a decision the Wyoming Conference endorsed at a subsequent meeting. Later in the same month, the Oneida Conference approved of the action taken at Syracuse and instructed the Rev. Daniel W. Bristol to visit Lima and inform the Trustees of the College as to Oneida's action and attitude. The Conference also supported a call for a general church convention to consider the problem and stated that if this convention should adjourn without taking any action, Oneida would allocate its Centenary Funds to Wesleyan University. A few days later the Black River Conference acted in a like manner.

During the months of May and June, 1866, there was considerable debate about Genesee College. The *Northern Christian Advocate* generously opened its columns and a number of letters appeared from interested parties. Most of these communications endorsed the idea of removal. Mr. Thomas Tooker of Rochester and a former trustee of the college declared he never had thought well of Lima as a site for Genesee; he was also of the opinion that the existing legal relations between the College and the Seminary had done neither much good.

A conflicting view was expressed by "B" who contended Genesee's record warranted its remaining at Lima. As for the charge Genesee had suffered because of its location in a small village, "B" wished to know if Wesleyan had been injured because of its association with Middletown. "And who," Genesee's champion continued, "had suggested moving Wesleyan to New York City?" More forthright was the Presiding Elder at Lima who thundered from his pulpit that Genesee College would not be moved from Lima "while the rocks stand and the stars shoot."

Shooting stars and standing rocks did not stem the onrush of the Syracuse group, representatives of which appeared at Lima in June, 1866. This visitation was timed to coincide with the annual meeting of the Trustees of Genesee College. The Board was a perfect host; it graciously received the brethren from the Central Conferences and respectfully listened to their pleas. The usual, but now familiar, arguments in favor of removal were repeated. A new note, however, was sounded when the delegates backed up their case with a concrete promise of $200,000 of Centenary funds provided the College was moved to a more central location. What attitude the Trustees might have taken had this offer not been made is pure speculation. In this respect, however, it is important to note that no public statement on removal had been made by them either as a body or as individuals up to the June meeting, unless one is to interpret Dr. French's letter as a reflection of their views. But once so attractive an offer had been made it was impossible for the Board to avoid taking sides in the current controversy. Accordingly, after some discussion, the Trustees by a vote of fourteen to one agreed to a change of location provided the *$200,000 was raised and no legal hindrances arose to block removal.* The existence of these conditions clearly revealed the presence of some doubt in the minds of the Trustees as to whether a change could be made. But as matters stood, the Trustees could ill afford to offend the Central Conferences; hence their answer was quite safe and sane. Moreover, to show their good will and to cement the growing alliance between them and these conferences, the Trustees offered the latter representation on the Board should removal not take place.

News of these talks and decisions within College Hall spread rapidly over the campus which, it so happened was preoccupied with commencement activities. Immediately these festivities assumed a different meaning and everyone's attention became focused upon the

question of removal. Visiting alumni proceeded to debate the issue at
their annual meeting and while deploring the thought of leaving Lima,
voted to support the action taken by the Trustees. Having reconciled
themselves to the idea of removal, the alumni allowed their imagin-
ations to soar, talked freely of the College's future, and pictured Genesee in a new setting, possibly at Syracuse or Canandaigua. Nor
could they understand why the citizens of Lima did not join them in
their new found happiness. Surely, no unprejudiced mind could deny
Genesee's destiny demanded a new and more virile residence.

We are not prejudiced, came the spirited reply, but we do deny
Lima's inability to provide for a greater Genesee. How, it was asked,
would the patrons and benefactors of Genesee react when they
realized their loyalties were being sacrificed for a new friend, Syracuse? How would Ezra Cornell feel if he were told that upon his death
Cornell University would be removed from Ithaca? And who seriously believed $200,000 could be raised in the conferences east of
Cayuga Lake? Moreover, what assurance was there of the Genesee
and East Genesee Conferences approving of the move, their consent
being implied by the charter establishing Genesee? Again, what of the
vested rights of past contributors, especially the scholarship donors,
whose gifts to the College were predicated upon Genesee *remaining*
at Lima? Finally, what of the Seminary? Had anyone remembered
the clause in the charter providing for the corporate life of the College and Seminary? How, in the face of this provision, could people
talk about moving the College without moving the Seminary?

Not waiting to answer these and other questions, the Trustees,
convinced of the sanity and security of their position, adjourned and
the visiting delegates returned home. Flushed with success, those favoring removal now issued a call for a joint meeting of the clergy and
laity of the Central Conferences. Representatives of the latter as well
as those of the Western Conferences met at Syracuse late in July. Rev.
D. W. Bristol, fresh with the laurels won as a delegate to Lima, outlined the history of Genesee, extolled its glorious past, but concluded
by insisting Methodism would never gain its educational objectives
except by moving the College to a centrally located site. Dr. Lore and
others warmly applauded these sentiments and Dr. L. Z. Paddock
moved the convention go on record as favoring removal.

Whereupon Rev. John Copeland, a charter member of the College
Board of Trustees, arose and vigorously denounced the motion. Cit-

izens of Lima, he declared, had entrusted him with the grave responsibility of presenting their case which, incidentally, was embodied in a series of resolutions recently passed at a village meeting. According to these resolves, which Dr. Copeland proceeded to read, the brief for removal was submitted to a most searching inquiry. Most determined was the assertion that removal was absolutely and unequivocally blocked by law—a point Dr. Copeland solemnly invited the convention to weigh before approving of Dr. Paddock's motion. Copeland was followed by a fellow Trustee, Dr. Luckey, who labored his colleague's arguments and belittled Lima's contentions in no uncertain terms. All of which was more than enough to convince an assembly in favor of Dr. Paddock's motion—an assembly that actually needed very little convincing. The Lima Resolutions were laid on the table and Paddock's motion was carried. Having voted for removal it was incumbent upon the convention to implement that action. Accordingly, the delegates from the Oneida and Black River Conferences promised to raise $80,000 each, those from the Wyoming Conference pledged half as much. Dr. Lore and his group were delighted with this committment and the *Northern Christian Advocate* fairly echoed with a song of victory.

A rising chorus of opposition, however, emanated from Lima whose enraged citizens girded themselves for battle. A second protest meeting produced a fresh batch of resolutions and a committee was appointed to present these before the fall sessions of the Genesee and East Genesee Conferences. In spite of this mounting tide of hostility which gained recruits from neighboring villages, those endorsing removal pressed ever forward and in October presented their case before the Genesee Conference. Lima's protest also was considered by the Conference but when all was said, the vote stood 77 to 4 in favor of the Trustee's action of the previous June. A little later, the East Genesee Conference arrived at a like decision, the vote being 105 to 21. Once again fortune smiled upon the Syracuse group which in its confidence may have lost sight of the conditions imposed by the College Trustees, conditions reaffirmed by both Conferences, or if remembered were dismissed as of no great importance. These difficulties, it was assumed, would be taken care of; sufficient funds already had been pledged, and a bill providing for removal would be introduced at Albany during the coming winter. Subsequent events revealed the hollowness of this false optimism.

During the months that followed these decisions, private individuals as well as committees of the various conferences were hard at work promoting the idea of a central location. Most outstanding was the labor of a self-appointed group of Syracusans. Possessed with vision and foresight, and realizing the many advantages of having Genesee College moved to their city, this group issued a call for a local public meeting to be held March 23, 1867. In announcing this gathering, considerable stress was laid upon the peculiar features enjoyed by Syracuse. Here was a city, centrally located, adequately serviced by railroads and the Erie Canal, teeming with activity, and endowed with a future—what more could one want? And to aid in bringing Syracuse to its new home, it was proposed the city bond itself for $100,000 on the condition the College be moved to Syracuse and the proposed endowment be raised to $400,000. Messrs. George F. Comstock, Elias D. Leávenworth, Charles Andrews, T. B. Fitch, Charles Tallman, Allen Monroe, Andrew D. White, and others, prominent in Syracuse business and religious circles, sponsored the call. The response was most pleasing. Not only did the public meeting endorse the bond issue but it adopted the draft of an act providing for removal.

During April, 1867, the Wyoming, Black River, and Oneida Conferences held their annual sessions. Foremost on the agenda of these gatherings was the moot college question. Would the Conferences officially endorse the action taken by their representatives at the Syracuse Convention of 1866? Rumor had it that while Wyoming was favorably disposed in principle, prior commitments in Pennsylvania might operate against a drive for funds within that conference. And this was the conclusion reached by the conference at its spring meeting. Black River, as was expected, warmly endorsed the findings of the Syracuse gathering, appointed a committee to cooperate with the other conferences, and pledged itself to raise the promised $80,000. Moreover, it hurried a copy of its resolutions to Utica where the Oneida Conference was sitting.

No conference ever faced a more delicate situation than that which confronted the Utica gathering. Fresh in the minds of all was the memory of the Syracuse Convention at which delegates from Oneida had endorsed the projected moving of Genesee College to Syracuse. Since that Convention, certain events had transpired which led many to question the wisdom of following the Syracuse proposal. Why, it had been asked, must it be assumed that Genesee has to be moved to

Syracuse? Is there any valid reason why it should not be located at Rome? To these questions, the Trustees and inhabitants of Rome had given an answer in the form of a bill, introduced in their behalf at Albany, providing for the removal of Genesee to Rome. Moreover, an obliging Senate had passed this measure by the time the Oneida Conference came to debate the action taken at Syracuse. Touched to the quick by the turn of events local pride demanded and secured the passage, by the Oneida Conference, of a resolution approving of Rome's desires. But hardly had the debate subsided before it was dramatically revived by the arrival of the Black River resolutions. It was now the turn of those who had supported Syracuse to have a full hearing. Finally, after prolonged discussion the Conference reversed its stand by declaring that while it was not ready to approve of one location to the exclusion of all others, it was nevertheless ready to cooperate in any practical way of establishing Genesee College at a place where the best inducements and endowment might be obtained. And in order to show its goodwill, a committee was created to work for that end in conjunction with the other conferences.

The decision of the Oneida Conference terminated all discussions of moving Genesee to Rome, and from that time on all efforts centered on Syracuse. Delegates from the Central Conferences hastened to Lima and aired their views before the College Trustees. At this meeting, the Board also reviewed a student petition relative to removal and the formal protest of the Lima group. The result of the deliberations that followed constituted a complete victory for the Central Conferences. Genesee College would be moved to Syracuse subject to state approval, a condition that probably implied among other things that removal was legal. Moreover, to meet the financial considerations agreed upon by the City of Syracuse, the Trustees promised to match the $200,000 which was to be raised within the four Conferences.

During the remainder of 1867 the endowment drive was pressed most determinedly in all quarters. Moreover, a committee of the Trustees waited upon the Seminary and obtained a complete release from all contractual and corporate relations. Particularly significant was the cancellation of the indenture of August 25, 1852 which had obligated the College to "forever keep and maintain and support a College, under their act of incorporation, upon the premises hereby granted." In other words, the College, having received property from the Seminary had bound itself to keep Genesee at Lima. But with the voluntary severance of this contract by the parties concerned and the return to the Seminary of all of the latter's property, the College Trustees believed themselves freed from all restrictions and obligations inherent in the original contract. Incidentally, it should be noted the Trustees of both institutions were of the opinion the Seminary was distinctly the gainer by the annulment of the indenture.

News of this action was officially laid before the College Board at their meeting in January, 1868. The committee also reported the receipt of a memorial from a large number of past contributors to the college favoring removal. Finally, it was stated, an application for removal had been made at Albany. The Trustees accepted the report. Whereupon Rev. John Copeland, who in 1866 had voted for removal, informed those present his views had changed. In view of which he now wished to have it recorded in the Minutes that he was strongly of the opinion removal was "wrong and impolitic." Several reasons may be assigned for Copeland's action. Possibly his conscience bothered him, or again he may have had an eye as to his future reputation at the hand of some historian. It might also be suggested that he hoped a public and official declaration in the transactions of the Board might add weight to the opposition outside. Copeland's request came as no surprise since everyone present had recognized him for some time past as the leader of the opposition. And while the Trustees considerably respected the wish of one who had done so much for Genesee, it refused to be deterred.

Copeland's stand, once it was aired throughout the state, did evoke comment. The "College Question" rapidly became a matter of deep importance throughout Methodist circles. Personalities and issues clashed as never before. Once again, the citizens of Lima registered a solemn protest and the *Livingston Republican* all but charged the people of Syracuse with seeking advancement at the expense of little Lima. Attention also was focused upon the vested rights of the donors of endowment and scholarship funds which, it was alleged, would be sacrificed if Genesee were moved. In answer to the latter accusation, Dr. Lore tried to make it clear that these rights would be respected; Genesee College, if moved, would still remain and be known as Genesee College.[1] Those who trumped up such charges, he insisted, were

1. At the February, 1870 meeting at Syracuse the question of what to call the new institution appears to have provoked debate. Dr. Daniel Steele in his Diary of February 24, 1870 says, "Had a hard contest to name the Syracuse University."

misinformed and guilty of placing individual interests above those of the Church. Lore's retort failed to convince those who believed there would be no Genesee College unless it remained at Lima.

On January 16, 1868, a petition of the Trustees of Genesee College asking for removal of the institution to Syracuse was received by the State Assembly. This request, along with a bill introduced by Mr. D. D. Lefler of Seneca County authorizing a change of location, was referred to the Committee on Public Education. During the course of the next six weeks a flock of petitions, for and against removal, also were placed before the Committee. In the meantime and while the Committee was deliberating, the din of battle at Lima reached even greater heights. Ira Godfrey, local postmaster, labored the neighboring postmasters with circulars invoking their aid in behalf of Lima. Heated meetings took place in various villages and the press throughout Livingston County generally denounced removal. The Trustees, it was declared, were required to keep Genesee College at Lima. No one among the Trustees, with the possible exception of Mr. Copeland, put much stock in these arguments. On the other hand, these gentlemen frankly admitted that their opponents thought differently, and not wishing to provoke dissension cautiously suggested the idea of a possible compromise.

Realizing he might be branded as a blind and bigoted partisan if he disdained this expression of good-will, Trustee Copeland inquired of the Board's President, Mr. Francis H. Root, as to the nature of the proposed compromise which, he stated, he would be happy to consider with an open and free mind. Root's reply blessed Copeland as a "peace-maker," but as the letter read on he discovered little that seemed to him to merit this beatitude. How could Root ask him to stop opposing the will of the Board or face the prospect of a refusal on the part of the Trustees and their friends to continue supporting the Seminary? Granted that Lima, which had furnished only a share of the funds that had kept Genesee alive, constituted the core of the opposition, the fact remained its citizens resented being told the future of their beloved Seminary was predicated upon the absence of such opposition. Nor did they relish the insinuation that their contributions to the College had been based upon selfish and speculative motives. And finally, what reason had Root, in spite of all his thousands invested in local Lima real estate, for predicting a rise in land values if Genesee were moved?

Root's views, carefully and precisely drawn, were presented in a circular letter issued by the Trustees late in January, 1868. This communication, together with Copeland's printed answer of early February, did little beyond revealing the sharp differences existing between Lima and the Board. There is reason, however, to believe the publication of both letters influenced the Committee of the Assembly, then engaged in drafting a measure favoring removal. Stout opposition greeted this bill when introduced in March. The bill, it was said, ignored basic issues and sacrificed the rights of the scholarship donors. More significant was the charge that the bill robbed the Seminary of its lawful funds and property. Mr. Lefler, champion of the measure, met the attack by accepting an amendment offering protection to the "holders of scholarships to tuition in the Genesee Wesleyan Seminary or in the Genesee College wherever located." But this did not satisfy the opponents who kept harping on the question of the legality of removal. Finally, in spite of what Dr. Lore bitterly termed "unscrupulous opposition," the bill passed the Assembly by a vote of 69 to 33.

Meanwhile, a similar measure had passed the second reading in the Senate. Here the opposition, led by Senator Wolcott J. Humphrey of Wyoming County, raised one question after another with the result, the bill was sent to the Judiciary Committee for clarification. In mid-April this committee reported a bill favoring removal, news of which cast gloom over the Lima group which now openly talked of carrying the issue to the courts should the Governor approve the measure. Mr. Humphrey straightway exerted himself to the utmost and succeeded in convincing a majority of the senators to delay action pending an arrangement with the citizens of Lima. As a result the Legislature adjourned without taking action. In commenting on the outcome, the *Northern Christian Advocate* questioned the sincerity of Senator Humphrey and called upon all friends of removal not to lose heart. The entire proposition, its readers were assured, would be brought before the new legislature. Finally, without wishing to intimidate or threaten the citizens of Lima, the editor expressed the hope that the latter would change their minds because if they did not and should another bill suffer defeat, a *new* institution would be founded *elsewhere*.

Shortly thereafter the Trustees of Genesee College reviewed the entire question. And if one may judge from the minutes of that body feeling ran quite high. Rev. John Copeland, seconded by Mr. J. Dennis, valiantly labored to stem the rising tide against Lima, but when all was said, resolutions favoring removal to Syracuse passed by a vote of seventeen to two. Nor were the feelings of Lima softened by the decisive manner in which the Genesee and East Genesee Conferences endorsed the findings of the Board.

Early in January, 1869, bills providing for the removal of the institution to Syracuse or its vicinity and the severance of existing relations between the College and the Seminary were introduced in the Assembly and Senate. In the latter, Senator Humphrey moved to have the measure referred to the Judiciary Committee, a device that had worked so well the previous session. The motion received scant consideration and by the middle of March the bill passed the upper house, nineteen to three. In the Assembly, Mr. L. E. Smith sought to sidetrack the measure by introducing a counter bill aimed at strengthening Genesee College and permitting removal only under certain conditions. Both of the Assembly bills were referred to the Committee on Public Instruction which, after much debate, rendered majority and minority reports. The former provided for outright removal to Syracuse subject to certain stipulations calculated to safeguard the interests of the Seminary; the latter was little more than a restatement of Smith's original bill plus reasons for its passage. The Assembly was in no mood to listen to the plea of the minority beyond ordering it to be printed. Having done this, it substituted the Senate's bill for its own and rejected, seventy-seven to fourteen, an amendment proposed by Smith for retention by the Seminary of the Agriculture Department and its $25,000 endowment. Finally, on April 13, 1869, the Senate Bill passed the Assembly, eighty-nine to two.

The minority report contained little that was new. One or two points, however, do deserve attention. In the first place, the contention was raised that inadequate provision had been made for the Seminary. Actually the bill as passed called for the transfer of real and personal property to the Seminary—property some competent persons estimated to have a value of $50,000. Moreover, the College Trustees were to invest, subject to the approval of the Seminary Board, the sum of $75,000, the income from which was to be paid annually to the Seminary. Finally, the College Trustees were to guarantee not less than six percent on this investment. Since the average annual expense of the Seminary for the past few years had been less than that amount it would appear as though Smith's contention, about inadequate provision for the Seminary, was a mild exaggeration. One may also dismiss without much hesitancy the minority report's charge that the Syracuse group intended to violate the charter of the college by transforming the latter into a theological institution. The subsequent chartering of the College of Missionaries in August, 1871, however, should be remembered in respect to this point.

Much more to the point was the charge of error leveled at the Committee on Public Instruction in rejecting a compromise bill sponsored by the citizens of Lima. Wishing to establish Lima's ability to maintain Genesee College through adequate endowments, the Legislature had been petitioned to allow the Town of Lima to bond itself at a regular or special election for the sum of $45,000 which was to be earmarked for the support of the College. Should the Town, however, fail to approve of such a bond issue, no obstacle would be placed in the way of removal by Lima provided the Seminary was protected to the extent outlined in the majority report. Nothing in the minority report, however, carried weight and in a short time, as has been indicated, the Legislature passed an act providing for the removal of Genesee College to Syracuse or its vicinity on the conditions as voted by the Trustees in 1866 plus certain provisions relative to the safety and security of the Seminary.

In all probability the detail incident to these conditions and provisions might have been resolved within the next few years had not the entire matter been referred to the courts. The legal aspects of the question, it will be recalled, had been raised in 1866 when Copeland and others intimated the likelihood of such an action. And this is precisely what happened on March 4, 1869. For on that day, Judge T. A. Johnson of the State Supreme Court sitting at Geneseo heard the complaints of Joel Daily *vs.* Genesee College. Evidently the plaintiff had the better of the argument since Judge Johnson issued an injunction restraining removal. Early in May the Trustees answered the complaints and prayed the injunction be vacated. On reviewing the evidence, Judge Johnson held that the certificates of scholarships, issued by the College, were binding contracts. Moreover, he ruled that the contributions to the College in 1850, and again in 1860, obligated the Trustees to maintain and support a college at Lima. The Court, he continued, was aware of no formal stipulation to that effect having appeared on the subscription blanks of 1860. Agents of the College, however, had obtained subscriptions on the verbal understanding

Genesee would remain at Lima and for the act of these agents the Trustees were accountable. In view of these and other reasons, Judge Johnson denied the defendant's prayer. Added strength would have been given to the decision had Judge Johnson known of Genesee's former President J. M. Reid's letter to the Trustees in which there was an admission of subscriptions having been obtained on the premise the College would be kept at Lima.

The impact of this decision upon the Trustees and the Syracuse group was tremendous. The drive for funds fell off and that in spite of renewed efforts on the part of the Conferences. As time went on it became increasingly apparent that all thought of moving Genesee would have to be abandoned. Taken back by the decision of the Court, the Trustees appear to have tried to gain a settlement out of court. At least this is an inference drawn from two unsigned and undated notes, written in pencil, to be found in the "Records of the Joint Executive Committee of Genesee Wesleyan Seminary and Genesee College." On the basis of internal evidence these notes must have been drafted after the issuing of the injunction but how soon thereafter is not known. Possibly they should be dated before the May session of the Court, though preference for a later date seems somewhat more logical. In either case these notes represent an attempt upon the part of the Trustees to arrive at a conclusion which might lead to a compromise between themselves and the Lima group. It is not known, however, that the conclusions reached were ever presented to Copeland and his colleagues but if they were, they most certainly failed to close the breach. An examination of the appended notes will bring to light the evident discrepancies between what Lima wanted and what the Trustees offered.[2]

2. The author has taken a little liberty in editing these notes in the interest of clarity; no fundamental change, however, in meaning has taken place.

The Com. propose the following as final arrangement between the Sem. & College Boards, to wit,

College Trustees should take Ag. Funds $25,000, College Library, $4,588, Chem. & Phil. Apparatus, $3,694, Cab. of Natural History, $3,500.

The balance of assets of college in real estate, and in bonds, mortgages, notes, subscriptions, and all other estimated assets as reported in the statement of the College Assets for the present year shall be made over to the Trustees of the Seminary, amounting, as estimated, to be about $50,000 more or less of productive capital.

The people of Lima shall herein concur and shall stay the legal proceedings which hitherto enjoined the Seminary to the removal of Genesee College.

Having failed in all attempts at conciliation and, so far as is known, having decided against continuing a defense of their position before the Court, the Trustees could only sit and wait. Nor did they have long to wait. In 1870 the Legislature provided for the establishment of Syracuse University. Thus it came about that while Genesee College was to remain at Lima, its life and utility were things of the past. The *Livingston Republican* might fill its pages with favorable predictions of Genesee's future but to the Trustees there was no future. Silent class rooms and a sadly depleted treasury were more convincing arguments than the pious wishes of a small town paper. The utter hopelessness of the situation was revealed in 1871 when three of the faculty accepted positions at Syracuse and when some of the students matriculated at the rival institution. Nor were conditions improved by the alumni accepting degrees from Syracuse. Trustees' meetings, however, continued to be held though nothing was done to revive a lost cause. Finally, after having gained legislative authority, the Trustees wound up the financial life of the College and then resigned as a body. The last meeting of the Genesee College Board of Trustees took place June 15, 1875. Citizens of Lima bemoaned the passing of their college. They never forgot to honor its memory, nor did they ever cease to view the founding of Syracuse with disfavor. They honestly believed they and Genesee College had been sacrificed for another community and institution.

The Cornerstone Year

3 Lima won the battle over Genesee College: the citizens
of a little village successfully resisted the combined efforts
of New York State Methodism. The proponents of removal had argued and, when that failed, pleaded with the inhabitants of the rural
community—but all to no avail. Lima honestly believed that given
proper support and endowment, Genesee College could become as
outstanding an institution at Lima as at Buffalo, Rome, or Syracuse.
Elsewhere, opinion differed sharply and might well have gained its
ends but for the strength of Lima's legal position. In all probability
the Syracuse group recognized the fact and decided not to contest
the issue. Although Judge Johnson had denied the motion of the de-
fendants in Joel Daily *vs.* Genesee College, the restraining order had
not been dissolved and, so far as is known, never was withdrawn. So
long, therefore, as Genesee College existed, and it was not dissolved
until 1875, the injunction remained alive; after that date it lost meaning and effectiveness even though it never was revoked. Had the
Syracuse group in late 1869 or early 1870 elected to contest the injunction and had an adverse decision been given, the dream of a centrally located Methodist university might well have vanished into
thin air. Wise leadership must have counselled against so hazardous an

undertaking. Let us ignore Lima for the time being! Let its people glory in their empty victory! But let us drive on with renewed determination to establish a university of our own! And who knows, Lima ultimately may see the folly of its action and approve of Genesee's removal to Syracuse?

Of course a decision predicated upon this line of reasoning was fraught with danger. What assurance was there the Conferences, which had pledged support for the removal of Genesee, would now aid in promoting a rival institution? And would the citizens of Syracuse renew their generous promise of financial aid? These and other questions must have arisen in the minds of Dr. D. D. Lore, Rev. J. B. Foote, Rev. E. Arnold and many more who still dared to exclaim, "We shall see in due time a magnificent university towering up on some of the high lands of our Central City, standing as a living record of constancy and perseverance, a blessing to the great State in which we live, a perpetual honor to the Church we represent, and an imperishable monument to the praise and glory of the great Head of the Church. God hasten the day when the vision shall be real!"

In spite of this optimism, the situation was none too promising and might well have discouraged leaders not possessed of sterner stuff. Although our sources are strangely silent as to the thought and activity of these men, the fact remains they were not idle. Careful plans were being made for a frontal attack and soon it was noised about that an all-state convention of Methodists would be held at Syracuse to discuss matters of general interest to the Church. Interest mounted rapidly and scores of the clergy and laity signified their intention of attending a meeting many knew would center about a college at Syracuse.

Washington's Birthday, 1870, was the date set for the opening of the convention, delegates to which began arriving the day before. Typical among those present was Rev. George Lansing Taylor of the New York East Conference, whose personal journal throws light on this historic gathering. Taylor reached Syracuse in the afternoon of the twenty-second and with others put up at the Vanderbilt Hotel. From the window of his room he looked down upon a city blanketed with snow through which he later trudged to Shakespeare Hall, where the convention was to convene. On arriving at the Hall—a short distance from the hotel—he found all in a state of noise and confusion. Such handshaking and greeting, one seldom experienced! But soon order was restored and under the master hand of Dr. Jesse T. Peck, the ensuing sessions were most successful. Taylor was so deeply moved by what happened that he was led to exclaim, "There is a manifest blessing from God upon the convention and I feel it in my soul." Additional inspiration came from Dr. Peck's great paper on "Our Rights and Duties as Christian Citizens," delivered the next morning. The climax, however, came the same afternoon for it was then and there that the "College Problem" was tossed into the lap of those present.

Dr. James E. Latimer of the East Genesee Conference led off with the key address. Others like Drs. Daniel W. Bristol, Daniel Steele, and George L. Taylor followed, after which it was resolved:

> That this State Convention of the M. E. Church of New York approves of the plan to establish, without delay, in the city of Syracuse or its immediate vicinity, a first class university and that we recommend that immediate measures be taken to raise at least $500,000 to endow the university.

Next in order was the appointment of a committee to cooperate with the College Commissioners of the Genesee and East Genesee Conferences who had in their possession some of the Centenary funds. The convention also agreed that should an agreement be reached with the Trustees of Genesee College and should the college be moved to Syracuse it was to be incorporated as an integral part of Syracuse University.

Evidently, there were some who still harbored the hope of capturing Genesee—a hope that had been quickened by the warm endorsement of Syracuse University on the part of the Genesee Alumni Association in 1866 and again in 1869. The full impact of this expression of good will, when announced to the delegates, stimulated the hearts of all. No one sensed the psychological significance of the moment more than the grand old man, Dr. Peck. "I have heard it said," he hastened to voice, "that talk will not build a college but that money will. I propose that you instruct Brother Ives to stand here . . . and see how much can be raised here and now." The proposition was unanimously endorsed and Rev. B. I. Ives hurried to the platform. In response to his call for pledges Dr. Lore rose and read a note handed to him by Dr. Peck. "I will be one of four," so the note ran, "to subscribe $25,000 each, making $100,000 towards endowing four professorships, when the University to be located at Syracuse, is legally and practically established; with the understanding that I with my good wife, appropriate the savings of a life-time to the payment of this subscription and make arrangements for any balance which may be unpaid at our decease to be paid from our estate."

Dr. Peck's generosity touched the convention to the quick. Here was one whose faith in an ideal was so overpowering as to induce him to pledge past and future income for the sake of Syracuse University. The effect was electrifying. In rapid succession, Eliphalet Remington of Ilion and Rev. J. F. Crawford of Syracuse promised sums equal to that of Dr. Peck while Francis H. Root of Buffalo pledged the interest on twenty-five thousand dollars for five years and George F. Comstock of Syracuse did the same for ten years. A torrent of smaller subscriptions followed ranging from a hundred to ten thousand dollars. Approximately $160,000 was promised for the new institution, which to many was already a living reality. "We could afford to sup on slim and airy things in the evening," so penned Dr. Taylor, "three such sessions would have turned all our heads. God's spirit was never more mightily upon any congregation under a subscription. Blessed be God for his love. A great Methodist University for the Empire State is now a certainty. Glory be to God!"

A few days later, March 4th, the College Commissioners headed by George F. Comstock obtained from the State Legislature authority to establish a university. News of this event was presented, late in the same month, to a joint meeting of the Commissioners and the University Trustees, the latter having been named at the February convention. Mr. Comstock also submitted articles of incorporation which were immediately adopted and ordered filed with the proper officials. March 30, 1870, witnessed certification by the Secretary of State and with that Syracuse was declared a university. According to the certificate the institution, known as "The Syracuse University," was chartered as an educational center at which "Christian Learning, Literature, and Science, in their various departments, and the knowledge of the learned professions shall be taught." The control and general patronage of the University was placed in the hands of the Methodist Church of New York, actual guidance being entrusted to a Board of Trustees.

Approximately a month thereafter, the Trustees met, reaffirmed the decisions made in March, and proceeded to organize. Dr. D. D. Lore was given the important post of secretary and vice-presidencies were judiciously allotted to George F. Comstock and Francis H. Root.

Gratifying as these elections were what pleased everyone was the naming of Dr. Peck as President of the Board. Peck's interest in the University had been kindled in 1866. Within the short space of four years, his enthusiasm had grown to greater proportions. And his noble utterances and generosity at the February convention marked him for all time as the true founder of Syracuse University. His election to the Presidency had been a forgone conclusion and now that he had accepted this post, the Board unanimously urged and obtained his spiritual translation to the recently established Centenary Church in Syracuse. Moreover, the Board without a moment's hesitation delegated to him the herculean task of raising the desired endowment and of erecting the necessary buildings. Assisting him in these tremendous undertakings was an Executive Committee composed of George F. Comstock, Thomas B. Fitch, Charles Andrews, Rev. A. J. Phelps, Rev. Ebenezer Arnold, Dr. D. D. Lore, and Rev. C. C. Curtis. Mr. Curtis also served as General Agent and Fitch gladly accepted the office of University Treasurer.

During the remainder of 1870, the fortunes of the young institution steadily advanced. The volume of subscriptions kept increasing and the patronizing conferences continued to pledge support. Encouraged by these and other expressions of loyalty, the Board cast about for a suitable location upon which it intended to erect a series of college buildings. After a preliminary survey, several sites were selected for final consideration. These in turn were reduced to one, namely, the so-called Comstock property which consisted of farm-land on high ground in the southeastern part of the city. Acting upon the advice of Dr. Peck, the Trustees accepted this site and instructed a committee to purchase a tract of fifty acres, most of which was owned by George F. Comstock.

Considerable time also was spent in negotiating contracts for the erection of the present Hall of Languages. Messers Randall and Nesdall, Syracuse contractors, won the award with a bid of $136,000. Again, the Board ironed out the financial arrangements heretofore existing between it and the College Commissioners and finally obtained, not without some public discussion and protest throughout Central New York, the proceeds of the City bonds which were paid to the Trustees in several installments. The electorate, it will be recalled, had agreed to bond itself so as to bring Genesee College to Syracuse. Genesee, however, remained at Lima; hence a legal question was raised as to whether the bonds could be allocated to Syracuse University. Ultimately, the issue was decided in the affirmative. Meanwhile, some agitation arose over the propriety of the Methodist Church accepting public funds. What, it was said, about the time-honored American principle of separation of church and state? Would not a dangerous precedent be established which Methodists of a later date might regret? Those who thought otherwise were in control and had their way and Syracuse University was aided in its start with a municipal grant.

Equally significant was the adoption by the Trustees of a body of University By-Laws. According to the latter, the administration of the University was to be lodged in a Board of Trustees, forty-one in number. Of these, six included a group of ex-officio members, one of whom was the President of the University—another title for the office of Chancellor. Nine others, all residents of the state but of whom six were to be non-Methodists, were to be chosen by the Trustees. In addition, each of the eight patronizing conferences was to elect three members. The Alumni Association also was to be represented by three elected members. The officers of the Board were to consist of a President, two Vice-Presidents, a Secretary, and a Treasurer, all of whom were to be chosen by the Board at its annual spring meeting. Assisting the Board was an Executive Committee.[1]

The By-Laws also provided for the establishment of the College of the University, later to be known as the College of Liberal Arts, and the Colleges of Medicine, Law, Industry, Fine Arts, and Letters. Other colleges, when needed, might be created by the Board. Each college was to be a unit unto itself and was solely responsible for all discipline and instruction within its jurisdiction. All-university affairs were subject to a Faculty of the University which consisted of the Chancellor, the President and Faculty of the College of the University, and the "first" officer of "each other faculty ordained by the Trustees." The University Faculty, the ancestor of the modern University Senate, passed upon all degrees voted by the colleges, subject to the approval of the Board of Trustees. Finally, it should be noted that little attention was paid in the by-laws to the important office of Chancellor. On the other hand, an examination of the University

---

1. On October 2, 1870, the Executive Committee made provision for the corporate seal of the University.

records extant for this period clearly reveals how significant and varied were the activities and responsibilities of that officer.

Although the by-laws envisaged the establishment of several colleges, which according to Dr. Peck were to be post-graduate institutions except for the College of the University, the Board elected to center its first efforts upon the latter. This decision may have been hastened by what appeared to be a demand for admission on the part of prospective students. Possibly, the Trustees would have preferred to have delayed the formal opening until a building had been erected and a larger endowment had been raised. Be that as it may, the Board announced the opening of college for the fall and at once made a search for temporary quarters. In May, 1871, a contract was signed for the use of the upper floors of the Myers Block, located at the southeast corner of Montgomery and East Genesee Streets, directly opposite to the present City Hall and across from the Yates Hotel.

The decision to open classes in September, 1871, probably explains why the offices of Chancellor and President of the College were not filled. Although there is no evidence to warrant any definitive conclusion, it does seem reasonable to assume that the Trustees realized the importance of obtaining the very best men possible and, since this end could not be attained at once, had made no appointments for the time being. However, by July of the year, a faculty had been engaged, of whom the Rev. Daniel Steele was appointed Professor of Mental and Moral Philosophy, and Vice-President of the College. Dr. Steele, therefore, became the first administrative head of Syracuse University. Rev. W. P. Coddington and Dr. John French, who together with Dr. Steele had been induced to leave Genesee College, were made Professors of Greek and Mathematics respectively, while Rev. J. J. Brown and Rev. Charles Bennett were assigned to the chairs of Chemistry and History. Each of these gentlemen was to receive an annual salary of $2,500, which in the case of Dr. Steele represented an increase of $600 over what he had at Genesee; for Drs. Coddington and French, it was a gain of $800 each. Having made these appointments, which as will be seen strained the purse strings of the institution, no attempt was made to fill the other projected professorships. The latter included chairs in Latin, English, Modern Languages, Astronomy, Oriental Languages, Natural Philosophy, Geology, Natural History, Elocution, Industrial Arts, and Fine Arts. In addition the Chancellor, when selected, was to direct the Department of "Evangelical Christianity," and the President of the College was to be the "Professor of Civil Liberty & Rights and Duties of Citizens."

A detailed statement of these various activities appeared in a modest but neat catalog which probably was published sometime in July. From this source an insight may be gained as to what faced the prospective students as they approached the Myers Block on the morning of September 1st. Coming into Market Square these young men and women saw a huge sign on the East Genesee street side of the Myers Block which read, "SYRACUSE UNIVERSITY," while another, "COLLEGE OF THE UNIVERSITY" appeared on that part of the building fronting on Montgomery Street. On reaching the entrance to the block, they climbed the stairs to the fourth and top floor, took seats in the Chapel or Assembly Room, laid out their paper, pen, and ink (all candidates for admission had been asked to furnish these supplies), and prepared to take a series of written examinations. Candidates for degrees in either the Arts or Science were excused from tests in geography, arithmetic, and grammar upon presentation of a certificate, issued by the Board of Regents, signifying these subjects had been successfully passed in high school. All, however, had to pass a formidable battery of examinations in American history, algebra, and plane geometry. In addition, those seeking the Arts degree were examined in the languages, grammar, antiquities, and geography of the classical world. Having cleared these hurdles the candidates were allowed to register for either the Classical or Scientific Course, the former being four years in length, the latter, three. Financial considerations, we are told, explain the lack of parity between the two courses. Moreover, it was generally understood that the entire curriculum was temporary in nature and that a better organized program would be instituted the following year. Similar information was given to those who, because of work done at Genesee College or elsewhere, had taken advanced standing examinations.

Having finished these various tests one may suppose the candidates availed themselves of the opportunity and inspected the various rooms in the Myers Block taken over by the University. On the third floor they found where classes in history, mathematics, philosophy, and chemistry (including a laboratory) were to meet. Other disciplines and subjects were assigned space on the second floor which also housed the library and reading rooms, the offices of the faculty, and several waiting rooms or parlors. All of the floors, walls and wood-work had been reconditioned and presented, so we are told, a most inviting appearance.

In the meantime, the Faculty held its first meeting, August 29, 1871, in the Myers Block. At this historic gathering, Dr. French was chosen secretary of the faculty, and the "inaugural" of Dr. Steele was read and approved. Following this, the Trustees were asked to provide instruction in French; and Professor George F. Comfort, "late of Princeton College," was recommended for the chair of Modern Languages and Esthetics. Early next morning, another meeting was held and final plans were made for the entrance examinations and the formal installation of Dr. Steele and the Faculty. The latter event was scheduled for the morning of August 31st, at Shakespeare Hall in the Bastable Building on Hanover Square.

Judged by present standards, the inaugural ceremonies may seem cold, unimpressive, and possibly meaningless. To those of 1871, they fairly pulsated with life and character. Appropriate scriptural readings, well selected hymns, and humble prayers provided a fitting background for the "charge" given by Dr. Peck to the Faculty and Trustees who, in deep respect, stood standing throughout the short address. Both the inception and the future of the University, Dr. Peck solemnly declared, rested in the hands of Dr. Steele and his colleagues. They were the stewards of a mighty undertaking in which the "old historical curriculum of the classics and sciences" were to furnish the basis for true learning. Proper respect, he admonished, should be evidenced for modern educational trends and the Faculty at all times were to "apprehend, thoroughly sift, and utilize for the benefit" of the student body, "all revelations in science." Nor was there to be any discrimination at Syracuse as to women or "persons of any nation or color." "Brains and heart," the speaker concluded, were to have a "fair chance, and we propose no narrow-minded sectarianism on the one hand, nor infidelity on the other. We are, in the words of our fundamental law, devoted to the promotion of Christian learning."

Complementing this able and balanced address was the reply by Dr. Steele. The University, according to Dr. Steele, was founded and built by a divine Providence to whom Trustees and Faculty had and must ever look for inspiration and guidance. For this signal manifestation of God's favor, reverent hearts and minds joined in one grand *"Te Deum Laudamus."* And with a humbleness that characterized both the speaker and the occasion, Dr. Steele prayed for God's grace to bless and nurture the stewardship which had been entrusted to him and his fellow teachers. At the same time, he continued, those who deplored the lack of a larger teaching staff, libraries, and laboratories should not lose heart; rather would they do well to remember that scarcely eighteen months had passed since the founding of the University. Given more time and increased endowment, and Syracuse could and would attain a vigorous growth and reputation.

In laying the foundations of the institution the Faculty, Dr. Steele insisted, had neither the desire nor the intention of discarding the wisdom of the past. Novelty in curriculum and change for change's sake were not to be followed at Syracuse. Yet all are aware that progress is the law of human society. Thus, while the University will hold fast to the older and well established theories and practices of education, it would carefully weigh "what the English style the new education." All of which was not so new as some might suppose. Had not Dr. Wilbur Fisk, the foremost educator in American Methodism, some thirty years ago introduced at Wesleyan University a science course and degree? And Syracuse was willing to follow where Dr. Fisk had led. In making this concession, the speaker continued, the Faculty realized it was departing from what most educators considered the best in education, a departure caused by the pressure of the times and the pecuniary necessities of many whose circumstances will not allow the "longer period and increased expense of the classical curriculum." But acting upon the principle that half a loaf was better than no bread, Dr. Steele commended the scientific curriculum to those who could not take the other.

Physical sciences and modern languages—the "new education"—would be pursued and respected at Syracuse. But the aim of the true college curriculum was not to prepare men for trades and professions; rather was it to fit men to be men, roundly developed, well cultured men, drilled to the most efficient energizing of their powers. "Discipline first and knowledge second is our motto." The mathematics and the ancient classics "have been proved by experience to be this grand palestra for the mind." Eighteen of the thirty-six whole term studies in the classical curriculum consist of philological and mathematical subjects. "We cannot without detriment to sound and true erudition abridge the amount of these drill subjects, however noisy the clamor for an abridgment." And then rising to still greater heights, Dr. Steele declared:

Well did Plato say, 'God geometrizes.' While the ancient classics, aside from their disciplinary value are the key to the vast tombs of buried thoughts, so long as Rome is the fountain of law and the center of history, the languages of Numa and Livy must be studied, and so long as Greece furnishes to the human race her matchless ideals in poetry, sculpture, oratory and philosophy; and above all so long as Jesus, the God-Man, speaks to His brethren after the flesh in Hellenic symbols, so long must we furnish instruction in the language of the majestic Demosthenes, the divine Plato, and the inspired Paul.

In conclusion, Dr. Steele reiterated with considerable thought and care the determination of the Faculty to conduct the University upon Christian ideals and principles. "We are most profoundly convinced that there is a God-Ward side to every human soul and that any process of education which ignores this great fact, whatever other excellencies it may combine, must be radically defective in its results." And in this summation the Faculty and Trustees unanimously agreed. Only a short time before in addressing the Trustees, Dr. Peck had presented them and the University with a beautifully printed and bound edition of the Bible which was to serve, so Dr. Peck stated, as the symbol of their office.

At the close of Dr. Steele's stirring address, which together with that by Dr. Peck might well be called a Magna Carta for Syracuse University, the Doxology was sung and the Benediction pronounced, after which the audience hastened away to prepare for the events of the afternoon. At three o'clock an immense gathering, five to six thousand persons we are told, assembled to witness the laying of the cornerstone of the Hall of Languages. According to the *Daily Journal* this, the first of seven buildings to be erected, was to have an ornate Chapel in the basement along with a dining room and kitchen, a library on the second floor, and an assembly room on the third. Subsequently, these plans were drastically altered but of this no one that afternoon gave a thought. Other and more important considerations were uppermost in their minds, not the least of which was the happy turn the weather had taken since morning. Up to noon, Syracuse had experienced its "usual, typical weather." The sky had been overcast and it looked as though it might rain at any moment. A brisk wind, however, scattered the clouds, partly cleared the sky, and lent a crispness to the air that foretold the approach of autumn.

It is extremely difficult for us to picture the scene as it unfolded that August afternoon. None of the sights so familiar today existed. Beyond an occasional farm shed there was not a building on what is the old campus, nor were there any streets leading to it from any direction. Most of the inhabitants of the present University district, then the old Eighth Ward, lived to the north of Adams Street which marked the southern limits of Crouse, University, and Walnut Streets. Even the latter bore different names: University, for example, was then known as Walnut, while Walnut was called Spruce, and Crouse, Chestnut. Farm roads and lanes most certainly existed and over these, shortly after one o'clock wound what seemed to be an endless procession of carriages and persons on foot. It was uphill all the way from the old Genesee Turnpike and many an individual, clad in the heavy clothes of that day, must have arrived at the "Hill" much the worse for the effort. Before them there spread an open stretch of abandoned farm land, dotted with a few trees, and overgrown with grass, weeds and hay. At its southern limit was a hill to which the name of Mount Olympus has been given; to the west was another hill on which John R. Crouse was to erect a splendid building at a later date. A third hill, somewhat to the east of West Hill, faced north and fronted on what now is University Avenue. Already the contour of the campus was being changed for ever since July 4th, when Dr. Peck had driven a stake on the east hill to mark the place for the future Hall of Languages, contractors had levelled that hill somewhat, depositing the surplus dirt in a deep gulley where now stands the Maxwell Building.

Amid huge piles of Onondaga limestone, large stacks of timber, and other building supplies, was a platform upon which distinguished guests and visitors took their seats. From Cornell University had come its great President, Andrew D. White. St. Lawrence College was represented by Dr. Wilbur Fisk. Then there was Dr. Joseph Cummings, one-time head of Genesee College and now in charge of Wesleyan University. Reference should also be made to Rev. Erastus O. Haven of Northwestern University, who in a few years was to be Syracuse's second Chancellor. The state and local bar was brilliantly represented by Chief Justice Sanford E. Church, and Judges George F. Comstock and Charles Andrews, the latter two being members of the University Board of Trustees. Others of the Board as well as selected representatives of the city churches and Common Council also were on the platform.

Once again, those in charge of the ceremonies took special pains through scriptural readings, hymns, and prayers, to impress upon those present the fact that Syracuse University was a Christian insti-

tution founded and favored by Providence. Nor was this theme slighted by Rev. A. J. Phelps in his well-delivered historical sketch of the
University. Dr. Haven also stressed the divine origins in an able speech.
Timely comments were added by President White and others, following which Dr. Peck solemnly laid the cornerstone of Syracuse University, dedicated, so he said, "to the diffusion of knowledge . . .
and the promotion of Christian learning, literature, and science." In
such a manner a great American University was started on its way.

Inaugural services over, it remained for the Faculty to put the
wheels in motion. The next two days, as has been noted, were spent in
examining prospective students, all of whom but one were certified
for admission. Forty-one students, of whom seven were "ladies," accordingly gathered in the College Chapel on the morning of September 4th, 1871. Chapel over, the students filed to their respective classes
which closed at one in the afternoon. The enthusiasm of this small
student body was more than matched by the citizens of Syracuse.
Everyone seemed proud of the new institution and was confident of
its future. Nor were the advantages of the University overlooked by
some local merchants, one of whom honored the day by announcing
the sale of a new cigar, the "University" by name.

In general, throughout the first year, a provisional and limited
course of studies was offered. The teaching load, shared by the original faculty, averaged fifteen hours a week. Of course, these gentlemen were quite unable to present all the various subjects listed in the
curriculum. Additions, therefore, were made to the staff in the persons of Dr. John H. Durston and Professor Foote, who taught classes
in Modern Languages, and Mr. S. Gurney Lapham, instructor in elocution. Later, Professor C. W. Winchester, one-time instructor at
Cayuga Seminary, did part time work in the classics and Professor
Heman H. Sanford offered special lectures in Latin. The activity of
the teaching staff ranged far and wide beyond the limits of the class-
rooms. Not a single phase of college life escaped their careful attention and scrutiny. On one occasion, they weighed with great care the
"disgraceful blackening of the signs of the University," on Christmas
Eve, by certain students. The latter promptly apologized, promised
to pay damages, and signed a paper admitting guilt. It may be that
some of the offenders were members of the Greek letter fraternities,
recently established at Syracuse with the knowledge and approval
of the Faculty. As another illustration of faculty activity reference

may be made to their decision of excusing a Roman Catholic student from attending chapel.

Greater in significance and more permanent in nature was the work relative to the curriculum. Several meetings were devoted to this subject and in February, 1872, a definite program, to go into effect the following fall, was adopted. Three regular fields of study, each four years in length, were offered, of which the Classical Course was viewed as the most important. Candidates for admission to this field were required to pass written examinations in seven different subjects: English Grammar, Geography, History, Mathematics, Natural Philosophy, Latin, and Greek. Certain exceptions were permitted those wishing to matriculate in the Latin-Scientific, and Scientific Courses. Provision also was made for advanced standing examinations. In general, each student who cleared these tests was required to carry fifteen hours a week plus assigned exercises in rhetoric. During the Freshman and Sophomore years there were no free electives though in the upper two years such an opportunity existed. The degree of Bachelor of Arts was conferred upon all who successfully completed the requirements in the Classical Course; those who did likewise in the Latin-Scientific received the Bachelor of Philosophy degree; while the degree of Bachelor of Science was given to those who passed the required courses in Science. Master's degrees in these three fields were granted to graduates of three years standing who had been engaged, during that period, in professional, literary, or scientific study. Finally, it may be noted that a Select Course existed for those who wanted complete freedom of election; a certificate of proficiency was given to these Select students.

Subject to the authority of the Trustees, the Faculty also evolved a unique system known as the "Gymnasia." The Gymnasia consisted of seminaries and academies whose academic standards had been approved of by the Syracuse Faculty. All registrants of these schools who passed certain written tests were admitted to the College of the University without additional examination. The Principals of these schools, who ranked as ex-officio members of the College Faculty, as well as their students appeared by name in the University Catalogue. During the course of the school year, 1871-1872, Gymnasia were established at the Hudson River Institute and Claverack College at Troy, the Central New York Conference Seminary at Cazenovia, and the Northern New York Conference Seminary at Antwerp. Other Gymnasia were founded at a later date at the Onondaga, Nunda, and

Amenia Seminaries. Ultimately, the relationships between the University and the Gymnasia were allowed to lapse and disappear though during their life they served as useful recruiting centers for the young University.

All of these activities received the warmest endorsement of the Trustees who in the meantime had become deeply concerned over more material matters. Uppermost was the ever bothersome question of finance. Subscription pledges, thanks to the untiring efforts of Dr. Peck and Rev. E. C. Curtis, continued to pour in and by the close of 1871 amounted to almost half a million dollars not including the contribution promised by the City of Syracuse. Payment, however, on the private pledges lagged and the Board became visibly agitated. And had it not been for the income from the City bonds plus the payment of a few large subscriptions, there would have been a deficit the like of which Genesee College never had known. Nor did conditions materially improve by the close of college in June, 1872. On the other hand, the total income from all sources, plus secured pledges and gifts of land, represented assets sufficient to justify a building program on the Hill, additions to the faculty, and an expansion of library and laboratory equipment. Among the tangible assets were the fifty acre campus and the eastern half of the old St. Charles Hotel property, the latter being located on West Washington Street between Bank Alley and South Warren. In 1871 the entire St. Charles Hotel property had passed into the hands of Eliphalet Remington, a Trustee of the University and a resident of Ilion, New York. Anxious to promote the fortunes of the new institution, Mr. Remington, aided by his brother, Philo Remington, provided for the transfer of the eastern half of this property to the University; the western half going to the College of Missionaries. This latter body, chartered in August, 1871, and having no legal connection with the University, was to train men and women for foreign missions and to educate the children of missionaries. The tangled and confused story of this college and the acquisition of its property by the University in March, 1877, may in part be found in the records of the University. It may, however, be noted that there is some evidence to warrant the belief that the patrons of the College of Missionaries, many of whom were Trustees of the University, hoped in due time to transform their institution into a theological seminary attached to Syracuse University.[1]

1. See page 43.

Approximately about the same time the University acquired its share of the St. Charles Hotel, the Trustees dug deep into pockets and established a small loan fund. The purpose behind this laudable undertaking was to provide financial aid, free of interest, to worthy students who otherwise might find it difficult to remain in college. Among the expenses was the item of tuition, set by the Board at $60 a year. Children of ministers were granted a fifty per cent reduction and the Faculty was empowered to remit tuition in whole or in part to any deserving student. A matriculation fee of five dollars was added in 1873; the following year a graduation fee of ten dollars was assessed. Of greater significance was the decision of the Board to accept the offer of the Faculty of the Medical Department of Hobart College to move to Syracuse and establish a College of Medicine.

Meanwhile, steps had been taken to fill the office of Chancellor. In part, this action was caused by Dr. Steele's announcement he would resign in June, 1872. Dr. Steele's devotion to Syracuse was beyond question. He had labored hard to help place the infant institution on its feet and had earned the thanks and respect of all concerned. At the same time, to use his own words, his "first love" was the ministry and when in January he accepted a call from the Tremont Street Church of Boston, he felt it was his duty to accept. Naturally, his colleagues and the Trustees wanted him to remain but when they realized how real and genuine were the Doctor's sentiments, they accepted his resignation with regrets and publicly extoled his services to Syracuse at the 1872 commencement.

It was highly fitting for the Trustees and friends of the University to honor Dr. Steele at this commencement. On Sunday, he delivered the Baccalaureate before a large congregation at the First Presbyterian Church. Later, he presided at the Annual Meeting of the Trustees to whom he rendered a report of his stewardship. The following day, June 25th, found him mingling among the alumni, many of whom had been his "boys and girls" at "Old Genesee." And finally, on June 26 and 27, he presided at the commencement exercises, the chief address being given by Rev. J. P. Newman. Nineteen students, including Syracuse's "first coed," Miss Mary L. Huntley, received Bachelor's degrees. Bachelor and Master degrees also were conferred upon one hundred and twelve graduates of Genesee, although most of these were not present. The degree of "Doctor of Philosophy in Course" was given to Dr. James H. Hoose, Genesee '61 and Principal of the Normal School at Cortland, New York.

And so the corner stone year came to an end. The year had been attended by many trials but it closed amid conditions that promised much for the future. The Hall of Languages was nearing completion, the Campus, though knee-deep in hay, was being graded and improved, and there was much talk about a College of Fine Arts under Dr. George F. Comfort from whom great things were expected. Far more important was the spirit and enthusiasm that had motivated these vast undertakings. It was a spirit that vibrated with pioneer courage and fortitude; it was enthusiasm that quickened an abiding faith in a greater and more splendid University.

Note on College of Missionaries

The idea and hope that Syracuse University might in part serve as a training center for prospective ministers was raised anew by Dr. Sims shortly after he accepted the office of Chancellor. In a letter to the Faculty of the College of Liberal Arts dated Brooklyn, New York, March 15, 1881, Dr. Sims submitted a plea and a plan for the establishment of a chair in "Sacred Literature." Such a course, which incidentally was to be offered by the Chancellor, had as its main objective the "training of young men for the ministry, especially such as have not the time nor means to attend a theological seminary." In response to this suggestion the Faculty after some discussion adopted the following answer:

> Whereas, at the time of the founding of the University, the announcement was publicly made that no theological movement was contemplated and a separate institution was therefore organized called the 'College of Missionaries' for the purpose of training persons for missionary work, and
> Whereas, the policy of the University thus far has been to so arrange the curriculum as to encourage rather than to discourage the attendance of our graduates at the theological schools, and
> Whereas, any important change in the policy of the institution should have the hearty concurrence of its trustees and patrons, therefore,
> Resolved, that in the judgment of the Faculty it would be wise to postpone any public announcement of the plan proposed until sufficient time can be had to carefully reconsider the matter and to ascertain whether it would meet the approval of the Board of Trustees and of the Patronizing Conferences.

In keeping with this resolution, to which the Chancellor seems to have made no direct reply the Faculty in May of the same year voted to strike from the post-graduate courses a course in Hebrew for the reason that it "is in the line of study usually required for a degree in theology."

Storm and Stress

4 Rev. Erastus O. Haven had recently resigned his presidency at Northwestern University when Syracuse sought him for its first chancellor. Dr. Haven had moved to Evanston in 1869 after having served as head of the University of Michigan. Prior to that he had been Professor of Latin, Language and Literature, and History at Ann Arbor, editor of the influential Boston newspaper, *Zion's Herald*, a Trustee of the Massachusetts Board of Education, a member of the Massachusetts State Senate, and the author of several well known books. Moreover, he was an intimate friend of Dr. Peck, personally knew a number of the Trustees, professors, and friends of the young university, and had made a most favorable impression on the occasion of his visit to the campus in 1871. The Board's decision in June, 1872, to offer him the chancellorship was greeted with applause and it was hoped an announcement of acceptance might crown the commencement festivities of that year. Unfortunately, Dr. Haven had already accepted, some few weeks before, the post of Executive Secretary of the Board of Education of the Methodist Church. Accordingly he declined the appointment and the Syracuse Board was forced to look elsewhere for a successor to Dr. Steele.

Among those whom the Board proceeded to investigate was Dr. Alexander Winchell whose life, ever since his graduation from Wesleyan in 1847, had been devoted to educational pursuits. Notable in a long list of impressive honors was his Professorship of Geology, Zoology, and Botany at the University of Michigan. Additional distinction had been won as president of the Masonic University at Selma, Alabama, editor of the *Michigan Journal of Education*, Director of the Geological Survey of Michigan, and as the author of several imposing and provocative volumes. And like Dr. Haven, Professor Winchell was well known at Syracuse. Dr. Steele, for example, was a "long-time friend" and had advised Winchell on the latter's *Sketches of Creation* which attracted so much attention in its day. Moreover, it was Professor Brown who in early March, 1872, had written Dr. Winchell inquiring as to whether he would consider the headship of the University.

This was not the first time Dr. Winchell had received such an offer. Several years before the Trustees at Madison had invited him to become the President of the University of Wisconsin. Winchell had declined the honor preferring, so he wrote at a later date, the role of a scientist and teacher to that of an administrator. Conditions, however, had since changed and in a letter to Dr. Haven asking for advice on the Syracuse overture, Winchell admitted his former preferences had weakened. And he might have added that their mutual friend, Professor Benjamin Cocker of Michigan, had urged acceptance of the Syracuse offer. How Dr. Haven or others advised is not known, though it is established, Professor Winchell replied to Dr. Brown in cautious but inviting terms. His knowledge of Syracuse, he wrote, was too general to warrant an affirmative reply nor would he promise acceptance if a definite offer were made. On the other hand, he was not so attached to Michigan as to shut his mind to a wider field of service and activity. This letter was written on March 11 but not answered. Evidently the Syracuse Board either found Winchell's reply none too encouraging or already had begun to center its efforts on Dr. Haven.

Dr. Haven's refusal quite naturally led to a revival of interest in Professor Winchell and late in July, 1872, Dr. Brown, in behalf of the Syracuse Faculty, telegraphed Winchell "to visit us." The following day another wire was received asking him "to come at once." "This raises," so Winchell recorded in his diary, "another question of great moment to me. I suppose they want to confer about the presidency and I shall be greatly tried to arrive at a decision." Tried though he was, Dr. Winchell hastened to board a Michigan Central train and arrived at Syracuse on the morning of August 1st, less than forty-eight hours after having received Brown's first telegram. Conferences were held that day and the next with various members of the Faculty and Trustees and sandwiched in were visits to Myers Hall and the Hill, where the Hall of Languages was in process of construction. Busy hours, crowded with meaning for the future, so Winchell thought as he journeyed back to his dear Ann Arbor. An annual salary of $5,000 was something not to be ignored and what wonderful things he might do with it for his beloved family! Nor would there be any expense incident to moving, for had not Brother Curtis, General Agent of Syracuse University, promised $1,000, $1,500, or even more? No worry over money matters, nor need he burden himself too much with "petty duties and details." What the Trustees wanted was one to administer academic life and "to travel and represent the University abroad—pursue science, etc., etc." And what a relief it would be not to leave Ann Arbor at once. Plan to leave, he had been told, at your leisure; take your time in saying farewells, assume your duties here in January or February of the new year—these and other pleasant recollections came to mind as he sped westward toward home.

Once back home, Winchell hurried to consult friends and colleagues as to what he should do. All agreed the offer was most flattering and should not be declined. Accordingly a wire was sent expressing a willingness to become Chancellor. Several days passed during which Winchell waited anxiously for an answer. Finally, on August 9th, he received official announcement of his election "as Chancellor of the University and President of the Faculty." After "two or three minutes deliberation," so he wrote in his diary, "I drew up the following reply: I accept the election . . . And so the die is cast." Within a few days, Winchell received many letters congratulating him on his good fortune and wishing him good luck in the new undertaking. All of which pleased him immensely and served to convince him he had acted wisely. Of course it would not be easy to leave Ann Arbor after a residence of nearly twenty years, but on second thought there was no cause to worry. Time and energy would have to be spent as never before but he still could and would remain the scholar and scientist.

Yes, the die had been cast and Dr. Winchell looked forward to his new life with great expectancy. In the meantime the Faculty at Syracuse began to labor the new chief with urgent and repeated requests for advice and counsel. Dr. Winchell's presence, it was argued, at the fall conferences of the church at Palmyra and Rochester would do much to enhance the fortunes of the University. Then, there was the pressing matter of the curriculum for the ensuing year, which the professors wished him to inspect in person before handing it over to the printer for publication. At first, Winchell turned a deaf ear to these requests. Why, he argued, could not the proposed curriculum be sent to him for inspection? "Petty duties and details—"? Nonetheless, early October saw Winchell at Syracuse where he helped with the catalogue and addressed the student body. On his way home he stopped off to attend the conferences. The cloistered scholar was being slowly transformed into an administrator.

During the remainder of the year, Dr. Winchell busied himself in many different ways. Box after box was filled with heavy tomes, relics, fossils and the like, while tables, chairs, and cabinets were crated and made ready for shipment. Meantime, a constant round of teas and parties tendered him by his Michigan friends made life easy and comfortable. Early in December, his peace of mind was somewhat shaken by the realization that beyond the telegram of August 9th he had no other evidence of his appointment as Chancellor. Moreover not a sign of a check from Brother Curtis for moving expenses. And so a cautiously worded letter was mailed to Syracuse, the reply to which dispelled all fears. By early January, his book shelves were about empty and "I could weep if I were not acting under my own will."

It was not until January 17, 1873, that Dr. Winchell arrived in Syracuse to assume his new duties. Syracuse outdid itself in welcoming its new executive. Bishop Peck, Professors Brown and French, and Agent Curtis greeted him at the depot and whisked him away to the Vanderbilt House which for the time being was to serve as a Chancellor's Home. Later in the same day, the Honorable James J. Belden, a Trustee, opened his elegant mansion on West Genesee Street and introduced Dr. Winchell to some three hundred of "the first people of Syracuse." A week later, Myers Hall was the scene of an elaborate reception accorded him by the student body. Professor Comfort, an old friend, welcomed the Chancellor and called upon him to respond to the toast, "Our Alma Mater." "This business of speaking to toasts," Winchell wrote in his diary, "is one in which I am so utterly without gifts that I made a complete failure. I omitted all of the gist of my intended remarks and said nothing that was worthy of note. All the other responses were remarkedly good."

Formal inaugural ceremonies were held in the afternoon, February 13th, at the Wieting Theater, following which in the evening a social levee was tendered Chancellor and Mrs. Winchell and their daughters, Jennie, Ida Belle, and Flora, at Convention Hall. And this time Dr. Winchell was not caught off balance. His address was such a success, the Trustees voted to have it printed and the *Daily Journal* published it in full. Nor was there any sniping evidenced because of the liberality of his views and purposes. Dr. Winchell entered upon his work with considerable enthusiasm and soon earned for himself the respect and confidence of both Trustees and Faculty. His skillful handling of the University's interest in respect to the Agricultural College Bill, then under debate at Washington, received much applause, and his repeated visitations throughout the neighboring conferences added to his prestige. Especially were the Trustees pleased with his endeavors to enlist the spiritual and material support of "local capitalists." Writing to good old Dr. Cocker in late May, Dr. Winchell was more than optimistic. Syracuse, he wrote, was moving forward.

During the summer of 1873, the Chancellor and his family were in Europe where he purchased a number of volumes badly needed for the University Library. Leaving his family in Germany, Dr. Winchell returned to Syracuse in time for the opening of classes, his first public appearance being at the inauguration in September of the College of Fine Arts. Shortly thereafter he began to realize the "honeymoon" of his chancellorship had ended. The financial outlook for the University was dark and dismal. The depression of 1873 had begun and threatened to drag the infant institution into oblivion. Greater exertions would have to be made and this, Winchell deplored, meant more canvassing on his part. Much as he disliked discarding the academic robe for the garb of a humble beggar, he might have answered the call of duty much better were it not for the deep indigo then settling around his home and family. From Germany came letters telling of his wife's need for additional funds and what was more alarming, of Flora's being none too well. Being short of funds and with "pay day" several weeks off, he approached Agent Curtis and Dr. Lore both of whom showered him with sympathy but nothing else. "I rather think,"

Winchell wrote, "Curtis doesn't care much. I can assure him that I shall look out for myself when hereafter he asks me for large contributions to his church." But Lore did help. On November 1st, for the tidy sum of five dollars, Lore arranged a three hundred dollar loan at a local bank, at seven per cent, for thirty days, by which time it was hoped Curtis would be able to meet the Chancellor's salary, now overdue.

A month later, with the campus agog with excitement over the approach of Christmas, the Chancellor felt as though the world was sinking beneath him. Letters from Germany told sad news: "Lotie," Winchell's pet name for Flora, was dangerously ill and late in the same month a cable brought word of her death on Christmas Eve. Dr. Winchell was stunned. Nor did the weeks lessen his grief as they sped by, crowded as they were with administrative duties. All of which was woven into a pattern of thought he translated into action by the spring of 1874.

Dr. Winchell's determination to resign from the Chancellorship most certainly was caused, in part, by domestic affairs. If the contrary were true, little space would have been given in this volume to such matters. On the other hand it is equally true that by themselves they would not have caused his retirement. Much the same may be said relative to the tardiness with which he received his compensation. Both factors most assuredly worried and depressed him. Basically, however, his decision to resign was predicated upon the conviction he was unequal to the task of shouldering the financial burdens of the University. Every inclination of his sensitive nature recoiled against the idea of drumming up funds. And when he did, he did so with little taste and tact. "It means," he wrote, "leaving my intellect to lie fallow." Then again, as he told his friends over and over again, the Trustees in 1872 had assured him others would do the disagreeable spade work. The truth was, he communicated in a letter to Dr. Cocker, they need a man here "to create a University, not to manage one and they can't afford a Chancellor and Creator both." Ever since arriving at Syracuse, he continued, he had been of the opinion the University had been "set in operation too soon." The financial instability of the institution clearly worried him and in a letter to Dr. Haven he expressed concern lest a mountain of debt would overwhelm Syracuse as it had the Methodist school at Troy.

Sentiments of this nature had been dropped from time to time by the Chancellor to certain members of the Board. It was not, however, until June 24th that an official resignation was presented. The Board was visibly agitated and pressed Dr. Winchell to reconsider. They then offered a professorship at a salary of $2,500, $500 additional for travel, and a six months leave. Before such a sincere demonstration of goodwill and conscious of the fact he had no other prospects of employment, Winchell accepted the offer. A public announcement to this effect was made by Dr. Peck following the commencement exercises of 1874. The audience was delighted with the news and "a cheer loud and long" rang throughout the hall. A few weeks later, Dr. Winchell left for Europe and on his return to Syracuse in December, 1874, entered upon his new duties as Professor of Geology, Zoology, and Botany. The following year, without severing his Syracuse ties, he assumed a similar position at Vanderbilt University. Finally, in 1878 he left Syracuse entirely, returning to what had always been home to him, Ann Arbor; here he died February 19, 1891.

Dr. Winchell's resignation caused no end of comment throughout the University and City circles. The impact of his retirement, however, was considerably softened by the knowledge he was to remain at Syracuse. More encouraging to those whose hopes for the University seemed endangered by Dr. Winchell's resignation was the timely news the new chancellor would be none other than Dr. Haven. Dr. Haven was present at the Board meeting, June 24, 1874, and expressed a willingness to accept the office should the Trustees make him an offer. Not a moment was lost, a unanimous vote amply reflected the desires of the Trustees and Dr. Haven was declared Chancellor of the University and President of the College of Liberal Arts.

During the administrations of Chancellors Winchell and Haven (1872-1880) the Faculty of the College of Liberal Arts, for so it was officially named in 1873, remained much the same. As is well known, Professors French, Coddington, Brown, and Bennett of the original staff served throughout the administrations of the first two chancellors with increasing efficiency and loyalty. Dr. French, later to act as Chancellor "*pro tem*", and Vice-Chancellor became the first Dean of the College of Liberal Arts in 1878, a post he most honorably filled until his death in 1897. Buried in the archives of the University is a stout box filled with the records of his Deanship—a mute but eloquent testimony to one known as a "University Builder."

Equally effective as teachers were Professors Heman H. Sanford of the Classical Department (1872-1877), John H. Durston of Modern Languages (1871-1878), W. Locke Richardson, popular instructor in Elocution (1872-1879), and George Fisk Comfort, better known as the first Dean of the College of Fine Arts. Others who joined the ranks for a short time were Professors George H. Hooper, G. G. Hapgood, and Assistant Peppion Melfi. Finally, it was in 1874 that Dr. Frank Smalley, Syracuse '74, began an association with the University that was not to be terminated until his death in 1931. The most outstanding fact about this able corps of teachers—and there can be no question of their ability—was that they gained the unending devotion and affection of their students. One can not read the Minutes of the Board of Trustees and the more informative student publications without coming to this conclusion. In a large measure the success of the University during these early years was built upon this student-faculty relationship.

In the hands of these loyal teachers, Syracuse prospered insofar as educational and spiritual values were concerned. Theirs was the unique privilege of serving without knowing what tomorrow might bring. Daily there came to their ears rumors, unhappily weighed with truth, of the University's financial troubles. Remington's gift of the St. Charles Hotel, it was said, was rapidly becoming a white elephant; annual deficits were eating up limited endowment; valuable University Avenue lots were being sold to meet current expenses; salaries for the time could not be met; the Hall of Languages had been mortgaged —these and many other stories freely circulated from Bank Alley in the City to the Hill. And yet amid all this depressing talk, the Faculty labored as though nothing was wrong.

Year after year these teachers reexamined the basic assumptions implicit within the curriculum of the College of Liberal Arts and while changes were made nothing was done in a hasty or careless manner. These assumptions may readily be found in the published and unpublished records of that college. In 1872, for example, the *Annual* in a reference to the courses of study stated:

The old Classical course is preserved in its traditional character, and is intended to afford as thorough a training in the classical languages of antiquity as can be obtained in any college. It aims, however, to be abreast of the educational thought and philosophy of the age, and yields as far as reputable precedent sanctions, to the valid claims of modern languages and sciences upon the attention of students seeking especially the culture to be derived from the study of the ancient languages and literature.

Eight years later the statement was modified as follows:

> The Classical course is substantially the same as pursued in the best American colleges for the degree of A. B., and is intended to afford a thorough training in the classical languages and literature and mathematics. It introduces also the study of modern languages and sciences in proper proportion.

Clearly little difference exists between the two. The language, however, varies and its tone is considerably softened. Evidently the classicist of 1872 had mellowed with the passing of time.

Between these dates Freshmen in the Classical course carried a total of forty-eight hours spread over three terms. Of this twelve to thirteen hours each were assigned to Algebra and Geometry, Latin, and Greek, while two to three hours each were allocated to History, Physiology, Elocution and Rhetoric; there were no electives. Sophomores devoted twelve hours to Trigonometry, Analytical Geometry, and Calculus, ten hours to German, eight hours to Medieval and Modern History, six hours each to Physics and Greek, and three hours each to Latin and Elocution, making a total of forty-eight hours; there were no electives. In the case of Juniors the yearly requirements varied in French from eight to nine hours, Chemistry from six to nine, Latin from three to six, Astronomy from three to four, while Logic, Psychology, and Elocution remained constant at five, four, and three hours respectively. Electives, which ranged over a wide field, varied from eleven to thirteen hours. In the senior year greater latitude was permitted, the electives ranging from sixteen to twenty-one hours out of a total requirement of forty-eight. In addition they carried, between 1872 and 1881, five hours a year of Geology, three of Constitutional Law, two of Art History, and one each of Philosophy of History and Esthetics. Moral Philosophy varied from six to seven hours, English Literature from five to six, and Christian Evidences from two to five. Elocution for three hours was required between 1872 and 1874.

The Latin-Scientific Course during the years covered by this chapter was substantially the same as the Classical Course except for the substitution of German for Greek in the Freshman year and other subjects for that language in the other years. It also required in the

Junior and Senior years a slightly wider range of literary and philosophical study. The Greek-Scientific Course was the same as the Latin-Scientific except that Greek stood in the place of Latin. The Scientific Course excluded both Latin and Greek, their places being taken by German and French and a more liberal range of Mathematics, Natural Sciences, Literature, History, and Philosophy. In recognition of the differing tastes and aims of students in these three sequences the number of free electives became larger in the Junior and Senior years.

Later, the Faculty revamped the requirements for graduate degrees and instituted instruction on the graduate level. Again, in 1877 a course in Civil Engineering was added. The present College of Engineering, Graduate School, the College of Fine Arts, and the School of Speech, therefore, had their inception with Liberal Arts. Finally, it should be noted that the Select Course, though continued was seriously restricted by a ruling that called for the approval of all registrations in this course by those professors under whom such work was to be taken. In the meantime, attendance at Chapel, though not required, was handled in such a manner that rendered absence almost impossible. Considerable attention was also given to student life and conduct. On one occasion, Dean French felt called upon to admonish the students against "snuggling" in the Library. Fraternities, which had been tabooed at Genesee College, were more than tolerated at Syracuse, and the Faculty openly endorsed the student publications and joined in the hope a School of Journalism might be established. Nor were athletics ignored and for many years the popular Professor Smalley usually appeared as referee at the annual Field Day contests.

Nor did the Faculty confine their activities to the Campus. A survey of the city papers during the 1870's reveals how active they were in local civic affairs. Hardly a Sunday passed but one of them occupied the pulpit of a Syracuse, Rome, Utica, Oswego, or Fulton Church. So effective was this Christian leadership that in one case, Dr. Coddington was invited to become the resident pastor of a nearby community at a salary three times as large as that earned as professor. Dr. Comfort, moreover, introduced and promoted a series of University Lectures which attracted more than ordinary attention in the city, and Professor Richardson's public readings, especially those on Shakespeare, received commendation. And in 1876, Dr. Comfort conducted what might be called the first Summer School. All in all, the Faculty demonstrated interest in adult education. The initiation and continuation

of these off-campus activities did much to enhance the standing of
the University among the citizens of Syracuse.

A striking illustration of the good-will engendered by those and
other civic undertakings occurred on May 8, 1873, when the City
joined with the University in the formal dedication of the Hall of
Languages. Classes were held for the last time in the Myers Block on
April 30th, the students gathering in the Chapel for prayer and last
minute instructions preparatory for the trek to the Hill. Following
these simple and informal ceremonies, the students joined hands with
the Faculty and sang a number of college songs such as "Auld Lang
Syne," "We Won't Go There Anymore," and the popular "Kefool-
seum." Meanwhile, stout trucks had hauled the library, museum,
chemical laboratory and other effects to the Hall of Languages and
on May Day, 1873, classes were held for the first time in the new
building.

The Hall of Languages, constructed out of Onondaga limestone,
was planned and executed in accordance with the best standards of
that day; the architect being Horatio W. White of Syracuse. In
general, the building occupied a rectangular area one hundred and
seventy-four feet from east to west by ninety-five feet, north to south;
the front and rear walls were set in on either side of the central section
forming, thereby, two recesses. The front recess was flanked by an
east and west tower; in the rear, the recess was partially occupied by
two structures consisting of coal houses below and porches above.
The two towers rose slightly above the central roof which like the
towers were finished off in the popular mansard style of that age. In
the western tower was a bell weighing six hundred pounds; there was
no central tower.

The basement floor was crossed from front to rear by two corridors,
each having north and south exits, which divided the floor into eastern,
middle, and western divisions. The room at the rear of the eastern
section (105), much larger than it is today, was the chemical laboratory; in the middle was a "weighing room" intended for "delicate
chemical manipulations" (104); and in the front or north end of the
section was a shop evidently designed for the physics department
(103).[1] The middle division of the basement was crossed by a hall that
connected with the two corridors. Part of the space in front of this

---

1. Numbers in parentheses indicate rooms as of 1947, except as noted.

hall, now occupied by rooms numbered 101, 102, 106 and a vault, was given over to Professor Brown's office and private laboratory; to the south of the hall was a science lecture hall (107), smaller than the lecture room on the floor above, behind which were the boiler pits in which was generated the steam that heated the building. Today (1951) the English offices and a small classroom occupy the space to the south of the center hall. To the right and left of the furnace room and directly under the stairs that led to the main floor were "little dens of Egyptian darkness," today occupied by the janitor and a faculty rest room. The entire eastern division appears to have been used as a natural science museum (110, 112, 113).

Similar corridors, hall, and divisions appeared on the first or main floor but with passages leading from them out onto the rear porches, thence down to the ground level; an east, west, and center flight of stairs provided exits at the front, and there were other stairs that connected with the basement floor. The eastern portion of the main floor consisted of class rooms (202, 203, 204, 204a, 205) as did the western division (209, 210) except for the men's waiting room (202) which in time became the Classical Seminar Room, and later the office of the Dean of Liberal Arts. The middle section was occupied by a large lecture room (207) and the main or center entrance at the front. The Registrar's Office (213, 214) and the Chancellor's Office (200, 201) were to the left and right respectively of this entrance. Two offices (206, 207) led from the corridors into the large lecture room.

Five flights of stairs led from the main floor to the one above. Two of these were continuations of the stairs starting at the basement level and another was a narrow winding flight midway between the former and opposite to the main entrance on the first floor. The other two led from the recesses formed by the passages which came from the east and west entrances to the Hall of Languages. Remains of these stairs may be seen in the old postal room (formerly the office of the *Daily Orange*, and now in 1951 a portion of the office of the Dean of Liberal Arts), and in an outer office of the Department of Philosophy. In all probability these latter stairs were used only on rare occasions and are not mentioned in any source after the building had been dedicated. In a short time the existence of these stairs seem to have been forgotten; precisely why is not known and conversations with alumni who knew the building at an early date reveal no knowledge on their part of these stairs.

On the second floor besides class rooms, offices, and the same halls as below was a ladies waiting room (306) in the northeast corner. A fine large room, known as the parlor, occupied the space directly over the Chancellor and Registrar's offices, while the present lecture room (207) housed the library and reading room. Over the library and extending from the front to the rear of the building was the chapel with a stage at the north end. The remainder of this top floor, namely that which represented the third floor of the eastern and western divisions of the building was occupied by offices, recitation rooms, corridors, and two stairs that led to the east and west towers. Also on the top floor were two large tanks capable, it is said, of flooding the entire structure in the event of fire. The balustrades of the stairways throughout the Hall of Languages were of alternate strips of ash and black walnut and the windows were provided with inside blinds of chestnut and black walnut. Surrounding the building was a campus still largely unimproved, only partly graded and with a higher ground level at the front than at present.

To return, however, to the dedication. May 8th, if one may trust the *University Herald*, was a dull drab day with the sky overcast and threatening rain. In spite of the inclement weather a large number of people assembled to witness the exercises. The College Quartette opened the ceremonies with selected musical compositions. Prayer and addresses followed, the chief speaker being the Rev. Edmund S. James, Bishop of the New York Conference. Bishop Peck then formally dedicated the Hall of Languages after which the ceremonies were concluded with the singing of the "University Hymn," composed for the occasion by Rev. George Lansing Taylor.

Later in the day the building was thrown open for public inspection. Few of those, however, who admired the spacious halls and well appointed class rooms and offices were aware of the financial uncertainties confronting the University. Indeed on the very day the Hall of Languages was dedicated, the Trustees after prolonged discussion came to the conclusion that it might be necessary to mortgage the building in order to meet the staggering demands of the University's creditors. The seriousness of the situation led to continued debate at the Annual Board Meeting in 1873. Nor was the matter settled at this gathering or at similar sessions for the next seven years. The minutes of these meetings, insofar as finances were concerned, might well have been written in red ink. At times a hopeful note was sounded when, for example, the Treasurer reported a slight increase in tuition payments or a two hundred dollar profit from the sale of hay cut from the campus which still looked more like a farm than an educational institution. Optimism of this type, however, was quickly erased when it was announced that necessary repairs on the Remington Block would more than wipe out the rentals from that property for the year and, in all probability, for the next two years. Retrenchment, repeatedly urged by loyal alumni and friends, was out of the question, as the University to all intents and purposes had operated on a hand to mouth basis since the day of its inception. Small wonder, Chancellor Winchell hazarded the opinion the University had been founded at the wrong time.

During these doldrums there was much talk of abolishing the office of General Agent, the cost of which did not exceed three thousand dollars a year. A small sum, it was admitted, but small as it was it represented an outlay that might well be applied toward interest charges on outstanding obligations. The General Agent, however, served as the University's most important contact with the Methodist clergy and laity throughout the state. Thanks to his efforts an appreciable share of the subscriptions and pledges had been raised. The office, in other words, was worth many times more than it cost and so the General Agent was retained. Attention was then focused upon the faculty which, it was suggested, might either take a ten per cent reduction or make a subscription of equivalent value. Chancellor Haven blocked this by pointing out how low salaries were and how little would actually be saved. In this respect it is worth noting that both the Chancellor and General Agent took a self-imposed cut in their salaries. The Board, however, did abolish the office of Registrar, the duties of which were assumed by a patient and long-suffering faculty.

Meanwhile, every nerve and fiber of the University was being stretched to keep the institution alive. Only the essential purchases were permitted and yet in spite of these drastic efforts current expenses continued to exceed income. Annual deficits, which since 1871, had averaged from ten to fifteen thousand dollars, were met only by generous gifts from the Trustees and friends. Temporary relief was gained in 1875 when two local banks loaned a hundred thousand dollars secured by a mortgage on the campus site and a note signed by Mr. Philo Remington. Hardly had this arrangement been negotiated, however, before another crisis had arisen. Finally, in June, 1879,

Chancellor Haven all but threw up his hands in utter despair and suggested that not only should the University Avenue lots, recently given to the University by Mr. George Comstock, be sold but that the College of Fine Arts might have to be abolished.

Information about the financial troubles of the University had been freely publicized by the Trustees in the hope of stimulating material aid from the patronizing conferences and friends of the University. Of course it was realized that such a policy had its dangers, especially when croaking voices from Lima were heard predicting the failure of an institution that "had been born in sin." As Chancellor Haven, however, so aptly said, "Retreat is disaster. Having received so much it would seem unworthy and almost thankless to doubt that it will also receive what is necessary to complete the enterprise." And so the University aired its troubles, trusting with an abiding faith in the prayers and subscriptions of its friends.

In reviewing the financial troubles of the 1870's one may be led to question some of the actions and undertakings of the Trustees. The assumption of the assets and liabilities of the College of Missionaries might be cited by way of illustration. But to have allowed that property to pass into the hands of an outsider might have endangered the University's interests in the Remington Block, the western portion of which belonged to the College of Missionaries. It is so easy to sit back today with the patent advantage of more than seventy-five years and criticize this or that feature of the University's administration. On the other hand it is quite sobering to realize, as one may from a study of the sources, that the Trustees of that age also questioned and that their decisions represented *considered* decisions for the future in which subsequent generations lived and prospered. Most certainly the Trustees might have handled things differently. They might have delayed construction of the Hall of Languages and continued to lease the Myers Block, but to have done so might well have spelled failure.

One should recall that the University had very few friends and benefactors to whom it might turn for help. Moreover, there was no appreciable reservoir of alumni to tap. Most of its sons and daughters were graduates of Genesee College and the Medical Department of Geneva College. Few of these had come from well-to-do homes and the same may be said of the handful of students that were graduated from Syracuse between 1871 and 1880. Even as late as Chancellor Flint's administration (1922-1936), the average income of the alumni was in the lower income bracket groups. Again, the greater share of the early graduates had entered the ministerial and teaching professions, generally considered dry wells when it comes to financial pumping. Time and time alone might rectify this condition, but for that decade no other outlook was possible. And it must be remembered without rancor that Central and Western New York families—yes, even those of the Methodist Church—preferred to send their children to older and better established institutions.

Finally, in any appraisal of the University's early history, ample consideration should be given to the over-all economic picture of that age. It was on September 18, 1873, the very day that marked the opening of the College of Fine Arts, that the great banking house of Jay Cooke and Company closed its doors. Two days later, the New York Stock Exchange suspended operations and in a short time the entire country was swept into the trials and uncertainties of the Panic of 1873. Bankruptcies became the order of the day, commodity prices skidded down and down, unemployment rose by leaps and bounds, and certain stocks and bonds took on the characteristics of Continental currency. During 1874, conditions went from bad to worse and it was not until 1878 that the climax was reached, following which men spoke hopefully about a return to normalcy. Certainly, the founding fathers of Syracuse University could not have foreseen the lean years ahead when they so optimistically announced the birth of the University. 1870 and 1871 were years of great prosperity and although no President talked of the speedy demise of poverty, it appeared as though a golden age had been reached in America's history. Unfortunately the exact reverse took place, and the life of Syracuse University hung in the balance.

Amid this crisis, Syracuse University was asked to make a tremendous sacrifice. The Methodist Church in 1880 in convention assembled, elected Chancellor Haven a bishop and assigned him to San Francisco. Haven's elevation necessitated his resignation from the University and there was nothing the Trustees could do about it. Nor was the blow softened by the numerous resolutions and complimentary remarks that echoed throughout the City and University circles. Chancellor Haven's unique qualifications for his new position, which was suddenly terminated by his death August 2, 1881 at Salem, Oregon, were repeated over and over again, and his valuable contributions to the life of the University were eulogized without stint. Moreover, suitable farewells and God's blessings were bestowed upon him with deep and heart-felt sincerity. But in spite of these demonstrations of good will toward one who had labored in season and out of season to maintain the University in the face of almost insurmountable obstacles and whose memory Syracuse will always cherish, the bold fact of impending misfortune hovered over the campus during Commencement Week, 1880.

Thirty-eight students, the majority of whom were of the College of Liberal Arts, received degrees that year. Although this amounted to a fifty per cent increase over 1872 it was below the record established in 1876 when a total of fifty-three were graduated. On the other hand it was above the average for the nine year period during which 294 persons were awarded degrees. Of the latter, 189 were of the College of Liberal Arts, 74 of the College of Physicians and Surgeons, and 31 of the College of Fine Arts. In the meantime, 1,941 individuals had matriculated in these colleges. Most of these, as might be expected, were residents of the State of New York with Onondaga standing first among the counties of that State. Registrations from other states, however, were increasing. In 1871, the total registration at Syracuse stood at 41; in 1880, on the eve of Dr. Haven's departure, there were 279 students in attendance. These figures, though modest in themselves, indicated a virility about Syracuse that promised better days ahead. Nor did enrollment at Syracuse suffer by comparison with the other institutions.

Equally encouraging was the fact that whereas in 1871 there was but one college, in 1880 there were three with some talk about a College of Law. Moreover, the curriculum of the three colleges had been broadened and enriched, thanks to the vision and understanding of a discerning faculty. Finally, among the educational and human assets of the University, there was the good will, loyalty and growing devotion of the alumni and student body. Fortified by these and other factors, the Trustees viewed the future with less alarm than might otherwise have been expected. The financial problems, it was frankly admitted, were serious and the resignation of Chancellor Haven was most inopportune. But the situation was not hopeless. The very presence of difficulty seemed to act as a stimulant rather than as a deterrent. The University was in danger, but there was no reason for believing disaster was inevitable.

Growing Pains

5 The immediate and most pressing problem, following the untimely resignation of Dr. Haven, was the selection of a new chancellor. Much thought was given to the matter and more than one candidate seems to have been considered, all of which was in keeping with a resolution passed by the Alumni Association at its June meeting. The Trustees were asked by the Association not to be hasty about the choice of a new chancellor so that its "selection may be one best calculated to conserve the highest interests of our Alma Mater." The summer of 1880, however, passed without an appointment having been made. Nor was the new executive at his desk when college opened in the fall and it remained for the ever faithful Dean French, now in his fifty-fifth year, to greet the new and old students. Of course, the faculty and student body were quite disappointed over the absence of a chancellor. Similar attitudes, moreover, were held by the Trustees who, while deeply deploring the situation, were determined to make no appointment until the right man had been found. And by the right man was meant one who could and would devote himself to promotional rather than instructional matters. Leave academic considerations and curriculum building to the faculty and allow the Chancellor to concentrate all of his time and energy upon the physical and financial life of the University! Such, in

brief, was the policy the Trustees had settled upon—a policy thoroughly endorsed by the faculty. Then there was the simple matter of tenure; two chancellors in eight years was not conducive to growth. Frequent changes might spell disaster; continuity of personnel meant development. "Growing pains," as Dr. Smalley so aptly phrased it in the *Golden Jubilee*, "possessed the institution." Small wonder, the Trustees searched diligently for one who, over a number of years, might ease these pains with increased endowments, and with new and more stately buildings.

Early in November, rumor had it the chancellor's mantle was to rest upon the shoulders of Rev. Charles N. Sims, pastor of the Summerfield Methodist Church of Brooklyn, and on the seventeenth of that month a definite offer was extended to him. Rev. Sims already had won considerable recognition for himself since graduating from Asbury (Indiana) University in 1859. In Methodist circles his reputation as a successful minister was established by various pastorates in Maryland, Indiana, and New Jersey. Nor was he unknown as an educator and administrator, having served as the Principal of the Thornton Academy in Indiana and as President of the Valparaiso Male and Female College of Valparaiso, Indiana. In the field of letters he had earned applause for several well written pamphlets and books, notably a *Life of Rev. T. M. Eddy*. All of these and other attainments marked and recommended him, but what pleased the Trustees most of all was Dr. Sims' willingness to assume the role of a creative builder. "I think," so he wrote to Dr. French, "the most strenuous efforts ought to be put forth by every man who can secure a dollar to secure the amount of our deficiency by the close of the college year. And there ought to be the beginning of actual endowment. . . . If the incoming administration cannot command sympathy and cooperation, the future of the institution will not be promising."

Dr. Sims was delayed in leaving Brooklyn and it was not until April 1, 1881, that he appeared at his office in the Hall of Languages. In the meantime, as had been true in the past, Dr. French shouldered the additional burdens of managing the University and kept in close contact with Dr. Sims who on several occasions visited Syracuse, each time receiving a rousing ovation from the students. During the remainder of the college year, Chancellor Sims taught classes in Senior English, visited the "Gymnasia," and frequently preached from local city pulpits. These practices and behaviors of Dr. Sims established a pattern he was to follow so well throughout his long and able chancellorship. The formal inauguration of the new executive took place before a large and attentive congregation at the University Avenue Methodist Church on June 28th. The next day, Syracuse celebrated its Tenth Annual Commencement at the Wieting Opera House where thirty-one students of the College of Liberal Arts received degrees. Earlier in the month, the College of Medicine had graduated twenty and the College of Fine Arts, fourteen. Out of the total graduating classes nineteen were women. Never before in the history of the University had so many degrees been granted—a fact not unnoted then.

No one was more cheered and heartened by this auspicious event than Dr. Sims who recently had asked for and obtained from the Trustees a definition of the Chancellor's duties and a statement of his relations with the Board, the faculties of the several colleges, and the agents of the University. Heretofore no sharp line of demarcation had been drawn, the absence of which probably accounts in no small measure for the halting steps of Chancellors Winchell and Haven. On the other hand with the University, in one sense, little more than a family affair during the administrations of the first two chancellors there was less need for precision. But with the coming of Dr. Sims and with the program he envisaged, boundaries and spheres of authorities needed clarity and limitation; particularly pressing were problems relating to the status of the Colleges of Fine Arts and Medicine concerning which comment appears below. It would be boring and would serve no useful purpose to list or describe all of the improved procedures that were introduced in 1881 or immediately thereafter, but much of the credit of the Sims regime may be assigned to these innovations and from that time on the hand of the Chancellor became increasingly more apparent in every aspect of university life. Ultimate authority and responsibility rested with the Board of Trustees as may be seen from an examination of the Minutes of that body. Not a penny, for example, was to be spent and no debts contracted "in or on account of the University" except by authority of the Board, though the Chancellor was to have general direction of the financial agents of the University and of all financial plans. Again, no degrees were to be conferred or refused by the Trustees except upon concurrence of the Chancellor. As a final illustration reference might be made to the

Board's decision in respect to the age-old question of academic tenure, though even here the Chancellor's influence must have been felt. Although no official position seems to have been taken by the Board relative·to instructors, all professorial appointments were limited to a six year period. In 1883, for example, professors of all ranks who had served for six years were reelected, and in 1887 the same procedure was followed in respect to the chancellor. To be precise, therefore, one might speak of the administrations, and not the administration of Dr. Sims.

Later in 1892 and upon the eve of Dr. Sims' retirement, a meeting of the Chancellor and the professorial members of the College of Liberal Arts reviewed the matter of tenure. The recommendation that developed from this gathering appeared as but one item in a larger report that embodied resolutions concerning the relations between the Chancellor and the Dean on one hand and the professors on the other. The first of these resolutions, all of which were adopted, provided that the Chancellor and Dean together with the Professor in charge of any given department were to be responsible for recommending to the Trustees for appointment all persons on the instructional level. However, only the Chancellor and Dean were to decide upon nominations for professorial appointments, though in both instances full consultation with the personnel of the department concerned should be held. In another resolution the Chancellor and Dean were to advise with any member of the teaching staff as to methods of instruction and management. And should these administrative officers believe that any professor or instructor was no longer of use in the University they should notify him "as early as the 1st of May in the college year." Again all recommendations for salary increases within the Colleges of Liberal and Fine Arts—nothing was said of the College of Medicine—were to be made by the Chancellor and Deans concerned. Finally it was resolved that should any member of the teaching staff desire a change in his salary he should feel himself free to consult with the Chancellor on the subject before the close of the college year.

It was also during his chancellorship that the charter of the University was amended so as to provide for the establishment of the University Senate, a reorganization of the Board of Trustees, the creation of a separate fund for endowments, and the incorporation of the Medical College and its property into the University. The assistance rendered by the Board of Trustees in these and other matters was of tremendous value. Naturally, the service of some of the members was more fruitful than that of others; in part this may be explained by the proximity of some to the seat of the University, in other cases it was due to ability and personality. Among those who held the office of President of the Board, special attention should be given to Mr. Francis H. Root of the Genesee Conference. Mr. Root was a leather manufacturer of prominence, residing at Buffalo, New York, and a charter member of the Board of Trustees. Tutored by men like Bishop Jesse T. Peck, Dr. Alexander Winchell, and Mr. David Decker—all former Presidents—Mr. Root presided over the meetings and activities of the Trustees from 1879 to his death in September, 1892; he was succeeded by the well known John D. Archbold. Assisting Mr. Root as First Vice-President was the Honorable George F. Comstock, also a charter member of the Board, and one time Judge of the Court of Appeals of the State of New York. Mr. Comstock was First Vice-President of the Board from 1870 to 1893. Mr. Francis H. Root was Second Vice-President, 1870 to 1879 and was succeeded by Chancellor Haven (1879-1880) and Mr. Erastus F. Holden (1880-1893). The office of Third Vice-President, created in 1892, was held by Dr. James B. Brooks for a period of one year. Dr. Dallas D. Lore was the Board's Secretary from 1870 to 1873. He was followed by Mr. John P. Griffin, Rev. D. W. C. Huntington, and Edwin Nottingham. Mr. Nottingham was graduated from the College of Liberal Arts in 1876 following which he began the practice of law in the city of Syracuse. In 1886 he became a member of the Board and in the next year assumed the office of secretary, a post he held until 1903. Mr. Thomas B. Fitch was Treasurer between 1870 and 1876 and was followed by Mr. Jonathan C. Chase (1876-1880), Thomas J. Leach, (1880-1884), and Thomas W. Durston (1884-1895). Financial agents included Rev. E. C. Curtis (1871-1884) and Rev. B. I. Ives (1879-1881). The office of Registrar and Receiver was held by Professor John P. Griffin between 1871 and 1876 and Dr. Frank Smalley between 1882 and 1894; Dr. Smalley was also Registrar at odd times.

The most outstanding achievements of the Board, insofar as this volume is concerned, came during the administration of Dr. Sims. Under his gentle but firm and directing hand the Faculty of the College of Liberal Arts grew in number and quality. To mention them all by name seems quite out of place and yet there were a few that deserve reference. First and foremost there comes to mind the towering figure of Dean French. Those who knew him, and in his day that included everyone on the Hill, had great respect for his teaching ability and skill in administration. Quiet by nature, he had the rare gift of being able to enlist the support and confidence of his colleagues and the unending admiration and devotion of the student body. During his long life at Syracuse he served as Professor of Mathematics (1871-1897), Chancellor *pro tem*, (October, 1893 to April, 1894), and Vice-Chancellor from 1895 to his death, April 26, 1897. Then there was Dr. Wellesley P. Coddington whose brilliancy as a teacher was attested by his Professorships of Greek, Ethics, Pedagogy, and Philosophy. Equally beloved by the students was Dr. John J. Brown, Professor of Physics and Chemistry. Nor could any student ever forget Dr. George F. Comfort who though translated to the Deanship of the College of Fine Arts continued to lecture in Esthetics and Modern Languages until his retirement from the University in 1893. Finally, there was Dr. Charles W. Bennett, Professor of Logic and History whose aid in obtaining the Ranke Library is told in another connection. Dr. Bennett moved to Evanston in 1884 where he became an honored member of the Faculty of the Garrett Biblical Institute. A few years before his death in 1891 he wrote as follows to his old friend, Dean French: "Fourteen years of struggle at Syracuse, I found left some scars upon me. Yet we did all learn to smile." What a splendid lesson to have learned!

In this respect learning was almost equivalent to earning. Syracuse in those days could do little more for its staff of hard-working and self-sacrificing teachers. The doldrums of the 1870's were gone but no material change was to be made in stipends for several years. Meanwhile the faculty, except for those who could not be censured for having accepted better and more profitable positions at other institutions, patiently waited for whatever the future might have in store for them. And when these days did arrive, late in the administration of Chancellor Sims, they found the Chancellor more than anxious to promote their petitions for small increases. Dean French, for example, asked for an additional $300, his salary having been frozen since 1871 at $2,500. In support of this request, the Dean reminded the Board he had served as Chancellor, Dean, Registrar, Professor, Bookkeeper, and local Fiscal Agent. Dr. French received his raise; so did the others. Although salaries during the Sims administration were not as high as some wished, they did not suffer much by comparison with the stipends paid at other comparable institutions. And it is sobering to note that between 1871 and 1893 faculty salaries amounted to about one-third of each year's expenditures.

What bricks were fashioned out of this straw? A partial answer may be found in a study of the curriculum of the College of Liberal Arts. If it be true that the life-blood of an educational institution may be measured in terms of its curriculum, Syracuse has every reason to be proud of its academic offerings. No one would want to deny the existence of defects and shortcomings and Dean French would have been the first to admit that some of the courses mentioned in the yearly catalogues seldom had any elections. Chancellors, Deans, and Professors, moreover, constantly bemoaned the painful restrictions imposed upon them by poverty. The Science Departments were always petitioning for a Hall of Science. The Fine Arts instructors wanted a building of their own, while those of the Classics and Humanities prayed for the day when the Hall of Languages would be purged of strange odors and discordant dins. And standing in the midst of this discontent was the Librarian whose humble requests received scant attention. But when has academic hunger ever been satisfied? No, the record at Syracuse was good. Improvement did take place and there was nothing to be ashamed of so far as the heart and core of instruction was concerned.

In 1881, the year that introduced Dr. Sims to the campus, appropriate degrees were awarded in the Classical, Latin-Scientific, Scientific, and Civil Engineering programs, each four years in length. Candidates for admission to these sequences were required to pass written examinations in substantially the same fields as listed in the *Annual* of 1871. English grammar led this battery of tests with questions based upon Sim Kerl's *Comprehensive English Grammar* while T. P. Allen's *Handbook of Classical Geography* or J. S. Baird's *Classical Manual* furnished materials for an examination in ancient geography; modern geography in its physical and civil aspects was also tested. In history the freshman was supposed to be prepared in the growth of the United States from the time of discovery to the close of the War of 1812; in addition the first twenty-five chapters of Charles Merivale's *General History of Rome* and the first fourteen chapters of William Smith's *History of Greece* were tested. Probably students of the present day if prepared in these fields would not find these examinations too severe though they would be highly embarrassed by the requirements in other fields. In Mathematics the examination was based upon arithmetic "entire", algebra—fundamentals, rules, fractions, simple equations, elimination, involution and evolution—, the calculus of radicals as treated in Horatio N. Robinson's *New University Algebra*, and the first five books of Adr. M. Legendre's *Elements of Geometry*. Dr. J. Dorman Steele's *Fourteen Week Course in Natural Philosophy* furnished materials for an examination of human thought and conduct. In Latin it was assumed the student knew Latin grammar, four books of Caesar's *Commentaries*, Cicero's *Orations against Cataline*, Sallust's *Cataline*, six books of the *Aeneid* and Joseph H. Allen and J. B. Greenough's *Latin Composition*. The requisite amount of Roman history and of Latin prose was not to be omitted as the college courses began in each case at the point indicated. Finally, in Greek, the student was tested in Greek grammar, three books of the *Anabasis*, two books of the *Illiad*, and prosody. But having laid down these requirements and mindful of human frailties, the faculty accepted Regents' certificates for all preparatory subjects covered; otherwise the mortality of entering freshmen even for that age might have been too severe. It should also be noted that if a student had not used a specified volume, such as Legendre's, a work of equivalent value was acceptable.

During the remainder of Chancellor Sims' administration no material change took place in the entrance requirements to the Classical course. Greek history and Sallust's *Cataline* were dropped, Cicero's *Orations* were increased to six, the *Eclogues* were added, and new text books replaced those of the earlier years. In 1881 candidates for admission to the Latin-Scientific course were examined in all of the subjects required for the Classical course excepting the test in Greek; nine years later these students were asked to show proficiency in German. Students in 1881 seeking admission to the Scientific course were examined in the same subjects as required for admission to the Latin-Scientific program. It is not clear from the sources whether Regents' certificates were accepted from candidates to the non-classical courses. On the other hand advanced standing examinations were open to all and provision was made for the matriculation of special students.

The Classical course at Syracuse was similar in most respects to that pursued at other American institutions and was intended to provide a thorough training in mathematics and in the literature, language and history of the ancient world. During the Freshman year (each year was divided into three terms) students were required to take forty-nine class hours, of which thirty-seven and one half were in Algebra, Geometry, Greek and Latin; the remaining hours were in Elocution, Ancient History, Rhetoric, and Physiology. Beginning in 1882 every Freshman was asked to enroll in a one hour course in English Criticism and in Elocution for three terms; in addition a term course (three hours) in English literature was required. At the same time certain other requirements were slightly lowered though the total hours to be carried now stood at fifty-one. During the decade that followed, no change was made except for the substitution of hygiene for physiology, a redistribution of the hours between English Criticism and literature, the lightening of the load to forty-eight hours in 1886 and to forty-seven in 1891; the following year it was raised one hour. At no time were there any electives.

In the fall of 1881 sophomores were required to carry a total of forty-eight hours of which twelve included Trigonometry, Analytical Geometry, and Calculus, eight in Medieval and Modern History, ten in German, six in a non-laboratory course in Physics, six in Greek, three in Latin, and three in Elocution. The following year the total load was increased to fifty-one hours by the addition of a three hour course in English Criticism. In 1886 the faculty reduced the requirements in History and Elocution one hour each so as to provide for a two hour course in Biology. No other change in the program took place except for the addition of an extra hour in Biology in 1891; this, however, lasted but for one year thus keeping the total load as before, namely, fifty-one hours. During the entire period from the fall of 1881 to the fall of 1893 sophomores might elect a course in Surveying and beginning with the fall of 1886 an additional one hour course in Elocution.

Juniors who registered in the fall of 1881 and who were enrolled in the Classical program were required to carry throughout the year a total of forty-eight class hours of which thirty-seven were divided as follows: nine in French, five in Logic, six in Chemistry, six in Latin, four each in General Astronomy and Psychology, and three in Elocution. No change took place in this program until 1886 when the required subjects were reduced to thirty-six due to a drop in Logic from five to four hours. In 1891 the total hours were lowered to thirty-four due to a reduction in Logic to three hours and Psychology from four to three hours. The following year Logic was removed entirely thus placing the hours of required subjects at thirty-one. Since each student throughout these years was required to carry a total of forty-eight hours the difference between that and the hours of required subjects was met by free electives. Here the Junior enjoyed a wide choice covering such courses as Hebrew, Spherical and Practical Astronomy, Greek Comedy, Physics, Mechanics, Constitutional History of England, the History of the Reformation, and many others. A much wider latitude in respect to course offerings and hours was accorded the Senior who in 1881 was required to enroll for seven hours of Philosophy, three hours of Geology, two hours of Art History, five hours of Christian Evidence, three hours of Constitutional Law, five hours of English Literature, and one hour each of Esthetics and the Philosophy of History. Balancing these twenty-seven hours were twenty-one hours of electives which included among others, courses in International Law, Revolutions of the Nineteenth Century, Jurisprudence, French or Italian Literature, History of Historical Writings, and Greek Tragedy. No change in the program took place until 1891 when the total number of required course hours was reduced to twenty-one; this included four hours in Ethics, six in the History of Philosophy, five in Christian Evidence, four in English Literature, and two in Geology. The following year the load was reduced to eighteen hours which was spread between Ethics, History of Philosophy, Geology, and English Literature. The electives in 1892, from which the senior selected courses to meet the requirements of forty-five class hours, included such disciplines as Political Economy, Mineralogy, Pedagogy, Constitutional History of the United States, Physical Astronomy, and a Seminar in American History. In all probability many of these electives were offered only in response to student interest or as an individual professor might wish. To have given all of these plus the regular required subjects would have necessitated a much larger teaching staff and this the finances of the university forbade.

The reductions in required courses and hours plus a corresponding increase in free electives reflected a growing desire on the part of the faculty to widen the scope and enrich the depth of education at Syracuse. Every change, be it ever so small, was the result of careful thought and study. One has only to skim the Minutes of the Faculty to realize that snap judgments were not made. Change did take place but each change was viewed as strengthening and not weakening the core of a liberal education. The ancient and honored literature of Greece and Rome, the immortal writings of a Shakespeare, Goethe, and Hugo, together with the disciplines of Mathematics, Philosophy, and History remained sacred and inviolate. In reviewing the offerings in the College of Liberal Arts for the college year 1892-1893, one is impressed by the seriousness and completeness of the program presented in the *Annual*. English Literature, it was stated, embraced the study of England's literature from the beginnings to the present together with so much history and languages as were thought necessary for an intelligent comprehension of the subject matter. Special consideration was given to Anglo-Saxon, Early English, the writers of the age of Queen Anne, and those of the nineteenth century.

The objective of the faculty in stressing Latin was listed as being threefold. First to secure the results and training of a scientific study of the language so as to instill into the mind of the student the values Latin presented as one of the finest fields for scientific study and of cultivating the faculties of observation, classification, and judgment. Second, to acquire an appreciation of the life and aspirations of a people through a critical study of their language. Third, to instruct the student not only in the principles of the language but to train him to read understandingly that language without translating. Much of the same was said for the Greek offered at Syracuse. Nor were the Modern Languages ignored. Here emphasis was placed upon grammar, conversation, and sight reading based upon textbooks such as Joynes-Meissner's German Grammar and the writings of Racine, Bossuet, Pascal, Daudet, Sand, Lessing, Grimm, Auerbach, and Heine. Equally broad were the offerings in Mathematics which ranged through College Algebra, Geometry, Trigonometry, Calculus, Mechanics, and Land Surveying in a most thorough manner. To illustrate, the classes in Calculus stressed the differentiation of single variables, the evolution of indeterminate forms, the cubature of volumes of revolution, and the study of the properties of curves. In support of these courses in Mathematics there were also offerings in Astronomy—General, Practical, Physical, and Spectrum Analysis. Lectures and laboratory work furnished the basis upon which Theoretical, Descriptive, Qualitative, Quantitative, and Organic Chemistry rested. Volumetric Analysis and Blow-Pipe Assaying were also given. In the field of Physics consideration was given to Mathematical Physics, Molecular Physics, Hydrostatics, Acoustics, Theory of Gases, Pneumatics, and

Hydrodynamics. Electricity and Magnetism "which have assumed such importance in modern times" were offered in the Junior year and were followed in the Senior year with a laboratory course in Heat and Light. Through the generosity of Mrs. J. Dorman Steele the laboratory was "fully equipped" with standard instruments— lathes, planers and other necessary tools—for the implementation of these specialized courses.

Biology, which in 1892 was a required course in the Sophomore year, stressed General Zoology, Embryology, Comparative Anatomy and Physiology, Osteology and Histology, Bacteriology, and Botany. The opportunities and facilities for work in these fields had been materially enlarged during the year preceding and it was with evident pride the *Annual* referred to "an importation from the best European makers of twelve microscopes; a new model Reichert Microtome, two latest improved Abbe camera-lucidas; Dr. Fleischel's "hemometer" and other apparatus such as thermostats, sterilizers, skeletons, models and charts. Equally impressive were the standards set by the Philosophy Department which offered instruction in Philosophy, Ethics, Evidences of Christianity, Psychology, and Pedagogy. In these courses, especially true of Ethics, a definite attempt was made to develop an insight into the foundations of moral obligation, moral law, and conscience. Nor was it all theory as considerable attention was given to the ethical and moral problems of that age. The significance of these problems in the minds of the faculty is attested by the fact that Ethics was a required course. All of which was quite in keeping with the aims and objectives of Syracuse University. For it will be remembered that Syracuse had been founded by men who were pledged to advance the Christian and religious life of the nation. And the faculty of 1892, constantly affirming their faith by membership in the local city churches, participating in Chapel, and joining with campus religious associations, were determined to keep the University a Christian institution. And it may well have been, aside from historical antecedents, that the ideal of Christian service prompted this department to undertake a teacher training program. So many students, so the *Annual* stated, have as their "purpose to make teaching their life work."

In the Department of English, which evidently was well organized and administrated, the stress was on Rhetoric, Criticism, and Oratory. So convinced was this department of the soundness of its position that it ran a special schedule in the *Annuals*—a privilege enjoyed by no other department. Here one reads of the various courses offered, of the text-books used, of the methods employed, of the essays written and of the preparation for public speaking. "All essays and orations," we are told, "are carefully revised by noting in the margin every principle of form or style there violated. The best of the Freshman and Sopho-more essays are read in class, and the essays and orations of the Junior and Senior years are delivered in chapel. Selections are made from the Commencement orations for delivery at Commencement."

Last, but by no means least in the estimate of other Universities of that age, was the Department of History and Political Science. Proud-ly did it state that it was prepared to offer unusual facilities for both undergraduate and graduate work. The presence of the "great library of the celebrated Von Ranke" provided source material in European history of great scope and value. Nor was American history eclipsed by the importance of the European field and students at Syracuse long remembered their hours in the American History Seminar. Actually nothing in the modern sense was offered in Political Science though several courses in American Political and Constitutional History pro-vided materials for that field. On the other hand three elective courses in Political Economy were given, the writings of Francis Wayland and William S. Jevons being among the required readings.

Reviewing these offerings from another angle and contrasting them with the requirements of other institutions of higher learning throughout New York one is impressed by the importance attached to the Social Sciences at Syracuse. Particularly worth noting were the number, variety, and breadth of the work in History, Govern-ment and Economics. In the field of Mathematics, Syracuse's concen-tration—seven full terms—was probably a trifle top-heavy; Rochester and Columbia, for example, requiring but six terms. Little difference, as might be expected, existed in Philosophy and the Classics, every institution within the State insisting upon a thorough grounding in these subjects. Syracuse, however, was weak in Modern Languages and English Literature, and was below par in the natural and physical sciences. On the other hand, Syracuse gained in academic stature by reason of its courses in Anglo-Saxon, Art, and Esthetics. Finally, it should be noted that Syracuse had not turned a deaf ear to the growing demand for more electives.

To fulfill the obligations inherent within the Classical Program as well as to offer an expanding battery of free electives, the personnel of the faculty was enlarged and enriched from time to time. History, for example, subsequent to Dr. Bennett's removal to Northwestern, prospered under the masterful hand of Dr. Charles J. Little, formerly of Dickinson College. Dr. Little was graduated from the University of Pennsylvania in 1861 and during the course of the next six years served as a Methodist minister in Delaware and Pennsylvania. In 1864 he received a master's degree at the University of Pennsylvania and in 1882 a doctor's degree at Indiana University; shortly before leaving Dickinson College he was honored with the degree of Doctor of Law. History, according to Dr. Little, was a discipline that merited a study of its principles as well as its facts. During the Freshman year, therefore, the students were introduced to historical methodology, historiography, and the necessary auxiliaries of history—namely chronology, geography, genealogy, and ethnography. In the remaining three years, specialized instruction was offered in various fields of history, such as the American Revolution, French and English Government prior to 1789, the Tribal Migrations, and the French Revolution. A series of lectures on the philosophy of history was presented in the Senior year; these lectures were designed to summarize "the principles and laws" that had been discovered and illustrated during the years preceding.

In 1891, Dr. Little left for Evanston where in time he became President of the Garrett Biblical Institute of Northwestern University. His place was taken by Professor William H. Mace of Depauw University. Thanks to the leadership and national reputation of Professors Little and Mace, and to the very fortunate acquisition of the Ranke Library, specialized and intensive work in selected fields appeared among the required courses and electives. Not satisfied with this growth, Dr. Mace early in 1893 addressed a lengthy communication to the Trustees asking for the appointment of an instructor to handle course work in Political Economy. In particular, he stressed the need of instruction in Jurisprudence, Social Science, International Law, Constitutional Law, Finance, History of the Tariff "and other kindred subjects." In support of his request he called the Trustees' attention to the fact that whereas students at Syracuse could find four professors each in science and language there was but one in history. So impressed were the Trustees that a special committee was appointed to investigate and in June of the same year a recommendation favoring the appointment of such an instructor, subject to the approval of the

Executive Committee of the Board, was voted.[1]

Meanwhile, the Department of Chemistry and Physics had marched forward under the direction of Dr. John J. Brown. Starting in life as a Methodist minister, Dr. Brown served the Genesee East and West Conferences of that church. Later, he taught natural science at the Falley Institute, Fulton, New York, and in 1870 went to Cornell University as Professor of Chemistry and Industrial Mechanics. The following year he accepted an appointment as Professor of Physics and Chemistry at Syracuse University. Under his guidance instruction was given in the History of Chemistry, Chemical Philosophy, Stoichiometry and the universal elements, and Analytical and Organic Chemistry. Those interested in physics secured training in the laws of solids, liquids and gases, heat, light and sound, and electricity. Clearly, as in the case of history, the Department of Chemistry and Physics was largely a one man affair. No one was more concerned over this than Dr. Brown and constantly he kept pleading for additional assistance and equipment. In June, 1887, he addressed himself to the Trustees and asked for the privilege of being allowed to employ an assistant on the understanding the "University was not to be responsible either in whole or in part for the payment of the wages of such an assistant." The Trustees agreed to the request and it appears that Mr. Joseph T. Fischer, an instructor in Modern Languages, was engaged as an assistant by Dr. Brown. Perhaps the arrangement was not entirely satisfactory or possibly the infirmities of age were becoming too heavy, because the following year Dr. Brown asked the Chancellor to accept his resignation. Dr. Sims thoroughly appreciated the situation and with Dr. Brown's evident approval requested the Trustees to appoint the latter Professor Emeritus and that he be assigned such work in his department as might be agreed upon by the Chancellor, Dean and Dr. Brown; in addition, Dr. Brown was to remain as College pastor and the Chancellor suggested that appropriate provision be made for Dr. Brown's future.

---

1. Difficulties arose and no appointment was made until June, 1894, when Delmar E. Hawkins became a member of the History staff; he assumed this position in the fall of the same year. In 1896 Dr. Mace studied at the Universities of Jena and Berlin, receiving his doctor's degree at the latter in 1897. On his return to Syracuse he introduced the German Seminar methods. Dr. Mace became Professor Emeritus in 1916 and for a number of years aided in the development of the Mace and Lincoln Library Endowments.

The Board's response to these suggestions was somewhat of a compromise. It honestly believed the financial conditions of the University could not stand the expense of a new appointment. Accordingly, the Trustees offered to reduce Dr. Brown's teaching load and to assume the cost of his assistant. Dr. Brown accepted the situation knowing that his action entailed a lower salary, a loss which his love and devotion to the University quickly balanced. And so for the college year, 1888-1889, Dr. Brown continued in charge of his department. In January, 1889, however, the Trustees announced that in the fall Dr. Eugene E. Haanel would assume the J. Dorman Steele Professorship of Theistic Science, a step that foreshadowed the establishment of a separate department of physics. Five months later the Trustees after publicly recognizing Dr. Brown's many contributions to the University, named him Professor Emeritus and placed him on retirement at a salary of $1,300. It may be he still continued to teach chemistry since no one is so listed in the *Annual* of 1889-1890; Dr. Haanel, however, might have assumed this duty. Certainly, he did not teach in the college year 1890-1891 as the *Annual* carries the name of Ernest N. Pattee as instructor in Chemistry. During this year Dr. Brown lived at his residence, 608 University Avenue where he died in August, 1891.

His successor, Dr. Haanel was born at Breslau, Germany. Here he attended the University of the same name and here he received his doctor's degree in 1873. Meanwhile he had moved to America and had taught at Adrian, Hillsdale, and Albion Colleges in Michigan. Later he became Professor of Science at Victoria University and in 1889 came to Syracuse. Dr. Haanel remained at Syracuse until 1901 when he moved to Ottawa, Canada. In the meantime, chemistry at the university was advanced by the young and promising instructor Mr. Pattee, who had been graduated from the University of Rochester in 1886. Prior to his coming to Syracuse, Mr. Pattee had taught at Heyward Collegiate Institute, Fairfield, Illinois.

A very close friend in those days to any and all members of the faculty was Dr. W. P. Coddington who, assisted by the ever popular Dr. Frank Smalley, offered instruction in Hebrew, Greek Comedy, Classical Literature, and the Bible. Dr. Coddington was the William Penn Abbott Professor of Greek and Ethics, and Dr. Smalley was Professor of Latin Language and Literature. Meanwhile, Dr. George F. Comfort, Dean of the College of Fine Arts, and Professor John

Haddaeus specialized in Modern Languages and Literature. The latter, a German by birth, received his doctor's degree at the New York University in 1891 and came to Syracuse the following year. Dr. Haddaeus remained at Syracuse for but three years. Assisting him and Dr. Comfort were Mr. Joseph Fischer, who in 1892 matriculated at the Syracuse University Medical College, and Dr. Franklin J. Holzworth, a graduate of the College of Liberal Arts and Graduate School and who in 1891 was appointed an instructor in German Language and Literature. This latter appointment signalized the establishment of the German Department of which Dr. Holzworth became the first chairman, a post he held until his retirement in 1937; he died at his home in Syracuse in 1948.

In the field of English Language and Literature, Professor J. Scott Clark, a graduate of the College of Liberal Arts in 1877, served as instructor in Rhetoric, English Criticism and Elocution between 1882 and 1886. The senior member of this department during these years was the Chancellor, Rev. Charles N. Sims. In 1886, Professor Clark was promoted to the rank of Professor, a position he continued to occupy until Commencement in 1892 when he moved to Evanston, Illinois, to become Professor of English Language at Northwestern University. It was the author's rare privilege to have been a student of his at Northwestern, thus he can vouch for the loss Syracuse sustained in Professor Clark's withdrawal from the University. During his last years on the Hill, Professor Clark offered advanced work in the History of the English Language, Anglo-Saxon, and Early English. His place at Syracuse was not filled until the fall of 1893 when William G. Ward, one-time Professor of History at Baldwin University, Berea, Ohio and President of Spokane College, Washington, joined the faculty of the College of Liberal Arts.

Finally, reference should be made to Dean French who took time out of a busy life to offer Spherical Astronomy and Dr. Lucien W. Underwood, Syracuse '77, who was singled out by Dr. Smalley in the *Golden Jubilee* for outstanding work in the Natural Sciences. Syracuse lost Dr. Underwood in 1891 to DePauw University, his place being filled by Dr. Charles W. Hargitt, one-time Professor of Biology at Miami University. Dr. Hargitt, a graduate of Ohio University and pastor in the Methodist Church presented at Syracuse advance work in Mineralogy, Botany, and Zoology. Those who enjoyed the benefits of instruction at the hand of these two men never ceased to admire and praise them. A tablet in Dr. Hargitt's honor may be found in Lyman Hall. Others who taught in the College of Liberal Arts during the administration of Chancellor Sims were Professor Edgar A. Emens of the Classical Department and Dr. Henry Allen Peck who was instructor in Mathematics and Astronomy. Finally, reference should be made to Mr. Orator Fuller Cook who during the college year 1890-1891 was an instructor in Biology. Later Mr. Cook became President of Liberia College in Africa.

The Latin-Scientific Course was substantially the same as the Classical Program; it employed the same instructors and used the same equipment. There was, however, one fundamental difference. In this sequence two years of Latin and German, and one year of French sufficed in respect to language requirements. Greek, moreover, might be substituted for Latin in which event the course was known as the Greek-Scientific. The Scientific Course generally paralleled the Latin-Scientific though German and French were taken in lieu of Latin or Greek and a broader system of electives was permitted in the Junior and Senior years. Judged by present day standards, the Scientific Course was much more classical in nature and substance than it was scientific, an arrangement that fitted nicely into the pattern of most curriculum builders of that age. The latter were willing to yield ground but they flatly refused to surrender the entire field to their rivals who were talking about specialization and the need for professional training. Herein lies the explanation for a program that entailed instruction in Christian Evidence, Constitutional Law, and Esthetics as well as Chemistry, Astronomy, and Calculus. No one, in short, presumed to think of the degree of Bachelor of Science as being professional in nature. Holders of the science degree were viewed as cultured men and women—possibly not as cultured as those who were graduated from the Classical Program, but nonetheless, cultured.

On the other hand the course in Civil Engineering was considered as being basically professional in substance and purpose. It was designed to acquaint the student with both the theory and practice of engineering. Actually, this course was little more than an introduction to the field of engineering—there being scant difference between it and the Scientific Course during the first three years. Here and there requirements and electives might vary but it was not until the Senior year that instruction was offered in Linear Projections, Strength of Materials, Roofs, Bridges, and Road Engineering.

In all probability more intensive work would have been undertaken in Engineering had the University possessed the equipment, faculty, and student body sufficient to warrant the necessary expansion. Certainly no great encouragement could be found in a study of enrollment figures. From the day Engineering was introduced in 1878 to the close of college in 1892, when the last engineering degree was granted by the College of Liberal Arts, a total of but twenty-five students had been graduated. Engineering, like the Sciences, was limited and overshadowed by the Classics upon which greater emphasis was placed. When one recalls that Dr. Haanel was Professor of Theistic Science, that the Chemistry Department, located in the Hall of Languages, was so stinted as to be almost useless, and that most of the Liberal Arts students were prospective teachers and ministers it is not difficult to understand why the Classical sequence was favored. The Sciences and Engineering were the "poor relations" of the more dignified disciplines included within the Humanities, Languages, Arts, and History. Additional evidence of the poverty of the sciences may be gleaned from an analysis of degrees granted by the College of Liberal Arts. During the administration of Chancellor Sims, for example, 452 diplomas were issued, of which 276 were Bachelors of Arts and 110 were Bachelors of Philosophy. In contrast there were fifty-two Bachelors of Science and but fourteen Bachelors of Civil Engineering.

The Faculty of the College of Liberal Arts readily admitted the existing disparities and repeatedly expressed the hope the Trustees might see their way clear to advance the fortunes of the sciences. Among others, a science building was requested in almost every report submitted by the Chancellor to the Trustees. Nor were these hopes and expectations altogether groundless. Student enrollment, often viewed as an index of institutional growth, steadily increased and each additional student meant more income, a part of which might be allocated to the sciences. In 1881, the year Dr. Sims came to Syracuse, the combined registration in the three colleges—Liberal Arts, Medicine, and Fine Arts—was three hundred and twenty-two. Twelve years later, on the eve of Dr. Sims' resignation, there were seven hundred and sixty-three students of whom the greater number were in the Colleges of Liberal and Fine Arts, with the former holding a comfortable margin over the latter. Included within the figures for Liberal Arts, however, were one hundred and twenty-nine students who today would be classed as Graduate registrants and were one to deduct these the difference in enrollment between the two colleges would be considerably narrowed. Generally speaking, throughout the administration of Chancellor Sims the enrollment in the two colleges was relatively the same.

More striking evidence of the University's advancement was shown by the demonstrations of loyalty and liberality on the part of alumni and friends. By 1881, the "Museum" of the Natural Sciences was receiving a steady flow of gifts from interested persons. Three years later, Bulletin Number One of the Biological Laboratory made its appearance. At the same time, 1884, the Natural Sciences were materially strengthened by the addition of the "Underwood Herbarium" and the "Banks Collection of Birds." A few years thereafter, Mrs. J. Dorman Steele endowed a chair in Physics and in 1893 the Board of Trustees voted increased appropriations for all the sciences. Meanwhile, the class rooms of the Classical Department were adorned with paintings, books, busts, and statues, and the College of Fine Arts received the valuable Woolf Collection of Engravings from Mrs. Harriet Leavenworth of Syracuse. The College of Medicine was also favored with the gift of a magnificent anatomical and physiological apparatus once the property of Dr. J. M. Wieting. Nor were the patronizing conferences tardy in bringing gifts: the Northern New York Conference, for example, pledged and ultimately raised thirty thousand dollars to endow the Gardner Baker Professorship. Numerous smaller sums were also received for other purposes. The Honorable Nathan F. Graves of Syracuse, to illustrate, presented ten thousand dollars in late 1892 for the founding of permanent Lectureship on Missions.

Equally impressive were the gifts ear-marked for endowment. The importance of the latter was not overlooked by Dr. Sims and from the day he threw his life and fortune into the University and its future he stressed the need for increased endowment. In his first message to the Board of Trustees he expressed himself in this manner: "In my judgment the time has come when the expense of the University should be placed where the current incomes and special contributions for current expenses should be made to cover all appropriations and that not a dollar of additional debt should be incurred, not a dollar of accumulated funds be applied to the current deficiency . . . . I would therefore recommend that the latter be carefully and absolutely reserved for paying mortgage indebtedness and for endowment." The wisdom and soundness of this advice was not lost upon the Trustees who at once adopted it as a plan for future action. And well they might in the light of what they heard from Rev. E. C. Curtis, the University's fiscal agent. His remarks are so significant they deserve direct quotation:

> At the last annual meeting of the Board . . . we had a floating debt of $31,651.00 which was provided for during the early part of the college year by converting . . . assets into cash and from new subscriptions secured for that object. That enabled me to pay up the Professors in full and thus release them from paying interest to the banks and your humble servant from the unenviable reputation of floating the University by the shining process, to say nothing of the time consumed thereby and the frequent difficulty of turning short corners in times of doubt and uncertainty as to the solvency of men or institutions. You will also discover that we have used up of available assets during the year over and above our regular income and from special subscriptions received for meeting current expenses $13,320.00.

A total, therefore, of $44,979.00 had been lifted from permanent funds and special gifts to meet expenses for the college year closing June, 1881. The assets of the University amounted to $552,274.00 against which there were mortgages of $141,077.00. Moreover of the total assets, $300,000 represented the estimated value of the University site, the Hall of Languages, the library, apparatus and other smaller items. Productive assets included the University Block, certain city lots and land in Iowa, Wisconsin, and various holdings in New York. The greater share, however, of these productive assets consisted of personal notes and obligations some of which, like the Alumni Subscription of $5,000, were of questionable value. Financially speaking the college year had not been a happy one. Nor was the blow softened by the knowledge of an indebtedness of nearly $173,000. But what of the immediate future? In answer to this query, Agent Curtis estimated total expenses for 1881-1882 at $41,000 of which the largest single item was $30,000 for salaries. Income he believed might equal $17,700 of which $13,400 might be expected from tuition and fees, $3,000 from the University Block, $1,200 from interest, and *$100 from campus grass* leaving a probable deficit of $23,000.

To wipe out these annual deficits, to stop periodic raids upon permanent funds, and to increase endowment became the primary objective of Chancellor Sims. How well he rendered his stewardship may be seen from the records of the Board of Trustees. Especially of interest is the fiscal statement made in June, 1893. Here one reads that the property of the University had a net value of $1,768,000 of which the chief items were University real estate, $1,052,000; stocks and bonds, $323,958; museums, library, and apparatus, $189,250; notes, pledges, bequests and subscriptions from neighboring conferences, $155,300; and land and city lots, chiefly in Syracuse, $100,000. Liabilities consisted of $77,600 of which a mortgage of $68,600 on the campus was the largest item. Total income for the year amounted to $94,646.48 against which there were expenditures equalling $87,870.64, leaving a balance of $6,775.84.

In commenting upon his chancellorship Dr. Sims said:

> At the time I entered upon my duties as Chancellor the University was employing two financial agents at a cost of $4,000 per year. One immediately retired . . . and the other ceased his connection with it about two years later, since this time the entire work of raising funds has fallen upon me in addition to my other duties . . . I have received more than 2,500 cash subscriptions, aggregating more than $600,000 besides the gifts which have come to us in buildings and equipment. The net increase of assets has been about $1,200,000 or $100,000 per year, in addition to the amounts raised for deficiencies ranging from $5,000 to $22,000 a year. Since I have been in charge more than $100,000 have been fully met.

Of course the record was not perfect but the overall picture was satisfactory. Significant as it was, and without the work of Dr. Sims the fortunes of the young university might well have been endangered, what cheered the hearts of all had been the inception and completion of a long awaited building program.

First in order of construction was the Charles Demarest Holden Observatory. Interest in astronomy had existed at Syracuse from the day of its foundation. Acting Chancellor Steele did all that was humanly possible to promote this interest but found himself frustrated at every turn by the absence of a telescope, the acquisition of which he rated as an "imperative necessity." Commendable as was the aspiration there was not the slightest chance of realizing the same so long as funds were lacking even for the bare essentials. And so the matter rested until 1884. In that year, Chancellor Sims, ever on the alert for everything and anything that might advance the fortunes of the University, informed the Trustees he had at length located a telescope he hoped the Board would purchase immediately. Precisely what happened is not clear. Evidently some difficulty arose since the telescope in question never appeared. Meanwhile, Dr. Sims was quietly cultivating the friendship of one of the most loyal Trustees the University has ever had, Erastus F. Holden, a prominent merchant and citizen of Syracuse. Late in the fall of 1886, Thanksgiving Day to be exact, Mr. Holden informed the Chancellor of his willingness to build and equip an observatory. Delighted beyond measure, Dr. Sims hastened to lay the matter before the winter meeting of the Board which lost no time in accepting the gift and instructing the faculty of the University to determine an appropriate site for the proposed building.

Acting upon the advice of the Chancellor, the faculty designated the south side of the hill directly to the west of the Hall of Languages, and as soon as weather permitted the masons and contractors were at work. By June, 1887, the building was all but completed. Summer witnessed the final touches and at the opening of college in the fall the student body, having been told of its benefactor, made the Chapel ring with cheers and songs one of which, "Here's to E. F. Holden, drink her down" must have seemed out of place to some. Meanwhile, Dr. Simon Newcomb of Washington, D. C., had accepted an invitation to speak at the dedication ceremonies scheduled for November 18th. Classes were suspended that day and most of the students joined with the faculty and selected friends from the city in attending the exercises. Dr. Newcomb's address, "The Place of Astronomy in the Sciences," was delivered, so we are informed, with telling effect and the audience was most attentive as Dr. Sims outlined the history of the gift. Whereupon a mighty round of applause followed which touched Dr. Holden to the quick, particularly since the observatory had been given in memory of his son. The Charles Demarest Holden Observatory was built of rock-faced gray limestone and was equipped with an eight inch Alvin Clark telescope, a three inch reversible transit, a comet seeker, a chronograph, and a chronometer. Later, a German made clock and a choice library was added.

Holden's magnificent gift, and it was magnificent for that day, was more than matched by the generosity of Dr. J. W. Reid, onetime President of Genesee College and now a faithful Trustee of the University, and the Honorable John Crouse, merchant and banker of Syracuse. Both of these gentlemen received a warm ovation from an enthusiastic student body in early October, 1887, when their names were coupled with that of Mr. Holden's as donors and friends of the University. Mr. Crouse's contribution came in the form of the Crouse College Building, a structure local critics affirmed was unsurpassed by any other college edifice in America. Nationally, the building attracted attention especially since it reflected the growing confidence in the future of Syracuse University. Dr. Reid's gift consisted of the celebrated and priceless library of the great German historian, Leopold Ranke. The acquisition of this internationally known collection did much to heighten the prestige and standing of the University throughout the American academic world. The acceptance of this gift necessitated the construction of a University Library Building, now used for administrative purposes. Both of these edifices, the story of which is told elsewhere, were formally dedicated in 1889 approximately two years before the erection of the University Gymnasium. Steady and ever mounting interest in athletics, plus a desire for the presence of a Christian center on the campus paved the way for a drive that culminated in the erection of a gymnasium, now known as the Women's Gymnasium, concerning which comment appears in a subsequent chapter.

The construction of these various buildings coincided with a campaign to improve and beautify the campus. In June, 1887, Mr. John D. Archbold indicated a growing interest in the University by meeting the expense incident to the grading of the campus in the vicinity of the Hall of Languages. Particularly significant were the stately trees that were placed in front of the building and the leveling of the area to the rear and east for an athletic field. Later, Mr. Archbold materially improved the latter and converted it into what became known as the Oval. Again, in 1889, Mr. William B. Smith of Syracuse came forward with a gift which together with other funds made possible additional improvement. All of the roads on the campus were graded and cindered, the gutters being filled with boulders. A terraced road, climbing the steep grade in front of the Crouse College Building, circled to the west of that structure, came out in the vicinity of the Observatory, and thence descended to a road that went by the Ranke Library. Ten thousand cubic yards of earth, moreover, were taken from the area in front of the Hall of Languages and deposited before and around the Library. The removal of this dirt, however, left the main entrance to the Hall of Languages in mid-air. A series of extra steps, therefore, were constructed and a stone walk was laid from the Hall to University Place. Meanwhile in 1887 the center tower of the Hall was erected.

Finally, the University Block on West Washington Street was renovated and improved in the spring of 1882. All of the stores on the street floor were enlarged and those portions above, once occupied by the St. Charles Hotel, were converted into offices. The old section that had been used by a printing establishment was torn down and a new building erected in its place. An elevator, moreover, was installed. Although these much needed improvements greatly enhanced the productive income of the Block, the Board was quite aware that sooner or later the entire structure would have to be replaced by a new building if the University intended to retain permanent ownership. During 1887 some thought was given to the matter and for a time there was talk of selling the Block. A price of $150,000 was placed upon the property, but no one seemed interested and the Board was left to struggle with a problem that was only partially solved in 1898 when the present University Block was erected.

Viewing the entire situation, however, Chancellor Sims had reason for feeling satisfied with the gains made since his coming to Syracuse. The hay field had become a campus dotted with four new buildings and alive with a student body that had more than doubled since 1881. Crowning all was a corps of teachers whose loyalty to the University and whose academic vision had never been found wanting. But none of these advances could have been made without an increase in income. And here it was the alumni and friends of the University rallied in splendid fashion. The total assets of the University in 1881 were slightly over half a million dollars; twelve years later the figure stood at over a million and seven hundred thousand dollars. In both years, the picture would have been brighter but for unfortunate mortgages on the University Block and Campus property, though these obligations had been cut in half during the administration of Chancellor Sims. On the other hand investments in Western Lands had boomeranged and the annual income from tuition and productive investments, though on the increase, seldom met current expenses. And it fell to the lot of the Trustees to balance accounts by personal contributions at the annual meetings. Had the University elected to mark time there would have been no question about balancing the budget. Such a policy was never followed. Both the Trustees and the Chancellor had faith in Syracuse and saw release from financial worries only through greater efforts and reasonable increases in expenditures. It was a gamble for many long and uncertain years. But who, on reviewing the evidence, will doubt the wisdom of having marched forward?

Tradition has woven a garland about Chancellor Sims that is as fresh today as when first conceived. One has only to chat with the rapidly thinning generation of his age to realize the love and admir-

ation his numerous friends had for him. Nor may one rise from a
reading of official University records, not to mention newspapers and
other contemporary sources, without the firm conviction that Dr.
Sims was a great chancellor. At no time did he harbor any illusions or
misgivings as to what his duties entailed. Academic considerations he
would not and did not ignore, but greater stress and energy were always bestowed upon the herculean task of providing the sinews for
the University he loved so well. Writing to Dr. French, shortly after
having accepted the chancellorship, Dr. Sims laid down two premises
upon which he believed the future of the University was predicated.
First and foremost there should be a separate fund earmarked solely
for endowment purposes, not a penny of which was to be spent for
current deficits. Heretofore, both principal and interest had been
used; in the future the principal was to be held inviolate. Second,
every friend of the University should give to its upkeep and having
given once, should give again and again. And it is gratifying to note
that the Chancellor counted himself as a friend of the University.

Today there are four buildings—Administration, Observatory,
Crouse and the Women's Gymnasium—that reflect to the credit of
Dr. Sims and to the generosity of the donors. The names of the latter
are written large in the books of the University Treasurer. Other individuals also are mentioned for having established a professorship or
for having presented to the University a choice painting, a collection
of rare fossils, or a priceless series of engravings. But no reference is
made, nor could it from the very nature of things, of the countless
others who gave so much as a widow's mite. For in his numerous and
repeated journeys throughout New York Methodism, Dr. Sims not
only made friends in the counting houses and market places but also
in the homes of the small shop-keepers, the humble wage-earners and
farmers. Year after year the stout hearted Chancellor travelled over
the lanes and back roads of New York in search of a dollar here and a
dollar there. Bit by bit these collections grew in size and all but measure the difference between life and death for the University. To say
that without Chancellor Sims' untiring efforts the auctioneer's hammer might have resounded over Mount Olympus, would amount to a
blushing exaggeration. At the same time it is a solemn thing to remember that Dr. Sims' efforts were "expendable."

After his retirement from the Chancellorship in 1893, Dr. Sims
moved to Indianapolis where for five years he served most success-

fully as pastor of the Meridan Street Methodist Church. Syracuse, however, never forgot him and in 1898 he was translated to the First Methodist Church in Syracuse and in 1903 became a Trustee of the University. After a few years of brilliant service, he retired from public life and returned to his old home in Indiana where he died in March, 1908. Syracuse honored its departed friend and Chancellor with fitting and appropriate services. "Syracuse University," so Dr. Frank Smalley wrote at a later date, "is great today because Chancellor Sims literally lived in a carpetbag. His trips around the country netted hundreds of dollars at a time that funds were imperative if Syracuse was to become a great institution. The University today is the fruit of Chancellor Sims' great loyalty, his great love for this institution. Chancellor Sims is one of the greatest men in Syracuse's history."

The Ranke Library

6 Most Syracuse alumni have long since forgotten the
national acclaim received by the University more than half
a century ago when it acquired the splendid library of one of the
world's most distinguished historians, Leopold von Ranke. The American Historical Association had proclaimed Ranke the "greatest living
historian," and elected him its only honorary member; American
historians who had gone to Germany to study under him were especially intrigued by the thought that the master's books were to
come to the new world. Stories about the library were so fanciful
that Chancellor Sims may be pardoned for the exaggeration with
which he told the Trustees of Syracuse University in 1887 that
Ranke's books were "the richest collection of historical material in the
world" with "fully fifty thousand bound volumes, besides many
thousands of pamphlets and manuscripts, the latter of inestimable
value." As a matter of fact, the books were still in Berlin, and Syracuse had not as yet the opportunity to evaluate its new treasure. Not
even Ranke had known what was in his library, for the books were
crammed in double rows from floor to ceiling throughout the second
story apartment which he rented for more than forty years. Many of
these volumes had been purchased during his extensive travels and re-

search, but if the impression of one of his secretaries is correct most
of the latter acquisitions were gifts. A catalogue kept at first was soon
outgrown and the confusion of the library became so great that even
Ranke had to confess his inability to cope with it. On one occasion
an ambitious visiting scholar spent *several days* in an energetic but
vain effort to find a certain work—one which numbered no less than
twenty-nine volumes!

Germany has not forgotten the Ranke Library. A German scholar
named Bernard Hoeft, who came to Syracuse to examine the collection, published in 1937 an interesting and painstaking study in which
he tried to answer the plaintive question: How could the Fatherland
possibly have lost the library of its great historian? Ranke had not
provided in his will for the disposition of his books, but he appears to
have made two things clear to his children who were his heirs: he
wanted the Prussian state to have the first opportunity to purchase the
books, and he did not want the library broken into fragments and
scattered. With these conditions in mind, his son Otto opened negotiations with the Prussian authorities in June, 1886, prodding them
along with the warning that already he had received an offer from
America.

But the Prussian officials were not to be rushed, even though the
Kaiser signified his desire that the library be acquired by the state.
The General Director of the Royal Library, Dr. Wilmanns, arranged
for a Berlin book dealer named Weber to catalogue the books and
estimate their value. Otto hoped to receive about $23,800 (100,000
marks), but Weber, after a detailed examination, concluded the books
would be worth only $3,800 in his business, though he would pay an
additional $350 because of the prestige of Ranke's name. The value
of the library, he wrote, was diminished by several facts: numerous
of the most important works had missing volumes; the books were
often either reprints or not the best available editions; and many of
the older secondary works had been supplemented by more up-to-
date volumes.

Despite Weber's discouraging report, Dr. Wilmanns recommended
that the state offer the Ranke heirs nearly $7,400 but on the impor-
tant condition that the library be broken up and distributed among
the royal and university libraries. This was a long way from the demand of the heirs. After further negotiations Otto reduced his price
to $11,900, an offer which met a varied reception. The Minister of

Public Worship and Instruction recommended that the state pay the sum demanded even though it was high. To support this view he asked for the report of another member of the Royal Library staff who emphasized the position of Ranke as a "national German intellectual hero;" the departure of the library from the homeland, he declared, would arouse widespread disapproval and regret. But such a sentimental argument made no headway against the realism of the Minister of Finance, who answered bluntly that the library was not worth $11,000, a fact which easily could be made clear to the public. Otto was informed at the end of March, 1887, that the state would not make the purchase.

It was Professor Charles Wesley Bennett who negotiated the purchase of Ranke's books for Syracuse University, a plan he had dreamed of for twelve years. As the first Professor of History and Logic in the new and struggling college, he had been acutely conscious of the tremendous need for adequate library facilities. The books of Genesee College had not been removed to Syracuse, and though a portion of the library of the Geneva Medical Department was brought in, it was kept separately in the Medical College. Nor were friends to be found like those who had just helped the neighboring Cornell University Library off to a good start. Something had to be done. So the Trustees provided a meager appropriation of $1,000 for the purchase of "library and text books," some of which arrived before the college first opened its doors in September, 1871. Further essentials had been provided by the appropriation of about $2,500 more by June, 1874, but the distressing poverty of the library is clearly revealed in the bare and cold figures in the annual financial reports to the Board of Trustees. The Panic of 1873 was a terrible blow but is not enough to explain the fact that for twelve of the next fifteen years the average annual expenditure for books and incidentals was the astonishingly low sum of $26.13. Only this poverty can explain such things as the library's loss of "complete files of the New York daily papers" for the Civil War and Reconstruction period. An alumnus had loaned these valuable files to the University with the hope that they might ultimately be purchased but when Syracuse failed to buy he sold them to Harvard University at a "handsome price."

University officials realized and occasionally called attention to this deplorable situation, but with annual deficits and salaries frequently unpaid they were naturally far more concerned with the immediate problem of keeping the University running from month to month. Vice-President Steele in the summer of 1872 made an appeal for a $25,000 library endowment fund and suggested "more deliberate efforts to secure donations from private libraries." But it was to be many years before such an endowment was created, and the donations from friends were mostly, as Bennett declared, "the lumber and refuse material of their private libraries."

When the librarianship was added to Professor Bennett's duties in 1875, he estimated the size of the library to be no more than 2,300 volumes. But a very bright spot in this dark story was about to appear —a godfather with money—in the person of Dr. John Morrison Reid, a former president of Genesee College. Since Dr. Reid wanted his role as benefactor kept secret, the details of his gifts are difficult to discover. From the correspondence of Chancellor Winchell it appears that as early as 1872 Bennett had found in Dr. Reid the man to "father" the "coveted" library by a contribution of $5,000. No immediate action followed, but in March, 1874, the former Vice-President of the University, Dr. Steele, told the Trustees he had received an offer of $6,000 "from a friend" to purchase a library in Germany; negotiations for this library, he reported, had failed but he expressed his "confident expectations" that such a purchase would be made in the future. The "friend" of this offer seems likely to have been Dr. Reid. If these conclusions are correct, Bennett's own version of the gift, written in 1889, is misleading. When the Reids were his guests early in 1875, he wrote, they asked the question: "What is the most pressing need of the university aside from general endowment?" Bennett answered, "an increase in the library," and soon received about $5,000 with which he was to visit Europe and buy books. He spent that summer in the book marts of Edinburgh, London, Amsterdam, Brussels, Berlin, Leipzig, and Paris, where he purchased 4,500 volumes covering a wide range of subject matter.

During the 1875 purchasing tour, Bennett learned that Ranke's great library might someday be sold. Since he was among the American historians who once had been pupils of Ranke, he found the news especially interesting. When he returned to America, he suggested that Syracuse University ought to have the library when Ranke died, a proposal to which Dr. Reid gave an encouraging response. Through two Berlin book dealers Bennett watched the development of the collection, learning that its price nearly trebled in the next ten years.

Bennett did not forget the Ranke books when he left Syracuse in 1884 to join the faculty of the Garrett Biblical Institute in Evanston, Illinois. Two years later, when news came of Ranke's death, he was on the verge of leaving the country to spend the summer doing research work in England. He went at once to Dr. Reid who told him to investigate the situation fully. In London, Bennett wrote to his Berlin agents but was informed that nothing could be done in less than six months. Impatient, and fearing the competition of several other American colleges, he telegraphed Otto von Ranke for a personal interview. According to Bennett, he saw Otto on July 2, 1886, and promised if Syracuse could have the collection it would be "safely housed as an entirety in a room built especially for the purpose," and would "be known forever as the Ranke Library." Otto received him cordially but expressed the confident belief the Prussian government was going to make the purchase. However, as a friendly gesture, he promised Bennett the chance to buy if the state did not, though Bennett learned later that Otto had no thought of such an eventuality.

In September, Bennett returned to America. Naturally impatient at the long delay in Berlin, he and Dr. Reid notified Otto in March, 1887, that their offer would be withdrawn unless a decision were made within two weeks. When Otto's final plea to the Prussian authorities brought a definite negative answer, he notified Bennett's Berlin agents that he was ready to sell, and the transaction was soon completed. The books were then carefully examined, worn and damaged volumes were repaired, efforts were made to complete imperfect serials and to classify and catalogue the collection, and a professional paleographer was employed to evaluate the 400 manuscripts. Syracusans soon learned the welcome news, although it was to be nearly a year before the books arrived.

The purchase price of the Ranke Library remains a mystery. No official records tell the story. According to Otto, Bennett had said Syracuse would pay a sum surpassing any European offer; it was Otto's understanding that this sum would be $23,800 (100,000 marks). Moreover, Syracuse University, in its financial report of 1888, listed the value of the collection at $25,000. But neither of these figures is conclusive evidence. Some unsubstantiated newspaper reports have put the purchase price around $10,000; unfortunately the flagrant inaccuracies of the local press in reporting on the Ranke Library undermine confidence in this figure. It is true that Otto cut his price in half as an inducement to the Prussian government, but there is no evidence that Syracuse got the benefit of the same reduction.

The secret of the purchase price was better kept than the identity of the donor. In October, 1887, a city newspaper stated upon the authority of a "Member of the Faculty" that Dr. Reid had bought the books; whereupon the Chancellor called the Liberal Arts Faculty together and got its authorization "to publish the fact that no member of the Faculty had ever authorized such a statement." Five men, he told the press, had been accused of the gift, but only two men beside himself knew who the donor was. Evidently, however, the revelation was too authentic to be denied, for eight days later it was confirmed by the *University Herald*.

Ranke's books, along with his massive desk, chair, life-size portrait, and other incidentals were shipped across the ocean on the steamer *Galileo* in eighty-three boxes weighing more than nineteen tons. Arriving in Syracuse, in March, 1888, they were simply stored in the basement of the Hall of Languages for still another year, pending the construction of a new home for the library. For Dr. Reid had made the gift on condition the University erect a fire proof building for the books.

Like most colleges of that day, Syracuse did not have a separate library building. The small number of volumes used by the forty-one students of 1871 had been kept in the Myers Block building down town, in which two rooms were set aside for the library and reading room. When the University moved into the new Hall of Languages in the spring of 1873 the books were placed in the central room (207) on the main floor. Here they remained for the next sixteen years until pleas for a new library began to be heard. One student, obviously without much appreciation of financial realities, suggested in a campus paper, *The Syracusan*, that an outstanding library building could be constructed for $250,000.

The issue was forced by Dr. Reid's demand for a new building to house the Ranke collection. Plans were begun during the 1887 Commencement ceremonies when, incidentally, Bennett was rewarded with the degree of Doctor of Laws. A Library Building Committee and a new Library Committee were created; to the latter Dr. Reid was added by special motion, a fact suggesting his role as benefactor was already known. Chancellor Sims, Dr. Reid, and Architect Archimedes Russell, one-time Professor in the College of Fine Arts, visited and examined numerous other libraries while the building was being designed. Sometime later Reid told the students in Chapel he had seen nothing in all his travels that came as close as the new Syracuse library to meeting his ideal of architectural beauty. Meanwhile, the Trustees began the difficult task of raising the necessary money by soliciting individual contributions. Occasional public reports showed how slow was their progress. Of the $40,000 estimated to be the total cost, only $12,000 had been raised by the beginning of 1888, so the Trustees voted to borrow the money, if necessary, in order to complete the building within the time limit set by the donor. For the date specified by Dr. Reid was November 1, 1888. Not even the arrival of the books in March seems to have helped, for the Chancellor reported at the June Commencement that only $16,000 had been pledged. To stimulate local interest some citizens of Syracuse were added to a reorganized Library Building Committee, and the laying of the cornerstone was publicized in a formal ceremony on June 25th.

Still another year was to pass before the building was completed and formally dedicated on June 24, 1889. The work of preparing the formal opening was in the hands of a new librarian who, unlike his predecessors, was not to be hampered by any other duties than the management of the library. At their January meeting the Trustees had elected to this position the "oldest member of the senior class" (he was 40), Henry Orrin Sibley, who was described in a student paper as a "phenomenal linguist." His linguistic facility must have pleased the Trustees, for they had specified that the new appointee, who incidentally was to be paid $800 a year, "should be able to read Latin, Greek, German, French and if possible, Hebrew." Though Sibley's term and salary were not supposed to begin until the following September, he went to work in March and April, with the help of other students, to remove the books from their storage place in the basement of the Hall of Languages. Dr. Reid had written him a few general comments on the contents of the eighty-three boxes, suggesting he first open Box 83 in which he would find the "catalogue in four paper boxes." Before Sibley had completed the last removals to the new building on May 6th, he realized the unhappy fact that the size of the library had been greatly exaggerated. *The Syracusan* reported the removal of about 17,000 "books and packages" totalling "about 20,000 volumes." Sibley now tried to cover up the disappointment by emphasizing the fine quality rather than the great quantity of the books. Reid wrote he had never dreamed that "the representatives of our agents and Dr. Bennett" were so wide of the mark, although he admitted he had "calculated the cubic feet" when the boxes arrived from Germany and had realized there could not be 50,000 volumes. Three weeks later he again expressed his distress, declaring he "would begin a grand disturbance at once in Germany," if he were sure Sibley was not mistaken. After a few months, however, he evidently reconciled himself to the truth, for he wrote that even though "those old Germans shaved me . . . the University has been the gainer and I don't mourn."

At the dedication ceremony on the occasion of the 1889 Commencement, Dr. Bennett was invited to come from Evanston to tell the story of his purchase of the Ranke Library. Illness prevented his attendance, but his manuscript was read by the Syracuse Professor of History, Charles J. Little, who also paid a short tribute to the donor's princely generosity and "golden silence." The annual financial report to the Trustees revealed that the new building cost $34,850.88, and was more than paid for by sixty-nine contributors totalling $35,028.62. Chief among the contributors was another great benefactor of Syracuse University, John D. Archbold, who gave $12,500. The seven other Trustees who had the fortune, good or bad, to be appointed to the Library Building Committee contributed another $8,200. Chancellor Sims, it is interesting to note, added $1,250 to the total, while Dr. Reid, with $100, was among sixty others whose contributions were as low as five dollars.

Later enlarged by the addition of a west wing along the front, the resulting building today serves as the headquarters of the University administration; for in 1907 the books were moved into their fourth and present home, the Carnegie Library Building on the south side of the campus oval.

With a large and valuable collection of books and a new building in which to house them, Syracuse University could indeed be proud. The logical complement to these two assets was soon forthcoming—a permanent library endowment fund for the continuous purchase of books in the future. Again it was the "godfather," Reid, who was the benefactor. Two separate gifts of $50,000 each, again anonymous, were made on annuity—that is, Dr. and Mrs. Reid were paid six per cent on the gifts until their death, at which time the money became without qualification the property of Syracuse University.

Some criticism of the Ranke purchase was heard because most of the books were written in foreign languages—twenty-two languages in all—thereby limiting their usefulness to students. It was his consciousness of this criticism that led Dr. Bennett to appeal to the teaching staff: "If the professors are continuously drinking at the living fountains of knowledge, the student himself will have a corresponding freshness of thought and purpose." Certainly the professors of history have found the collection full of treasures. The sixteenth, seventeenth, and eighteenth centuries were best represented with German, Italian, and French history foremost. Probably one of the most valuable parts of the collection for purposes of historical research was the remarkable number of original pamphlets printed in France during the early seventeenth century and during the French Revolution. But the most valuable "manuscripts" in the library turned out to be copies made for Ranke rather than originals, though of the latter there are many. Finally, in addition to the strictly historical works, Ranke's books included the Greek and Roman classics, medieval and early modern theology and philosophy, and modern literature.

The acquisition of the Ranke Library seems to have brought about an influx of gifts from other sources too, for the official report of 1893 credited the library with 42,356 volumes and 9,705 pamphlets. Aside from the Ranke collection and the 4,500 books purchased during Bennett's 1875 European tour, the library of 1893 was made up mostly of gifts, some large and some small. It is true that Chancellor Winchell had bought a few items in Europe, and a small number had been bought with money appropriated by the Trustees, but most of the rest came from different friends and alumni. Many documents were contributed by government officials until 1878 when the University became an official depository for copies of all United States government documents. Some valuable books also came from private libraries; the Reids, for example, must have given several thousand volumes of their own. Many of these donations are mentioned either in the Trustees' Minutes or in the student papers, though usually only the number of volumes and the name of the donor is listed. Rarely does one find a record of what the books were—almost the only such case is the Librarian's report to the Chancellor for 1877 which is scarcely worth mentioning because the title of the book is seldom given unless the donor gave but one book. In other cases only the number of volumes is stated or, perhaps, the volumes are collectively classified as "standard works," "sacred poetry," or "from the library of" the donor. Unfortunately many of these early Librarian's Reports are missing, a fact which further limits our knowledge. Doubtless the library staff was too small to keep adequate records. Certain manuscripts of Dr. Sibley, largely personal in nature, add little to the information gleaned from more official sources.

Not only was the library organization inadequate but the system of rules left much to be desired. The old ideas of library administration emphasized rigid regulations to protect the books, rather than liberal rules to encourage their use. A student editorialist wrote in the *University Herald* in 1888 that if the present policy continued, "we shall expect to see a high wall around it [the library], mounted with well manned guns, and uniformed sentinels stationed at short intervals to give warning of the approach of any deluded mortal who still clings to the old idea that libraries are to be *used* and not simply *kept*." This rigid policy originated under the supervision of John P. Griffin, who served as librarian, and also registrar, until 1875, though it was the faculty which was responsible for the rules. The system they set in September, 1871, prevented students from taking periodicals from the library or reading room at any time; moreover, only the librarian was permitted to remove books from the shelves. Naturally irritated at such restrictions the students found still further reason for complaint in the limited hours. For the library was to be open less than three hours a day (8 to 8:30 a.m. and 2 to 4 p.m.) and the reading room less than six hours (8 to 12 a.m., except during Chapel, and 2 to 4 p.m.). The moving of the library to the Hall of Languages brought only a slight change in this system; the hours for both library and reading room being set from 9 a.m. to 1 p.m. Students, often in class during these hours, continued to protest. One student also objected to the poor seating facilities: "Are the authorities aware that even in a 'mixed college' twenty-five chairs can accommodate but few more than twenty-five students . . . ?"

Student gibes brought some results; at least the library hours were lengthened in January, 1874, three afternoon hours (2 to 5 p.m.) being added to the morning schedule. Agitation for withdrawal of books was to be unsuccessful for many years. Probably a little too tactless was the suggestion of one student that the regulation prohibiting withdrawals ought to be changed because there were from twenty-five to fifty volumes constantly missing in spite of the law. One complained that even the high school library on West Genesee Street was much "more desirable to use" because it had better hours and allowed withdrawals.

No fundamental changes were brought about by the advent of Dr. Bennett as librarian in 1875 though some minor improvements were attempted. In answer to student complaints, the new librarian began a better system of cataloguing to facilitate use of the books, and the library staff was increased by part-time employment of some men students. The periodical room also benefited from Bennett's efforts: he made a proposal that each alumnus contribute one periodical to the reading room along with money to bind it. Rev. M. J. Wells of the Class of 1875 had already offered to pay for the binding of the accumulation of past periodicals. Perhaps these improvements were in part responsible for the fact that use of the library more than doubled.

Apparently the students were really interested in the periodicals. At least they were inspired to make several suggestions when some of the papers and magazines were discontinued. One student proposed a donation from each graduating class, another suggested a ten cent a month payment, and still another proposed the raising of funds by admission charges on special lectures. However, no action resulted from these ideas, nor was the administration stimulated to increase the periodical offerings. The Senior Class of 1881, it seems, did set a precedent for future classes by making its class gift in the form of money to purchase books on American poetry.

It is not surprising if Dr. Bennett, busy with his duties as Professor of History and Logic, was unable to keep order in the reading room. If the complaints of one student in the *University Herald* be correct, things were pretty bad at times. When the librarian was busy elsewhere, students invaded the forbidden wire "cage" where the books were kept; periodicals and newspapers were not returned to their proper places; and upperclassmen dumped their coats in the crowded reading room. Even worse, there was too much "vociferous soliloquy, boisterous conversation, or gymnastic creation," such as clearing two tables at a single bound, mimicking the cry of a savage. The conduct of the gentlemen seems to have upset at least some of the ladies, one of whom protested that the men crowded them from the tables and even stared at them! Another complained that every morning after Chapel, the gentlemen were admitted to the library at once, while the ladies had to stand out in the hall exposed to "frightful din" or even take refuge in the dressing room until the door on their side was opened.

When Bennett left the University in 1884, an informal ballot in the Liberal Arts Faculty elected Dr. W. P. Coddington (six votes), over Professor Frank Smalley (one vote) as librarian. Early the next year, the faculty again took up the question of liberalizing the rules, but voted to maintain its rigid policy. Little record exists of Coddington's activities as librarian; presumably his work was overshadowed by the great achievement of Reid and Bennett in bringing the Ranke books to Syracuse.

Not even the advent of the first man to spend his whole time at the task of library supervision brought about a break in the iron clad rules. Henry O. Sibley, who entered the position when the Ranke collection was brought into the new building, worked in close co-operation with Dr. Reid, who became a leading member of the Trustees' Library Committee. New recommendations of this committee, as reported by Dr. Reid, provided first, no book could be taken out of the library; second, only library officials could enter the library alcoves; third, books might be used by faculty and students, and other persons who got the consent of the Library Committee and paid an annual fee of five dollars. In the spring of 1890 the faculty profited from the establishment of a "consulting room" to which each faculty member could take as many as twelve books at one time from the stacks. The students, who still received no concessions, kept up a running fire of protest until their first great gain came at the beginning of 1894, when they were permitted to take out one book overnight at 5 p.m., if they first obtained a written order from the professor in charge of the work for which the book was desired. This entering wedge soon led to the breakdown of the old rules and the great transition to a circulating library which came in 1895 during Chancellor Day's administration.

"I hope to have a great library and a great librarian, and I want to help all I can toward it." Thus did Dr. Reid sound the keynote of his thought. The history of the early library would be incomplete without special mention of his enthusiasm and energy. A remarkable testimonial of this work has been found recently in some ninety letters and postal cards from Reid to Sibley, which have been dug out of a mass of disorganized old library records scattered through dusty cardboard boxes in the library basement. Dr. Reid had "made fortunate investments in Chicago and Cincinnati real estate . . . for which he gave God the credit, and therefore had all of his estate with the exception of some small items, given back to religious interests." As a former president of Genesee College, and missionary secretary of the Methodist Church for many years, he felt that the Methodist College at Syracuse was the proper place for a large share of his benefactions. Even more remarkable than the money he gave was the actual work he did to improve the library. Primarily interested in Methodist journals, minutes, reports, and periodicals, he made prodigious efforts to fill the gaps in the Syracuse collections. Sometimes he would make personal calls on friends and acquaintances to persuade them to donate books, sometimes he would trade books from his own library for items needed at Syracuse, and sometimes he would visit the second hand dealers. "But I am getting my eye teeth cut," he wrote Sibley, "as I frequent these dusty, dark holes and cellars. I am persuaded these traffickers in old books grasp all they can get. If they imagine you want to buy . . . they ask you four prices—nay ten prices for what you want."

To keep track of correspondence regarding missing items at Syracuse, Reid had Sibley prepare an elaborate "business book," and even paid ten cents an hour to his wife's nephew, Rev. W. M. Fenton, '92, a student at the University, to help Sibley. Though Methodist literature was his prime concern, he did not neglect other fields entirely. When Sibley somehow got the wrong idea that Reid wanted a Methodist department in the library, Reid emphatically denounced any such thought, saying he was merely "bent on having Methodist literature prominent." On one occasion he expressed the wish to enrich the American history collection, and somewhat later he announced his intention to try to find four or five thousand dollars to buy such books on modern science as the professor in each department would select. Surely this was a remarkable record.

Though the library has since grown tremendously, it was these great achievements during Chancellor Sims' regime that placed it in the front rank. According to a study of 456 libraries of institutions of higher education, published in 1893, some 253 of them had less than 5,000 volumes, the quality of which was usually no better than the quantity—and which were often crowded into one or two out of the way rooms. But the students at Syracuse University in 1893 had the privileges of a library totalling 42,356 volumes and 9,705 pamphlets, and a separate library building in which to house them. Probably fewer than twenty-seven other institutions had as much in which to take pride.

The College of Fine Arts

7 Among the several colleges envisaged by the founding
fathers of Syracuse University was one devoted to the
study and promotion of the Fine Arts. No University worthy of the
name—and Syracuse was to be precisely that—could afford to ignore
a field of learning so ancient and honorable. The affinity of the Fine
Arts to the Classics was time-honored; its value as a discipline was beyond question. Trustees and Faculty of Genesee College, burdened as
they were with financial worries and all but buried within the confines of a rural community, had sensed the significance of the arts by
providing descriptive and cultural courses in that field. Moreover at
New Haven an attractive building "adapted to the purposes of the fine
arts in Yale University" was completed in 1866, and thirteen years
later upon the appointment of John F. Weir as Professor of Painting
and Design, the Yale School of Fine Arts was formally opened. A
certificate was given each registered student upon the successful completion of a prescribed sequence of study. It was not, however, until
1891 that Yale University began granting the degree of Bachelor of
Fine Arts. Another illustration of the trend toward instruction in the
arts appeared in the School of Design of the University of Cincinnati
which announced an intensive program in Fine Arts shortly before

the establishment of Syracuse University. Nothing, however, in the way of a degree seems to have been granted by that institution and the evidence seems to warrant the conclusion that the idea of work in Fine Arts at Cincinnati was still-born.

No institution, however, had sensed the full implications of this trend. Nowhere in America had the Fine Arts been raised to the rank and distinction of a degree conferring college. Manifestations of a drift toward that end begin to appear only as the impact and value of the arts become more and more apparent. Especially, as at Yale University, was this true during the years that immediately followed the close of the Civil War. Added stimulus came in 1869 with the establishment in New York City of what now is known as the Metropolitan Museum of Art.

Prominent among those who had a guiding hand in the inception of this great undertaking was George Fisk Comfort, born at Berkshire, New York, in 1833, and whose preparatory school days had been spent at the historic Wyoming and Cazenovia Seminaries. Later, as did so many Central New Yorkers of that age, young Comfort journeyed to Wesleyan where in time he earned the Bachelor and Master's degrees in the Liberal Arts. In 1857 he embarked upon his life's work when he accepted a position as a teacher of drawing and painting at Amenia Seminary, Amenia, New York. The following two years found him instructing in these same fields at the Fort Plain Seminary, after which he travelled extensively throughout Europe and to a lesser extent in Asia. The wanderlust seemingly satisfied, Mr. Comfort returned to America in 1865 and became Professor of Modern Languages and Esthetics at Allegheny College. Skill and reputation as a teacher came to him, but far more significant was the niche he carved for himself throughout the nation as being one of the foremost promoters of the Fine Arts. Additional recognition was showered upon him when he was invited to be the principal speaker at a meeting that led to the founding of the Metropolitan Museum.

Dr. Comfort's rising fortunes brought in their wake an ever increasing circle of friends and acquaintances, one of whom was Andrew D. White, first President of Cornell University. President White, deeply attached to the City of Syracuse, since it was the place of his birth, and knowing of the likelihood of a university being established there, introduced Professor Comfort to Rev. Jesse T. Peck, then busily engaged in the herculean task of promoting the foundation of the future

Syracuse University. Bishop Peck, whose enthusiasm for a truly great university included the notion of a College of Fine Arts, eagerly embraced the opportunity of stimulating Dr. Comfort's interest in the project. Though the details of their conversations and correspondence appear to have been swept into oblivion, it is clear from other sources that Professor Comfort welcomed the chance of fulfilling a long cherished dream, namely of organizing and founding America's first degree conferring College of Arts. Added incentive and spirit arose from the fact that the contemplated adventure was to be under the aegis of his own beloved Methodist Church.

Additional meetings and conversations between the two gentlemen must have followed in rapid succession, for how else may one explain an entry in the Minute Books of the Trustees of Syracuse University for August 31, 1871? Here one reads of a communication recently received from the Faculty of the College of the University warmly endorsing the candidacy of Professor Comfort for the Professorship of Modern Languages and Esthetics. As anticipated, the Trustees applauded the suggestion and extended an invitation to Mr. Comfort to assume this chair in June of the year following. In such a manner did Syracuse University obtain the services of one of its most outstanding teachers, educators, and administrators.

Nothing, it will be noted, had been said about Professor Comfort's appointment to the projected College of Fine Arts; every reference having been to his relations with Liberal Arts. During the college year 1872-1873, Dr. Comfort taught classes in Modern Languages and Esthetics, introduced courses in Drawing and in the History of Art, and laid the foundations for an art museum by loaning to the University his personal collection of engravings and photographs. But never once did he or his associates in Liberal Arts lose sight of the object dear to them all, namely of establishing a College of Fine Arts. Stimulated by this welcome support, especially that shown by Chancellor Winchell, who among other things was somewhat of a friend and student of the arts, Professor Comfort kept himself eternally busy. Determined to make both the Campus and City art-minded, he instituted a series of University Lectures on Fine Arts during the winter of 1872 and 1873. And in the spring the first University Glee Club made its appearance. In the meantime plans for a College of Fine Arts were gradually unfolding. Several meetings of the University faculty had been held for the purpose of discussing the project and in May,

1873, a unanimous vote of approval was given to a plan drawn in part
by Professor Comfort. As finally adopted the College of Fine Arts
was to consist of courses in Architecture and Painting. Each program
was to cover four years and graduates were to receive Bachelor degrees in either Architecture or Painting. Fortified by this action the
Chancellor laid the entire scheme before the Trustees who on June
25, 1873, gave their hearty consent. Professor Comfort was named
Dean, and the Executive Committee of the Trustees was empowered
to complete all necessary details and arrange for the College's installation.

During the course of the summer that followed, the Executive
Committee appropriated small sums for the purchase of essential
equipment and furniture, set the tuition and fees at a level comparable
to those of the College of Fine Arts, and appointed the original
faculty—all of whom except for Dr. Comfort, were to serve without
pay. It seems, therefore, reasonably clear that the Trustees were determined to keep expenses down and to recruit a corps of teachers from
local city talent. In brief, there was to be a College of Fine Arts for
art's sake, an arrangement Dr. Comfort appears to have accepted without so much as a frown. He felt confident support would be forthcoming as soon as the new college had demonstrated its right to live.
As to the ultimate outcome, he entertained no doubts. For the time
being, however, he would not risk the success of the University by
insisting upon an ambitious and expensive program. Accordingly, he
contacted local artists whose faith in an ideal constituted their sole
immediate compensation. Archimedes Russell and Horatio N. White,
architects, Sanford Thayer and George K. Knapp, portrait and landscape painters, Henry C. Allewelt, decorator, and Ward Ranger, pho-
tographer, offered their services, while Drs. Brown, Bennett, Coddington, Durston, and Richardson opened their courses in Liberal Arts to
the students of the new college.

On September 18, 1873, the Chapel in the Hall of Languages was
the scene of the formal opening of the College of Fine Arts. Before
an enthusiastic audience that completely filled the Chapel, Chancellor
Winchell, Dean Comfort, and the Rev. Dr. Calthrop, pastor of the
Unitarian Church of Syracuse, as well as certain others, honored the
occasion with appropriate remarks. Judging from an entry in his diary,
Chancellor Winchell was tremendously delighted; his administration
was off to a fine beginning and he was very proud of the fact. And

what of Dean Comfort who left no record of his sentiments? Clearly, no definite answer can be given. One may be certain, however, that his was the joy of knowing he had been largely responsible for having established at Syracuse University, America's first degree conferring College of Fine Arts—a distinction recognized at the time by the New York *Nation.*

Admission to the College of Fine Arts depended upon the passing of entrance examinations in English Grammar, Arithmetic, Geography, Elementary Drawing, and Elementary Physics.[1] Having cleared these hurdles, and nothing was said about Regent's certificates, students might register in either the Department of Painting or the Department of Architecture. An analysis of the curriculum of these two disciplines reveals a determination on the part of its framers to afford a broad and liberal culture in the field of esthetics. Instruction was not to be limited to mere exercises in art; nor were the theories and principles of the arts to be unduly stressed. Laudable and essential as these were, Dr. Comfort's vision was not so narrowly circumscribed. An imposing number of sustaining courses in fields vital to the appreciation of the arts and to the training of accomplished artists and critics were required of all students.

In the Department of Architecture first year students were required to carry forty-seven hours spread over three terms of which eighteen were in elementary drawing as well as in drawing from cast and nature; five additional hours were in architectural drawing. Of the remaining hours eight were in Algebra, four in Geometry, ten in German, and two in Ancient History. Sophomores carried twelve hours in Perspective, Nature, and Ink and Sepia Drawing, four hours of Water Coloring, four hours of Trigonometry and Surveying, four hours of Calculus, four hours of Analytical Geometry, seven hours of German, six hours of Physics, three hours of Artistic Drawing, and two hours of Illumination and Lettering, making a total of forty-six hours. Juniors were required to take forty-nine hours of which fifteen were in Architectural Drafting. Of the remaining hours French and Modern History accounted for eight each, and Esthetics, Chemistry, Strength of Materials, and Oil Painting one hour each. During the Senior year forty-five hours were required of which fifteen were in

---

1. Special students, or those not intending to graduate, might enter at any time and elect desired courses.

Architectural Drafting. Of the remaining hours, Political Economy accounted for six, Italian four, Geology and History of Civilization three each, Rhetoric, Geology, and Decorative Art two each, and the History of Art, Engraving, Sculpture, Painting, Modern Art, Art Criticism, Art Literature, and Landscape Gardening one hour each. Seniors were also asked to take a non-credit course in the Essay of Art. Those whose interest led them to enroll in the Department of Painting pursued a sequence that embraced most of these same subjects, additional work being required in Physical Geography, Physiology, Natural History, Botany, Mythology, History, and extra Painting. During the remainder of the period covered by this chapter, constructive and well advised improvements were made in all sequences.

Fifteen students matriculated in the College of Fine Arts during the college year, 1873-1874, of whom all but one were enrolled in the Department of Painting. Measured by present day standards of registration such a start would be considered disappointing, but to those of 1873 it was a most auspicious beginning. Dean Comfort and his staff of faithful teachers were stimulated to greater efforts and the optimism they radiated inspired all with whom they came in contact. The students rallied and formed an Aesthetic Society; others joined in reorganizing the University Glee Club. Meanwhile, Dr. Comfort presented a series of stereoptican lectures on art at the Park Presbyterian Church. And in 1875 instruction was offered leading to the degree of Bachelor of Engraving. A year later classes were formed. The course in Engraving was identical with that in Painting except that in the last two years classes in engraving were substituted for those in painting.

Considerable attention was also given to the field of music. A University Chorus was established and in June, 1877, Dr. William H. Schultze was placed in charge of the recently established Department of Music. In this discipline, instruction was offered in Piano, Voice, Violin, Ensemble Playing, and Organ, with supplementary work in History, Physics, English, and Appreciation of Art. Formal dedication of the Department of Music took place in the fall of the same year. And it was at this ceremony that Dr. Calthrop, pastor of the May Memorial Church at Syracuse, most appropriately remarked, "Professor Comfort is always doing new things and in my opinion every new thing is a good thing." Encouraged by this and other expressions of good will, the College of Fine Arts took on renewed vigor and life. The students reorganized the Glee Club, which had developed the unfortunate habit of disbanding at the close of each college year. More, they founded the Euterpean Society, and warmly supported a series of Musical Soirees presented by various members of the faculty and visiting artists. Not to be outdone, the students in Architecture established the Ictinus Society. Meanwhile, the public lectures on art were continued much to the enjoyment and satisfaction of the University student body and the citizens of Syracuse.

It should not be forgotten that the founding of the College of Fine Arts coincided with the Panic of 1873. As one reviews the hectic happenings of the sad seventies, one may be pardoned for wondering why the College of Fine Arts was not nipped in the bud. As is well known, the Trustees of the University were at their wits' end to keep the College of Liberal Arts intact and loathed to divert so much as a penny toward the new venture beyond what was absolutely essential. Nor were conditions improved by the discovery of certain laxities existing in the administration of Fine Arts, the chief complaint being that too many students paid only part tuition while others, through negligence, managed to avoid meeting these obligations in whole or in part. The seriousness of the situation could not be denied though an optimistic note was sounded by Chancellor Haven when, at a meeting of the Trustees he expressed the opinion that ordinary expenses might be met provided full tuition was paid. But as for additional expansion, the Chancellor continued, new sources of revenue would have to be discovered and if the latter were not forthcoming in the near future the College of Fine Arts would have to be disbanded. Precisely what the Faculty of Fine Arts thought of the situation is not known as no records of any meetings of that body are available. Nor is it known that any meetings were held, the absence of which might explain in part some of the difficulty the College had gotten itself into.

Financial and administrative factors were not the only disturbing elements though probably they were by far the more important. Many persons honestly believed the seat for all the trouble lay in the intimate association that existed between the College of Fine Arts and the College of Liberal Arts. Like near relatives, blood ties engendered discord. Echoes of ill will bobbed up at the Alumni meeting in June, 1880. Here, after some discussion the following was adopted:

Whereas: We believe that the intimate association of the College of Fine Arts with that of the College of Liberal Arts is detrimental to the best interests of this University, and Whereas the relation of the College of Fine Arts to the University should be the same as that of the College of Medicine, therefore, Resolved that while we rejoice in the success that has thus far attended the establishment and maintenance of the College of Fine Arts connected with this University, We commend to the attention of the Friends of Art in this City of Syracuse and vicinity the enterprise of erecting a suitable building in which the College of Fine Arts may be better accommodated.

A copy of this resolution was directed immediately to the Trustees of the University who were then in session. To which the Trustees replied by instructing its Executive Committee to locate any such building as contemplated by the resolution on the grounds of the University. They did not, however, register any opinion as to the Alumni belief that present arrangements were unsatisfactory and that Fine Arts might be placed in the same position to the University as the College of Medicine. As will be shown in a later chapter the College of Medicine was all but a detached unit at the time, collecting its own income, paying its own bills, and graduating students without so much as the blessing of the Board of Trustees. If the action of the Alumni meant anything it would seem as though they favored a comparable scheme for Fine Arts which if adopted would release certain sums for the growth and expansion of Liberal Arts. And it should be remembered most of the alumni were graduates of that college.

This event, explosive in more ways than one, preceded the resignation of Chancellor Haven. His successor, Dr. Sims, most certainly must have been duly informed of the problem that faced him and in his report of June, 1881, he asked the Trustees to define more carefully his relation to the College of Fine Arts which in his opinion needed "more definite organization." Silence may have been golden to the Trustees but to the historian it is most provoking for though the matter was referred to a select committee, no report seems to have been rendered. Possibly the Trustees hoped that time would solve all of Syracuse's problems. If so they must have been more than startled to have heard of the commotion the question caused at the 1881 meeting of the Alumni Association. At this gathering the problem of the two colleges became the subject of much debate. Professor Comfort, so one reads in the diary of Mr. Eudelmer F. Cuykendall, '76, appeared "uninvited" and spoke in a manner that aroused considerable feeling. The discussion, Cuykendall recorded, was "most spirited even verging upon bitterness." Turning to the brittle minutes of the meeting one reads, "After a somewhat extended discussion of matters

and things in general and of the Fine Art College and of the previous
action of the Association in relation thereunto in particular the following resolution was adopted: Resolved that we have heard Professor
Comfort as to the successs of the Fine Art College and the Chancellor
as to the condition and affairs of the University in general, and that
we wish the Fine Art College and all the other Colleges of the University large prosperity." And so what might well have split the Association was turned by someone's gentle hand into a happy love feast.

Supporting evidence, however, that the issue was by no means
settled may be found in the *University Herald* whose editors never
for one minute questioned the educational value and merit of the Fine
Arts. At the same time they deeply deplored the silent invasion of the
Hall of Languages by the College of Fine Arts. Originally, classes in
art had been assigned two rooms in the college building, but now, so
the editors asserted, the entire Hall had all but been transformed into
a Hall of Fine Arts. In the basement we are told was the modeling
room while the rooms and even the corridors of the second floor were
occupied by art classes. And on the top floor the din arising from
classes in music had become so loud as to silence instruction in elocution. On the other hand the Minutes of the Faculty of the College of
Liberal Arts have little to say about these commotions and inconven-
iences but that is not to say all was at peace. Clearly what was needed—
and this probably was the crux of the problem—was a building devoted solely to the Fine Arts, a proposition the alumni and others kept
bringing before the Trustees on more than one occasion.

The Trustees quickly registered approval but did little to translate
the latter into action. Nor may they be blamed for not having done
more. A casual glance at the financial reports of the University for
these stormy years should convince the most determined critic that
there were no funds available for so vast a project; nor were there any
benefactors in sight whose gifts might warrant such a program. An
honest attempt, however, was made relative to the administrative aspects of the College of Fine Arts. The thorny question of tuition was
adjusted and an improved system of accounting was introduced.
Favorable results followed in the wake of these innovations and in
1884 Chancellor Sims in a speech that reviewed the unhappy and uncertain past expressed his faith in the future of the college which now,
he said, was a "going concern." He did not, however, wish to be misunderstood; his optimistic comments should not be interpreted too

generously. The College of Fine Arts most certainly had a future, but that future was dependent upon the satisfaction of its pressing and patent needs, none of which, however, should be met at the expense of the College of Liberal Arts for which the University had been founded.

Foremost among the needs of the Fine Arts was the small matter of an organ, the absence of which sorely tried the patience of the students who perforce did their practising at neighboring churches. But now this avenue had been closed by these churches whose increased use of their organs precluded concessions to the musical students. Touched to the quick by this action, Chancellor Sims, upon the advice of the Trustees, personally assumed responsibility for the purchase of an organ. At this juncture an unknown friend of the University came forward, paid two thousand dollars for an organ Dr. Sims had located, and in June, 1885, a twenty-two stop pump organ, manufactured by Johnson and Company of Massachusetts, was installed at the north end of the Chapel. Shortly thereafter, January 16, 1886, the organ was formally dedicated by a musical soiree. Professor George A. Parker entertained with eleven different numbers on the organ, while Dr. William H. Schultze, Professor Otto K. Schill and Kate E. Stark, and Miss Ella I. French furnished vocal, violin and piano music.

The reception accorded these artists exceeded all expectations and the editor of the *University Herald* predicted that it could be only a matter of time before the College of Fine Arts would outdistance those of Liberal Arts and Medicine. Dr. Schultze and his students were delighted with the rising fortunes of the Department of Music and so were many others for the time being. Soon, however, Liberal Arts classes were seen retreating before the din of organ and piano, from the top floor of the Hall of Languages. All of which occasioned an outburst of complaints that echoed through the columns of the *University Herald*. Meanwhile, and possibly by way of retaliation, the demonstration and modeling rooms of the art classes mysteriously became disarranged. Chairs and tables were not in their usual places, while exhibits and models were shoved hither and yonder. Rumor had it that certain ill-advised "frosh" of the College of Liberal Arts were guilty of this and other like offences though only the uninitiated were misled; those informed knew only too well that freshmen often have been accused of the misdeeds of their elders. Continued depredations followed: still-life classes, for example, assembled only to find models, such as fresh fruit, stolen. Trivial as these disconcerting affairs were, they were definite signs of a situation sadly in need of immediate correction. The truth of the matter was patent. The College of Fine Arts had outgrown its cramped quarters within the Hall of Languages. Continued expansion of both Liberal and Fine Arts argued for the speedy erection of another building but how to finance so vast an undertaking no one knew. Here it was that Chancellor Sims once again came to the rescue of the University.

Precisely when the Chancellor first approached Mr. John Crouse, honored citizen of Syracuse and Trustee of the University is not known. It may have been during the summer of 1887 since by the fall of that year Mr. Crouse had signified his desire to the Chancellor and Trustees of presenting to the University a building to be known as the "John Crouse Memorial College for Women." Little time was lost in accepting this most generous and timely offer. Moreover, Mr. Crouse was told that his wishes, including the name and location of the proposed building, would be respected. Actual work on the edifice began on New Year's Day, 1888, in accordance with and under the direct supervision of Mr. Crouse himself. Not a single item, we are led to believe, relative to the construction and equipment was handled by either the Administration or the Trustees of the University. In all probability, their advice was frequently sought and followed, but the thing to be remembered is that it was Mr. Crouse's project from start to finish. He simply moved in and onto the campus with his architect, contractors, masons, and carpenters, and proceeded to erect a building as though he were on his own property. Day after day, we are told, he took a direct part in the undertaking and when it seemed advisable to alter original plans he willingly assumed the additional expense. Fortune played a mean trick upon him for on June 27, 1889, with the building all but completed, Mr. Crouse died. His role as a benefactor was immediately assumed by his son, D. Edgar Crouse, who signified his intention of finishing the "John Crouse Memorial College for Women" in accordance with his father's wishes.

Twice within the space of two years, the donors had specifically spoken of the building as a memorial college for women. Their desire to have it so named is also attested by the inscriptions to that effect which they had placed over the entrance to the building and upon the largest of the bells that made up the Crouse Chimes. And not a murmur of dissent arose from the Trustees, Administration, Faculty,

Genesee College Hall (1951) erected in 1852

Genesee Wesleyan Seminary (1951) erected in 1842

Dr. Alexander Winchell
Chancellor, 1872-1874

Dr. Erastus O. Haven
Chancellor, 1874-1880

Dr. Charles N. Sims
Chancellor, 1881-1893

Dr. Frederick Hyde

Mrs. John M. Reid

Reverend John M. Reid

Bishop Jesse T. Peck

George F. Comfort

William P. Coddington

Charles W. Bennett

John J. Brown

John R. French

Hall of Languages, 1880

University Avenue, north from Hall of Languages, 1881

Alumni, and Students, all of whom repeatedly referred to it as the Crouse Memorial College for Women. No other title was used. There can be no question, therefore, as to what name the building was to bear and not one shred of evidence has come to light to warrant the title now in use, namely the Crouse College of Fine Arts.

But some doubt does exist as to what Mr. Crouse had in mind when he spoke of his gift as a memorial college for women. By memorial, Mr. Crouse meant a building "in memory of his wife;" later, his son said it was a memorial for both "father and mother." But why a "college of women?" Was he thinking in terms of a women's college at Syracuse? An affirmative answer fails to make sense in view of the University's avowed and determined declaration of 1870 in favor of coeducation, though this announcement in no wise stood in the way of an arrangement similar to that now followed at Duke University, Hobart College, and at one or two other institutions. A women's and a men's college, both on the same campus, was not an impossibility. It may be that this was what the Chancellor had in mind when he referred to the new building as a women's center for specialized study. Again, the *Annual* of 1887-1888 stated that the Crouse Building was "intended chiefly for the use of ladies." On the other hand, the University Senate at the request of the Chancellor was assigned the task of deciding what classes and departments were to occupy Crouse College. In resolving this matter, the Senate appears to have limited its attention to the College of Fine Arts. Moreover, the interior arrangements of the edifice, particularly the unique construction of the auditorium and galleries, and the installation of an organ, clearly points to an occupancy by the Fine Arts. Finally, since a Victorian interpretation of education might well consider a College of Fine Arts as an appropriate home for women students there was nothing incongruous in calling that domicile a "college for women."

The John Crouse Memorial College was constructed of Long-Meadow red sandstone bolstered and ornamented with stout granite foundations. It was four stories high, 162 by 190 feet in extreme dimensions, and was crowned by an imposing and lofty tower in which were hung the Crouse Chimes. The latter consisted of nine bells set to E flat, the largest bell weighing three thousand pounds. Equally impressive was the Roosevelt organ which was of the latest and most modern design and which was operated by a ten-horse Baldwin engine. Six distinct bellows provided the air needed for the organ's seventy-four stops and 2,591 pipes. The organ was placed at the north end of the auditorium, which had a seating capacity of one thousand, and whose carved and decorative wood-work was singled out by art critics as worthy of special commendation. The entire cost of the building and the equipment was in the neighborhood of a half a million dollars. Many critics hailed it as the best college building in America and Chancellor Sims declared it to be the "finest college edifice in the world." And it was all that and much more so far as Dr. Sims was concerned who saw in this magnificent structure the fulfilment of a cherished dream. For it was Chancellor Sims and Chancellor Sims alone who had been chiefly responsible for persuading Mr. Crouse to make this very remarkable gift. One can well understand and appreciate the sense of pride the Chancellor must have experienced on witnessing the formal dedication of the building on the afternoon of September 18, 1889. The entire student body marched from the Hall of Languages to the West Hill where an interested throng of friends had already gathered. Mr. Francis H. Root, President of the University Board of Trustees, graciously received the gift, and suitable addresses were delivered by the Chancellor, Dr. Charles J. Little, and others. In the evening, Professor George A. Parker entertained with an elaborate organ recital.

During the remainder of Chancellor Sims' administration, the College of Fine Arts continued to prosper and grow under the guiding hand of Dean Comfort and his staff of loyal and self-sacrificing teachers. Among the original members of the Faculty of the College of Fine Arts mention should be made of Professor George K. Knapp who for six years was in charge of the classes in Drawing and Painting. Professor Knapp was well known in his day for his portraits in oil and many historical paintings. Closely allied in interest was Professor Ward V. Ranger who was in charge of the courses in Photography from 1873 to 1877. Professor Ranger's reputation was attested by a Federal appointment to observe the eclipse of the sun and the transit of Venus in 1864 and 1874 respectively. Next in order of seniority was Professor William H. Schultze who, after a brilliant career in European and American concert halls, became Professor of Theory and Practice of Music at Syracuse in 1877. Dr. Schultze rapidly became a favorite among his colleagues and students, and his sudden death in 1888 was a serious blow to all. Student regard was shown by the *University Herald* which in addition to a glowing tribute provided an elegant etching of Dr. Schultze.

Among his many friends was Professor Newton A. Wells, Chairman of the Drawing Department from 1879 to 1888. Professor Wells frequently exhibited his paintings in Philadelphia and New York and was the author of several articles on art which were published in leading American magazines of that day. Highly favorable comments as to his artistic skill appeared in art reviews and the daily papers of metropolitan New York. Locally, he was known for his historical paintings and sketches of Onondaga County. One of these paintings, the "Weigh Lock" is a treasured possession of the Onondaga County Historical Society. In 1888 Professor Wells resigned to accept the position of Dean of the School of Art at Western Reserve University.

Mention should also be made of Professor Robert F. Dallas who was in charge of Oil Painting and Modeling between 1886 and 1893. Ella I. French, daughter of Vice-Chancellor French, was Instructor in Piano from 1884 to 1893, after which she was promoted to the rank of Professor of Piano. In Water-coloring, there was the genial instructor Mr. Hiram S. Gutsell who, after having served at Syracuse from 1882 to 1887, resigned to take a similar position at Cornell University. Reference also should be made of E. Eli Van DeWarker, Professor of Artistic Anatomy (1874-1881); Peter H. Stuart, Professor of Engraving (1874-1877); Charles F. Webber, Professor of Vocal Music (1887-1888); Isaac V. Flagler, Professor of Organ (1879-1884); Percy Goetschius, Professor of Music (1890-1892); Edgar M. Buell, Instructor in Architectural Drafting (1881-1883); George H. Liddel, Instructor in Drawing (1883-1886); Frederick Carr Lyford, Instructor in Drawing (1888-1891); and Arthur B. Clark, Instructor in Architecture (1889-1892). Finally, there was George A. Parker, Graduate of the Royal Conservatory of Music, Stuttgart, Germany, who in 1892 entered upon his life's work as Professor of Piano and Organ at Syracuse. Dr. Parker, well-known and honored by all Syracusans, married Miss Mary D. Sims, daughter of Chancellor Sims. During the years 1896 to 1898 Dr. Parker was Acting Dean of the College of Fine Arts.

The indebtedness of Syracuse University to these men and women of the College of Fine Arts is nothing by way of comparison with that owed to Dean George Fisk Comfort. His had been the driving force that led to the growth and expansion of that college. Starting as a one man department within the College of Liberal Arts, the Fine Arts waxed in stature and achievement. In prominence and reputation, at home and abroad, it soon rivalled its Mother, the College of Liberal

Arts who, though grumbling at times as its lusty and overgrown off-spring jammed and crowded the corridors and rooms of the Hall of Languages, was always the first to recognize the value of Fine Arts to the University. Repeatedly did the officials, teachers and students of the University honor that College and praise the Dean who had accomplished so much. He was an organizer and creator of unusual gifts. "No man," so Dr. Smalley once wrote, "of the early days of the University could reach and interest so many men of the highest standing and the largest influence as he."

It was, therefore, with genuine and deep regret that the University heard of his decision to leave Syracuse in the spring of 1892. Dr. Comfort, it seems, had received an offer to visit La Porte, Texas, where a group of enterprising educators were contemplating the establishment of a Southern College of Fine Arts. Thoroughly impressed and with his imagination challenged by the opportunity, Dean Comfort informed Dr. Sims of his determination to leave Syracuse. Several courteous letters passed between the two gentlemen and in June of the same year the Trustees, being told of what had happened, accepted Dr. Comfort's resignation. Nothing, however, was said as to the date when this resignation was to become effective, Dr. Comfort having indicated his willingness to retain nominal direction of the College of Fine Arts until after the opening of the winter term in 1893. Executive burdens at La Porte forced Dean Comfort to ask for an earlier release and in September, 1892, the Executive Committee of the Board of Trustees granted the request.[2]

In the meantime and with the blessing of Dr. Comfort, overtures had been made to the Rev. LeRoy M. Vernon, pastor of the First Methodist Church in Syracuse since 1888. Rev. Vernon had received his Bachelor and Master's degrees from Iowa Wesleyan in 1860 and 1863 respectively. Since then he had served as minister of Trinity Methodist Church in St. Louis, Missouri, and as Presiding Elder of the Springfield, Missouri, District. Between 1866 and 1868 he had been President of St. Charles College in Missouri, following which he was a missionary in Italy for eighteen years. During this busy and varied

2. Admiration and respect for Dean Comfort were evidenced in a printed letter issued by the Alumni Association, addressed to the Board of Trustees, urging the return of Dr. Comfort to the University. It was their hope the Trustees would be able to provide him with a lectureship or a professor's chair in any one of the University's Colleges.

career, Rev. Vernon had become considerably interested in the Fine Arts and while at Syracuse had impressed Dr. Comfort with his abilities. It would, however, be distinctly unfair to Rev. Vernon to rate him as a scholar in the Fine Arts and at no time did Dean Vernon ever entertain such an opinion of himself. It was his other qualifications that earned for him the appointment of Dean of the College of Fine Arts, a position he began to fill in January, 1893. The story of his deanship, unfortunately terminated by death in 1896, will be told in a subsequent volume.

The Geneva Medical Faculty

8 The antecedents of the Syracuse University College of Medicine may with certainty be traced to the establishment of the Medical Faculty of Geneva College in 1834. To indicate an earlier origin is replete with difficulties that sentiment rather than reason alone may bridge. It has been suggested, for example, a "legitimate relationship" may be found between the Syracuse College of Medicine and the College of Physicians and Surgeons which was chartered in June, 1812; the latter's home being at Fairfield, New York. Sponsored by those who in a previous decade had established Fairfield Academy and supported by occasional grants from the State Legislature, the Fairfield Medical College continued to function until the spring of 1840. During its early life, the College had benefited from a corporate connection with the Academy which numbered among its friends and patrons the influential and wealthy Trinity Episcopal Church of New York City. The keen interest displayed by this parish, it should be noted, centered about the Academy where much emphasis was laid upon training men for the priesthood of the Episcopal Church. And with the founding of an Episcopal College at Geneva, New York, in 1825, the support of Fairfield by Trinity Episcopal Church came to an end.

The effect of this upon the fortunes of the Medical College was nothing in contrast to that which must have attended the inception of the Geneva Medical Faculty in 1834. Nor should one forget the increasing prosperity of an older rival, the College of Physicians and Surgeons of New York City, or the chartering of the Albany Medical College in 1838. Student enrollment at the Fairfield Medical College declined and in 1840, with the removal of Professors James Hadley, John Delameter, and Frank H. Hamilton to Geneva, and of Professors Beck and McNaughton to Albany, the Fairfield College closed its doors.

The arrival of Messrs. Hadley, Delameter, and Hamilton at Geneva strengthened that institution and did much to enrich its historical heritage. Moreover, their presence at Geneva kept alive the traditions of Fairfield. But to predicate a "legitimate relationship" between the two colleges on the basis of the removal of some of the Fairfield faculty to Geneva seems unwarranted. A careful appraisal of all available evidence fails to establish any organic connection between Fairfield and Geneva. And without such a nexus the attempt to trace Syracuse to Fairfield becomes meaningless.

Equally unconvincing is the story that ties the Syracuse College of Medicine to the abortive medical school established at New York City in 1826 by Dr. David Hosack, one time a member of the Faculty of the New York College of Physicians and Surgeons. Dr. Hosack, it seems, parted company with the New York institution and during the school year, 1826-1827, conducted a medical college at New York under the patronage of the Trustees of Rutgers College. Shortly thereafter, for reasons that do not concern this narrative, the connection with Rutgers College was dissolved. Disappointed by this turn of events, Dr. Hosack approached the Trustees of Geneva College hoping they would lend a willing ear and helping hand to his pleas for the founding of a Geneva medical school. After some deliberation, the Geneva Trustees voted, October 30, 1827, to create such an institution. According to the Trustees' Minutes, the Geneva College was to consist of two branches, each having an initial faculty of six professors. One of these schools was to be located at Geneva—an intention, however, that never materialized. Certain unspecified difficulties, according to the Geneva *Gazette* of November 14, 1827, forced one delay after another with the ultimate result that the venture was abandoned. The second branch was established at New York City under the direction of Dr. Hosack and was known as the "Rutgers Medical Faculty of Geneva College."

The doors of the New York branch were opened in early November, 1827, amid a barrage of criticism on the part of the New York College of Physicians and Surgeons. The latter declared that the "Geneva College, Rutgers Medical College" was of no standing, that its degrees were worthless, and that the charter of Geneva College distinctly forbade the founding of a New York branch. Dr. Hosack and the Trustees of Geneva College denied these charges, which incidently received some publicity in the *New York Statesman*, and battled for their rights in the State courts. The latter ruled against them on the ground that the college's charter restricted its educational life to the corporate limits of the Village of Geneva. Whereupon, Dr. Hosack announced in November, 1830, the suspension of the medical college—a suspension that has continued, it is believed, from that day to this. And what of Geneva College? An examination of the Trustees' Minutes reveal that it quietly accepted the decision of the court. The "Geneva College, Rutgers Medical Faculty" had ceased to exist.

The memory of the New York branch, however, persisted at Geneva and it was not long before voices were raised advocating the establishment of a local medical college. The matter came to a head in August, 1834, when the Trustees of Geneva College appointed a committee to confer with a number of interested parties relative to the formation of a "medical faculty." Although there were some throughout Geneva and Seneca County who questioned the expediency of the proposed undertaking, the committee, on September 15, 1834, brought in a report favoring the creation of such a faculty. The Trustees immediately endorsed the recommendation and in the same month issued a prospectus in the form of a *Circular and Catalogue of the Faculty and Officers of the Medical Institution of Geneva College*. Classes, we are informed, were to be under the guidance of Dean Edward Cutbush, one time a member of the United States Medical Corps, and Professors Willard Parker, Thomas Spencer, John George Morgan, Charles B. Coventry, and Anson Coleman—all licensed doctors. Formal installation of the Medical Faculty took place on February 10, 1835 and on March 27th of the same year, the State Legislature gave the enterprise its blessings.

Nothing, it should be noted, is said in the act of the Legislature about the chartering of a medical college. Recognition of Geneva's right to create a medical faculty under its charter is admitted, and provision is made for the granting of degrees by the Trustees upon the recommendation of the Medical Faculty. Beyond this, the act is silent. Nor do the regulations and organic rules established by the Trustees for the governance of that faculty warrant a different conclusion. No one would care to deny the fact that the terms "Medical College" and "Medical Faculty" were used interchangeably by the local press and Geneva College authorities, but so for that matter was the description, "Medical Department." Nor would one question the statement that the medical faculty, regardless of title, functioned as though they were self-contained members of a college. But this does not justify the oft repeated comment that a *medical college* was chartered at Geneva. Common usage has established a tradition historical research is obliged to contradict.

In creating the Medical Faculty, the Trustees of Geneva College carefully outlined the former's authority, the status of its faculty, and a score of administrative details. Particularly significant was the provision obligating the Medical Faculty to handle and assume responsibility for all financial matters. The Trustees, in brief, while anxious to promote a medical center did not wish to jeopardize the life of Geneva College by shouldering the expenses of the Medical Faculty. Thus it was the Medical Faculty that charged and collected all tuition and fees, bought and sold property, and erected, with State appropriations, the Medical Building on Main Street.

Thirty-three students matriculated when the Medical Department opened in February, 1835; the following year there were sixty-eight— all of whom received instruction in a three story brick building situated between Geneva and Trinity Halls. Continued success followed during the course of the next few years. So flattering were the prospects that the Faculty launched a program of expansion, sold the "old Medical Building" (often known as the "Middle Hall") to the Trustees and by the fall of 1841 were the proud owners of a handsome four story brick and stone building, seventy-six by forty-four feet in dimensions. Fortune continued to smile upon the Medical Faculty. In January, 1844, the Faculty reported to the State Board of Regents that during the previous year one hundred and ninety-five students had been in attendance and of this number forty-five had been graduated. Moreover, the total value of the Department's property amounted to over nineteen thousand dollars. During the remainder of the 1840's, thanks chiefly to state aid, the Medical Department's record and condition remained good. Student enrollment, though not up to the banner year of 1844, was relatively high and a note of optimism permeates throughout the annual reports.

Beginning, however, with 1851—the year Geneva College became known as Hobart College—things took a turn for the worse. The recent establishment (1846) of a Medical School at the University of Buffalo touched the fortunes of Hobart to a marked degree. So serious did the situation become by 1851 that Dr. Sumner Rhoades, one-time a member of the Geneva Medical Faculty, published an open letter in the Geneva *Gazette* advocating the dissolution of that faculty. In its place, Dr. Rhoades favored the founding of an agricultural college. Bishop DeLancey of the Episcopal Church opposed the plan, but when the Medical Faculty gathered in the fall of 1853 they found no students had registered in medicine. Whereupon, the Faculty resigned and for a year no instruction in medicine was offered. In 1854, a new faculty was organized, but even this effort failed to check the downward trend. Enrollment soon fell below the one hunded mark and by the close of that decade had dropped to twenty-two. By this time expenses had outdistanced income and the Faculty were greatly concerned as to the future. And yet with a patience that did them much credit, they managed to carry on and to keep the Department alive.

Each succeeding year, however, brought new trials and uncertainties. Finally, in January, 1869, the Trustees of Hobart College were forced to give careful consideration to the problem and for a time actually debated the question of abolishing the Medical Faculty. Unfortunately, our sources do not disclose the outcome of this debate. Two factors, however, do suggest that a negative decision had been reached. First of all, it was currently reported throughout Geneva that clinical instruction was going to be provided at Willard Asylum located at nearby Ovid. In the second place, a campaign for an endowment for Hobart College was scheduled for the near future within the village of Geneva and it was hoped that this effort would bring timely relief to the Medical Department.

Nothing, it would appear, ever materialized in respect to the projected clinic at Willard Asylum. On the other hand, the endowment drive yielded some ten thousand dollars. Grateful as were the Trustees for this demonstration of local good-will, the amount raised was by no means sufficient to care for the over-all needs of the College; thus the fortunes of the Medical Department remained precarious and uncertain. Nor did conditions improve as the college year progressed. The fate of the Medical Faculty hung in the balance and it was not until July 12, 1871, that the Trustees of Hobart, acting upon the request of that faculty, voted that the "Medical Department of the College be discontinued after the first of February, 1872." A public statement to this effect appeared in the *Annual Announcement of the Geneva Medical College* for the year 1871-1872. Accompanying this announcement, there appeared a brief resumé of the Department's history and contributions. From this, as well as from other sources, we are informed that the Faculty had spent upwards of thirty thousand dollars in the erection of buildings and in the purchase of a museum and library. It was a record of which the Faculty and Trustees of Hobart might well be proud. During its life, 1834-1872, a total of 721 students were graduated. Among the alumni, reference should be made to Dr. Charles L. Wells, prominent in the history of Minnesota medical circles, Dr. Darwin Colvin, founder and one-time President of the New York State Medical Association, Dr. Corydon LaFord, who for many years was Professor of Anatomy at the University of Michigan, Dr. Bleecker L. Hovey, who earned a name for himself among the doctors of Rochester, New York, and Dr. Elizabeth Blackwell who had the distinction of being the first woman in the United States to receive a degree in medicine. These and many others did honor to their Alma Mater which after nearly forty years of meritorious service was forced to close its doors.

Among the several reasons assigned for the suspension of the Medical Department of Hobart College, some emphasis has been placed upon the establishment of a similar department at the University of Buffalo. To assume that the latter institution in no wise affected the fortunes of Hobart would be equivalent to saying that there is no competition among American colleges and universities. Beyond these considerations, no other evaluation, for the present, ought to be given to the argument that the existence of a medical unit at Buffalo was a contributing factor for the decline of the Hobart Medical Faculty. Equally difficult to determine as to its validity is the view sometimes expressed that had there been less change in the presidency of Hobart College between 1858 and 1871, the lot of the Medical Department might have been different. During these years there were three presidents of whom Dr. James K. Stone served for but one year (1868) and Dr. James Rankine, for the years 1869-1871. Evidence as to the influence of these changes in personnel upon the College may be gleaned from scattered references in the Minutes of the Trustees of Hobart College and the Geneva *Gazette.*

Regardless of the strength of these contentions, greater attention has been paid by past historians to the quality and type of instruction furnished at Hobart. Generally speaking, degrees in medicine were granted to those who had successfully pursued their studies for three years under a competent doctor and who were twenty-one years of age. In addition, each candidate was required to attend two full courses of lectures at the Medical Department and to submit an appropriate dissertation upon some phase of medicine. There was nothing reprehensible in this program. "Given the right student and the right preceptor," so Dean Heffron of the Syracuse University College of Medicine wrote in 1920, "and a course of lectures such as given at Fairfield and at Geneva, and no more ideal plan could be conceived by which a young man could assume gradually the duties of a general practitioner." Moreover, as Dr. Heffron pointed out, the program of studies pursued at Geneva conformed with State requirements—requirements that were not materially altered until 1891.

Unfortunately, the State law did not insist upon a degree in medicine as a prerequisite for practicing medicine. Most of the medical students, therefore, throughout the state never were graduated from a medical college. Rather did they acquire the status of "doctor" by merely passing an examination given by the censors of the local county medical societies. Judged by the standards of the early nineteenth century, this arrangement was less bad than one might suppose. But what had been normal in 1810 was rapidly becoming an anachronism by the middle of the century. Dean Heffron quite aptly summed up the situation when he wrote:

> With a rapidly increasing population, with the multiplication of means of more rapid transportation, and with the extraordinary financial development of the country, practitioners became too busy to serve as preceptors effectually, medical schools were multiplied out of all proportion to their need, courses were shortened, while the number of subjects upon which lectures were given was increased, examinations in consequence of which became a farce, and worst of all the system of personal instruction under leading practitioners degenerated into a nominal registration with any doctor just to keep within the letter of the law, and many students romped through the lecture courses required, in order

to get the diploma of a college with its license to practice in the least possible time and with the expenditure of the least energy and the least money.

By 1870 most of these defects and evils were more than apparent at Hobart and no one was more conscious of the same than the Medical Faculty of that institution. In all probability it was the realization of these facts that prompted that Faculty to hope for clinical instruction at the asylum at Ovid. Buffalo, a serious rival, had a large public hospital to assist in the training of prospective doctors. Geneva had none and because of the size of that village the Hobart Faculty could not hope to provide what many now believed to be "an indispensable adjunct" of a successful college. Death came swiftly to the Medical Department of Hobart College and there were few at the College or in the Village of Geneva that seem to have mourned its departure.

Meanwhile, throughout Central New York there had been much talk about a new institution—Syracuse University. Citizens of Geneva read in their local *Gazette*, the *Northern Christian Advocate*, and other papers of the chartering of this university in February, 1870. And as they read they must have noted the announcement that the Trustees of Syracuse intended to promote the establishment of a college of medicine. A medical college at Syracuse! Syracuse—a prosperous and rapidly growing city of over forty thousand persons, situated on the main line of the New York Central Railroad, and blessed with one of the state's most progressive hospitals. What a splendid location, so thought certain members of the Hobart Medical Faculty, for a medical college! And having so reasoned, the contrast between their own checkered existence at Geneva and the glowing prospects of a college at Syracuse became more and more apparent. Moreover, if the Syracuse Trustees mean what they say why should we not try to make capital out of the situation? Let us convince these Trustees that a Syracuse Medical College established upon the foundations of the Medical Faculty of Hobart is the sole answer to their problem. But what of the Hobart Trustees, would they approve of the moving of the Medical Department to Syracuse? Why not ask and find out? Accordingly, a committee of the Medical Faculty waited upon the Trustees.

Conscious of their own limitations and inability to adequately provide for the needs of a medical department, the Trustees appointed a committee to confer with the Medical Faculty. At this gathering the Faculty formally requested permission to "transfer the *Medical De-*

partment [italics mine] with the Library and Anatomical Museum to the University of Syracuse." Whereupon, the committee of the Trustees replied that they "could not recommend any such action" but that they would endorse "a sale of the Medical Library and Anatomical Museum to the Medical Faculty or to the University of Syracuse or to any other parties at a moderate price." The Medical Faculty expressed satisfaction and on July 12, 1871, the Trustees of Hobart College accepted the recommendations of their committee authorizing the sale of the library and museum. Ultimately, these units were purchased by Professor John Towler of the Hobart Medical Faculty.

Although no source casts any light upon the motives that prompted the Hobart Trustees to retain the Medical Department but permitted its personnel and equipment to be moved to a new location, the question may be raised as to whether the Trustees hoped to start afresh once the dissatisfied elements had disappeared. There is not a shred of evidence to warrant an affirmative answer; on the contrary, everything points to an opposite conclusion. At the same time the Trustees must have been aware of the privileges afforded them by the college charter which, it will be recalled, permitted the granting of any degree common at that time to American colleges and universities. Such a document, unique in itself, had potential values no Board of Trustees would care to tamper with and any action on their part authorizing the removal of the Medical Department would of necessity involve legislative action and might lead, therefore, to a revaluation of the charter. Surely, wisdom must have counselled a "hands off" policy and since no serious opposition arose within the Village of Geneva and, so far as is known, among the alumni, the Trustees acted so as to avoid trouble for themselves and the College. All of which may be written off as mere speculation. History, however, does record that the Medical Department of Hobart College never was moved from Geneva.

Once an understanding had been reached with the Trustees of Hobart College, the Medical Faculty of that institution was at liberty to make overtures to Syracuse University. What must have been a carefully worded letter, therefore, was drafted by Professors John Towler and Frederick Hyde sometime in the late summer of 1871. Presumably, the communication was directed to Rev. Peck, then President of the Board of Trustees of Syracuse University. Neither the original nor a copy of this letter has been found but one may surmise its general nature from what followed. Dr. Peck was delighted with the prospect of a medical center being established at the University and straightway invited Drs. Hyde and Towler to confer with the Syracuse Trustees at their next meeting scheduled for August 30, 1871.

At this gathering, Dr. Peck informed the Board of what had transpired and, after having introduced Drs. Hyde and Towler, threw the matter open for general discussion. Considerable questioning then followed with the fortunes of Hobart representatives rising every second. Anxious to advance the well-being of Syracuse and conscious of a clause in the charter providing for a medical unit, the Syracuse Trustees viewed the Hobart request with interest and favor. And when the meeting finally broke up, the Hobart men departed for home carrying with them the welcome news the Syracuse Trustees had voted to found a medical college and that in all probability the Hobart Medical Faculty would be asked to direct the venture. Moreover, a committee of the Trustees would correspond with them as to details and general policies.

It is unfortunate the University records do not disclose the nature of the conversations and communications that ensued between the Trustees' committee and the Hobart Medical Faculty. Reference, however, may be had to local newspapers and to the Minutes of the Syracuse University Medical Faculty. From these sources it is clear that the initiation of the removal question stemmed entirely from Geneva. It was Professors Towler and Hyde who directed the thinking of the Syracuse Trustees toward that end and it was these men who stressed Syracuse's advantages as a medical center to Dr. Peck and others at a meeting of the Onondaga County Medical Society in mid-November. Enthusiasm ran high, if one may judge from the speeches made at this gathering. During the course of the discussion that followed two significant comments were made. The first of these came from Dr. Hyde who pointedly remarked, "We . . . at Geneva simply propose to come with the material which is in the Geneva Medical College, the Library, the anatomical specimens, and other appliances." Nothing, it should be noted, was said by Dr. Hyde about the removal of the Geneva Medical Department. Dr. Peck's remark, however, contained an admission that it was because of the University's poverty Professor Towler, and not the University, had bought the equipment of the Geneva Medical Department. Incidentally, this remark by Dr. Peck may disclose knowledge on his part of the action taken by the Hobart Trustees in July. Neither of these comments, though important for this narrative, dampened the enthusiasm of the moment and the Onondaga County Medical Society endorsed the establishment of a College of Medicine and pledged its support for that end.

In the meantime, the visit of Drs. Towler and Hyde to Syracuse in late August had become common knowledge throughout that city. Reference, in this respect, might be paid to a letter of Dr. Sumner Rhoades of Syracuse, published in the *Journal* for September 4, 1871. In this communication the doctor warmly approved of the steps taken by the Syracuse Trustees in promoting a medical college at Syracuse. Rhoades' letter evoked some comment in Geneva where the editor of the *Gazette* reminded the Hobart Trustees of the recent endowment drive which in part had been predicated upon the needs of the Medical Faculty. This, it is believed, was the only sour note sounded at Geneva relative to the dissolution of the Medical Department. Nothing more appears in that village paper until December when the *Gazette*, still leaning upon the *Journal*, referred to a report about the removal of the medical unit to Syracuse. "We know nothing," the editor concluded, "of the alleged transfer," but later in the same month he informed his readers of the dissolution of the Geneva Medical Department.

By this time, Drs. Towler and Hyde had successfully completed their conversations with the Syracuse Trustees for the medical college at Syracuse. Among other things the Trustees agreed to accept "the proposals of Professors Towler and Hyde to transfer the Museum and Library of the Geneva Medical College with the understanding that this virtually removes the College to Syracuse without expense to Syracuse University." This agreement was dated December 4, 1871. The following day, however, a new and different understanding was reached. Possibly the Board realized the action taken the previous day might be interpreted to mean the Geneva Medical Department was to be moved to Syracuse—an interpretation the Trustees knew to be unwarranted. Be that as it may, the Board reconsidered the clause in question and after some debate, adopted a substitute provision that placed everything in its true and proper light. The new clauses read as follows: "Resolved that we accept the proposal of Professor Towler to present the University with *his* Medical Library and Museum."[1]

1. Italics are those of the author.

On the basis of this agreement, which nails down the misstatement that a Geneva Medical College was moved to Syracuse, a majority of the Medical Faculty of Hobart College—Drs. Towler, Hyde, Nivison, Eastman, and Ryder—became members of the College of Physicians and Surgeons of Syracuse University.

The original appointments to this faculty consisted of eighteen persons, nine of whom were known as "Adjunct Professors." The latter included Drs. John Van Duyn, Professor of Histology and Microscopy; Joseph P. Dunlap and Henry Didama, Professors of Clinical Medicine; Roger W. Pease and Alfred Mercer, Professors of Clinical Surgery; J. Otis Burt, Professor of Materia Medica; Wilfred W. Porter, Professor of Midwifery and Diseases of Children and Women; William T. Plant, Professor of Medical Jurisprudence; and John Lawton, Professor of Clinical Ophthalmology. The others, or full professors, were Drs. John Towler, Professor of Chemistry, Pharmacy and Toxicology; George K. Smith, Professor of General, Special and Surgical Anatomy; Nelson Nivison, Professor of Physiology, Pathology, and Hygiene; Hiram Eastman, Professor of Materia Medica and Botany; Caleb Green, Professor of Obstetrics; Frederick Hyde, Professor of Surgery; Harvey B. Miller, Professor of the Diseases of the Mind and Nervous System; and Charles E. Ryder, Professor of Ophthalmology and Diseases of the Ear.

These appointments, as stated, were made on December 5, 1871 the understanding being that each member was to serve without expense to the University. Had these gentlemen insisted upon remuneration in whole or in part there is every reason for believing the establishment of the Medical College would have been postponed. The truth of the matter, as was well known to all, was the stark fact the Trustees had no funds for a medical college. More disappointing was the realization there was no immediate prospect of conditions improving for some time. Practically every cent and resource the Trustees had at their disposal and all they hoped to raise in the near future was pledged, and rightly so, to the College of the University. All of which the medical staff appreciated and accepted. At the same time it should be remembered a somewhat similar arrangement had existed at Geneva —a procedure that may have conditioned the Faculty to the practice of looking out for itself.

The College of Medicine

9 The initial meeting of the Faculty of the College of Physicians and Surgeons of Syracuse University took place January 2, 1872, at the office of the University in the Myers Block.[1] Dr. Hiram Eastman acted as chairman and Dr. John Van Duyn as secretary. Uppermost in the minds of those present was the pressing need for class rooms, laboratories, and offices. After some discussion, Dr. Roger Pease offered the use of the second and third floors of his block on Fayette Street. So attractive did the suggestion appear that a committee was immediately sent to investigate the proposed site. Unfortunately the rooms were found to be inadequate. Attention then focused on the old High School Building on Warren and Fayette Streets which, it was rumored, might be rented for six hundred dollars a year. With no other suggestions before them the Faculty appointed a committee to look into the matter. It was also at this meeting that Dr. Frederick Hyde was chosen Dean of the College and Dr. John Van Duyn, Registrar. Evidently, the Faculty entertained democratic notions relative to the filling of administrative positions.

At a subsequent meeting held in April it was decided to abandon the idea of using the old school building. Cheaper and better quarters had

---

1. In February, 1877, the name was changed to the "College of Medicine."

been found in the Clinton Block on whose site now stands the United States Federal Building. The following month a formal contract was signed between the owners of the block and the medical staff, the latter agreeing to pay an annual rent of four hundred dollars for the use of the second and third floors. Meanwhile and during the ensuing summer and fall months, efforts were made to remove the library and museum which, for some unknown reason, were still at Geneva. Dr. Towler who had purchased this property and who in one sense should have arranged for the transfer apparently did not accomplish much. Dr. Eastman then tried his hand but he too did little and the college opened in the fall without either library or museum. Handicapped by the absence of this equipment, a special meeting of the Faculty was held to discuss the problem. Nothing, however, materialized for the time being though in a few months the library did arrive. When the museum was brought to Syracuse is uncertain; probably not before 1873 though even as late as 1876 and 1877 the Medical Faculty and the University Trustees expressed concern over the absence of some of this property. Nothing more is known of this matter and it may be that portions of the museum never were transferred to the University.

During the course of this troublesome episode the question was raised as to the approximate value of the library and museum which, it will be remembered, had been given by Dr. Towler to the University. By way of reply, Dr. Eastman expressed the opinion that it might be in the neighborhood of a thousand dollars. Although this was not a large sum even for that day its significance increased as those present remembered to what expense they had gone to rent and remodel the rooms in the Clinton Block. Some of the staff openly questioned the justice of the situation and pointedly inquired why the University had not made a contribution toward meeting these various costs. To Dr. Eastman it seemed peculiarly queer in view of a promise, he understood Dr. Peck had made, the Trustees would assume the expense of the rooms in return for the library and museum. Whereupon Dr. Towler frankly corroborated his colleague's statement by admitting Bishop Peck had promised the college rooms "would be furnished free of rent to the College as compensation of the Geneva property. And that no mention was made of that in the writing drawn up, out of deference to Dr. Peck's wishes." Possibly Dr. Peck's enthusiasm in 1871, the year the promise had been made, exceeded the bounds of good judgment or it may be the good Bishop had not expected the

Medical College would open until the fall of 1873 by which time adequate space might be allotted to it either in the Myers Block or in the Hall of Languages. Of course it is possible Bishop Peck never made such a promise or that if made it was misunderstood by Dr. Towler. The argument, however, seems unconvincing in the face of Dr. Peck's silence on this matter.

Bishop Peck's inability to make good his promise caused the medical staff considerable embarrassment as may be seen from an examination of the college's fiscal statement issued in October, 1872. Nor did conditions improve during the course of the next few weeks. Soon the poverty of the Medical College became common gossip and a plea for financial assistance was made by one of its friends in the Syracuse *Standard* for December 9, 1872. In spite of this and other trials, Dean Hyde and his staff of loyal teachers pressed forward and on the evening of October 3, 1872, formally opened the College at its quarters in the Clinton Block. Most of the city's medical profession, the entire Faculty of the College of Liberal Arts, representatives of the Board of Trustees, a number of leading citizens, and twenty-three medical students were present at the gathering. Rev. J. J. Bacon, pastor of the Fourth Presbyterian Church, invoked God's blessing upon the new college, after which short talks were given by Bishop Peck and Dean Hyde. The following morning classes were begun for the first time.

Although nothing appears to have been said at the installation ceremonies of the relationships existing between the College and the University, those informed knew them to be but nominal. All questions about finance and curriculum were entirely within the jurisdiction of the Medical College. Degrees were to be conferred by the Board of Trustees but beyond this and one or two other items the College of Physicians and Surgeons was a unit unto itself. In a gesture of sincere friendship and in accordance with a precedent adopted in respect to graduates of Genesee College, the Trustees in 1873 voted that alumni of the Geneva Medical college could, upon application, become alumni of Syracuse University. Unlike the Genesee Alumni, a large number of whom sought and obtained alumni standing from the Trustees, not a single request from the much larger Geneva alumni body is recorded in the Trustees' Minutes for the years 1872 to 1893.[2] More-

2. Research beyond the year 1893 may disclose the granting of alumni standing to some Geneva graduates.

over, it was not until February, 1875, that the Medical Staff concerned itself with the status of the Geneva students. Then it was the Medical Faculty voted Geneva graduates should be received as "alumni of this school in conformity with action taken by the other departments of the University." Actually, this vote added little to what the Trustees had done. It should be noted, moreover, that the Trustees had extended an invitation in terms of University Alumni standing whereas the Medical Faculty acted only in respect to the Medical College. An Alumni Association of the College of Physicians and Surgeons of Syracuse University was formed in February, 1875.

The entire episode illustrates quite well the detached and independent status of the Medical College. Other examples exist. On February 8, 1876, the Medical staff voted that Geneva graduates in good standing and upon payment of a five dollar fee might receive a Syracuse University diploma—a diploma, however, that carried an endorsement certifying graduation was from *Geneva*. Now the interesting thing about this decision is not that a diploma was granted but rather that the Minutes of the Trustees of Syracuse University contain no reference to the affair. It is, of course, difficult to believe the Medical College would have presumed to have made this offer without first obtaining the consent of the Trustees, and it may be that such was done but if so there is no record of such action. More illuminating is the fact that of the one hundred and fifty names given in the *Annual* as having received degrees in medicine between 1873 and 1886 inclusive, only twelve are mentioned in the Trustees' Minutes. And it was the Trustees and not the Medical Faculty who by law awarded degrees. On the other hand since the conferring of all degrees was by the hand of the Chancellor it may be assumed all degrees in medicine were in good standing even though the procedure followed was somewhat irregular.

No one was more conscious of this irregularity than Chancellor Sims who, after a preliminary investigation, laid the matter before the Trustees in June, 1885. One of the southern states, so Dr. Sims reported, had questioned the validity of Syracuse's degrees in medicine —a charge which, if true, should be cleared up immediately. Although the Trustees referred the matter to a committee little if any progress was made and in January, 1887, the Chancellor repeated his request. During the course of his remarks, the Chancellor made this significant statement and admission: "While our by-laws require all degrees to be acted upon by the Board of Trustees, in fact no degrees conferred upon medical graduates have ever been passed upon. Some evil disposed persons have attempted to discredit the validity of our medical degrees. It would seem wise to ask for legislation on this subject." Thoroughly aroused by this forcible recommendation, a select committee of the Trustees waited upon the Albany authorities and on May 11, 1887, the State Legislature obliged with an act which declared valid all degrees heretofore granted by the College of Medicine. In the future, however, all degrees in Medicine were to be granted by the Board of Trustees.

The implications of this legislation involve more than the matter of degrees. By placing responsibility where it rightly belonged, the act shattered in part the autonomy of the Medical College and paved the way for the ultimate union of that college with the University. To a thoughtful administrator like Dr. Sims the existence of an independently operated college within the University was a problem calling for immediate correction. Seizing the opportunity afforded by the question of the degrees, the Chancellor urged the Trustees to embark upon a policy aimed at the merger of the two institutions. Such a merger, however, could not be a one-sided affair. The assets of the Medical College could not so easily be bargained away. And it was high time the Trustees assumed financial responsibility for the well-being of a college within the University.

The issue was by no means new. It most certainly existed when Professors Towler and Hyde talked with Dr. Peck in 1871 and would then have been resolved had the University's financial cupboard not been bare. Thus the Medical College was launched without a penny from the University treasury. For a brief spell Dean Hyde was able to keep the college out of trouble but when in the winter of 1873 and 1874, with the students petitioning for better and cleaner quarters, it became apparent the Clinton Block would have to be abandoned in favor of a larger and better building, the question of financial aid from the University came to the front. At a meeting of the Medical Faculty, January 24, 1874, the matter was thoroughly aired, special reference being paid to the "pledged faith of the President of the Board of Trustees." After considerable discussion a committee was appointed to investigate and report on a "college building."

News of these happenings spread rapidly throughout the campus and city. Among others, the editors of the *University Herald* heard of it and, after reporting the Medical College would leave the Clinton Block by the fall, suggested that temporary quarters might be found in the Hall of Languages. Meanwhile the Committee of the Medical College discussed the issue with certain of the Trustees resident in Syracuse. A report of these conversations was presented to the Medical Faculty. Most of this report and the discussion that followed centered about the problem of a new college building. Two sites were considered, the Hoyt property on Orange (McBride) Street, and the old Park Presbyterian Church building on Mulbery (South State) Street. The former consisted of a lot, one hundred by two hundred feet in size, sufficiently large for the eventual construction of a hospital and two buildings. The price asked for the property was high—$15,000—and possession could not be had until May, 1875, in view of existing leases. Should the property, however, be purchased the Committee believed the occupants might be induced to leave.

In opposition was the Park Church lot for which the owners wanted $30,000. From point of view of location and investment there was much to recommend it and had it not been for the price might have been purchased at once. But the Medical Faculty were neither in the mood nor did they possess the financial resources necessary to negotiate such a proposition. But what of the Trustees, it was asked? Whereupon the Committee expressed the belief assistance might be forthcoming from these gentlemen. Reassured, the Medical Faculty voted to place all the facts before the Trustees; they said nothing, however, about the erection of a hospital though emphasis was laid upon the need for additional funds once either lot had been purchased. All of which was brought before the Trustees in March, 1874. To say the latter were embarrassed would be no exaggeration, for where in the face of the depressing report of University finances just rendered by the Treasurer could sums be found for the Medical College? The best they could do, and it was most important something be done, was to promise to encourage but not to initiate a drive for funds. In such a manner were the hopes and aspirations of the Medical Faculty deflated.

Two months later, the Liberal Arts Faculty offered their colleagues in medicine space in the Hall of Languages and for a time Chancellor Winchell thought the proposal was going to be accepted. But at a meeting of the medical department in May, the proposition was rejected—primarily, it was said, because of the distance between the Hill and the City. Attention then focused upon the Hoyt property and a committee was appointed to buy the same and prepare the buildings thereon for the fall term; *the expense to be assumed by the University*. Although the latter declined the responsibility, and it is difficult to see how any other answer could be given in view of the March decision on the part of the Trustees, the committee refused to be downed. Nor was their discouragement registered when aid was not forthcoming from the "well-to-do" in Syracuse. Girding themselves with additional personal self-sacrifices, a bid of $15,000 was made in July for the Hoyt property. Occupancy, however, could not be had until the following spring and with that the matter rested during the ensuing fall and winter.

Sometime early in 1875 negotiations with the owners of the Hoyt lot were renewed and certain verbal commitments were made. In order to implement the latter the Medical staff met on April 28th and agreed to organize themselves into a joint stock company "to pay for the . . . property . . . on Orange Street and to construct and furnish the necessary building or buildings for the purpose of the Medical School." Styling themselves the "Syracuse Medical Library Association of Reference," three hundred shares of stock, each valued at fifty dollars, were subscribed. Of this number, sixty-one shares were to be paid for by May 1st, the date set for a down payment of $3,000. On that date the contract of sale was duly signed and the Hoyt property, subject to a sizeable mortgage, passed into the hands of the Library Reference Association; the purchase price being $15,000. Early in the summer plans were drawn and accepted for the remodeling of the buildings and on October 8, 1875, the Medical Faculty held its first meeting in the "nearly completed College of Medicine." One of the buildings, a former carriage factory, was rebuilt to accommodate the lecture rooms, museum, library, amphitheater, dispensary, and laboratories. The amphitheater, though not the largest, was claimed to be "as cheerful and as well lighted as any in the country." The dispensary rooms were placed on the ground floor. The other structure, a blacksmith shop, was converted into a chemical laboratory. According to a public statement made by Dr. Plant both buildings "will be open to the public soon and will be kept open during a part of each afternoon throughout the year, Sunday and holidays excepted."

The decision to undertake this venture amply reflects the vision and courage of the Medical Faculty. It was by no means a light obligation these men had assumed, particularly in view of the "depressed financial condition" of the Medical College. But their devotion to the medical profession and their desire to train worthy successors dispelled all fears. At the same time their purchase of the Hoyt property, now part of University College, appears to have made an impression on the University Trustees who in January, 1876, came forward with a plan of assistance. Numerous difficulties arose but thanks to the untiring work of Chancellor Haven sufficient funds were subscribed and in December, 1877, the Medical Faculty voted to transfer the "real estate" owned by the Library Association to the University. For some unknown reason the transfer did not take place. It is difficult to believe misunderstandings developed over the meaning of "real estate" and it is not likely that men such as Horace White and John Crouse reneged on their subscriptions. A more tenable assumption may be found among the records of the Medical Faculty where there is reference to the fact that the total sums raised fell short of what was needed. In part this was due to some not meeting their pledges; it was also because the needs of the college increased as the drive for funds progressed.

Between 1878 and 1886 little if anything was done to correct the anomalous relations that had existed between the University and the Medical College since 1872. Had there been greater continuity of personnel in the Office of Chancellor and had there been fewer problems in the administration of the College of Fine Arts, not to mention the usual and routine matters of Liberal Arts, more time and effort might have been given to the Medical College. Basically, however, it was a matter of finance and so long as the University was forced to live on a day to day basis nothing could be done for the College of Medicine. With the advent of Chancellor Sims in 1881 some improvement in University finances took place but it was not until January, 1886, that Dr. Sims was able to devote any serious consideration to the problem. Then it was he asked the Trustees to review the entire situation and explore the possibility of obtaining title to the Medical School property.

In reply to this request the Trustees instructed its Executive Committee to join with the Chancellor in a careful survey of the existing relations between the University and the College of Medicine. Out of this investigation emerged a series of propositions which Dr. Sims presented to the Medical Staff in the fall of 1886. The property of the College, it was suggested, should be deeded to the University in return for which would be made an annual appropriation of three hundred dollars to the Medical Faculty. An equivalent sum would be voted each year for scientific apparatus and equipment—an amount the Medical College was to match. All entrance examinations were to be held on the Hill and all medical students were to attend Chapel once a month. University scholarships were to be honored by the Medical Faculty and a University rather than a College diploma was to be issued at commencement. Nothing, it would seem, was said about tuition or whether such income was to go to the College or University treasurer.

One may safely assume that a number of questions were raised following the presentation of the scheme to the staff of the Medical College. Certainly there was ample room for discussion over each item outlined by the Chancellor. But perplexing or irritating as these matters may have been they constituted little more than detail in a broad and comprehensive plan the significant part of which was the offer of the University to be of positive help and assistance. Here in brief was something which might serve as an approach to a long standing problem and the Medical Faculty wisely voted to appoint a committee to confer with the Chancellor upon the proposals he had submitted. Unfortunately other matters arose on the campus to delay final settlement—a delay that tended, it would seem, to widen rather than narrow the gap between the two institutions. Evidence of injured feelings was voiced at the gathering of the Medical Alumni in June, 1887. Much of this centered about the sharp indictment of the University at the hands of Dr. John L. Heffron. Dr. Heffron complained of the lack of contact between the University and the College and called attention to the fact that in spite of promises made in 1871 and 1872 no financial help had been given to the Medical Faculty. "We are gathered ," he said, "under her wing once a year and left to scratch for ourselves the rest of the time."

Those who listened to these charges, which were true in themselves, must have wondered what Chancellor Sims, who was present, would have to say. And on being called to address the alumni the Chancellor pointedly remarked that only of late had the shadow of poverty vanished from the campus. A brighter day, however, had arrived and the University was now both willing and able to be of help. But nothing, he continued, could be done so long as the medical property was held by a society, the "Library Association of Reference." University assistance, in brief, was dependent upon the University owning that property. In conclusion, Dr. Sims predicted a splendid future for the Medical College if the Library Association were to sell its property and erect a new and modern building on the campus.

The Chancellor's balanced and thoughtful statement created a favorable impression. The University's position had been made clear. Sins of omission were to be atoned for and financial aid would be forthcoming upon the deeding of the Association's property to the University in the event the College did not care to move to the campus. The Medical Faculty, it transpired, did not care to move but it eagerly entered into a series of conferences relative to transferring the Orange Street property to the University. Finally an agreement was reached in June, 1888. According to this understanding transfer would take place subject to certain conditions. First, the Medical Faculty was to retain control over the property, pay interest on all debts, meet taxes and operational costs, and receive any income that might arise from rents. Second, the University was to grant to the Medical College an annual subsidy of five hundred dollars. Third, no disposition of the property was to be made without the consent of the Medical staff. Fourth, should the property ever be abandoned by the Medical Faculty or the Medical Department of the University the faculty was to "lose all control over the property." Fifth, details as to other matters were to be worked out at a later date.

What these details were is not known; possibly they referred to such matters as attendance at Chapel and the like. If so, it was the University that yielded ground since nothing as to this or other requirements appears in subsequent publications of the University. Nor was anything said about tuition—the financial reports of the University treasurer show no tuition receipts from the College of Medicine. These details, whatever they may have been, were not allowed to block negotiations and on April 10, 1889, the Library Reference Association empowered Dr. Didama to dispose of its holdings to the University. Five days later, the Executive Committee of the Board of Trustees directed a sub-committee to "procure the extinguishing of all claims . . . and to draw on the Treasury of the Syracuse University for a sufficient sum . . . not exceeding one thousand dollars for the extinguishing of such claims if they find it practical to procure a title or titles which in their judgment will be carried." All of which was done as ordered and in May of the same year the medical property, lot and buildings, were deeded to the University. Immediately thereafter the Trustees voted a grant of five hundred dollars to the Medical

College; additional grants and other services were made available during the remaining years covered by this volume.

During the course of these protracted negotiations, which culminated in the merging of the Medical College and University, the Medical Faculty never once faltered in its teaching program. An examination of the latter is interesting and suggestive. It will be recalled that
one of the reasons prompting the abandonment of the Hobart Medical
Department and the establishment of the Syracuse University Medical College sprang from the department's inability to maintain a sound
curriculum and a high academic standard in a small and relatively
isolated community. The Syracuse location made the realization of
these ends possible. For some time the members of the Hobart Medical
Faculty had been aware of the existence of a three year graded course
at the Chicago Medical College, now an integral part of Northwestern
University. Later, in 1871, and while plans were under way for the
inception of a medical unit at Syracuse University, Harvard announced a graded course of medical instruction. An analysis of the Harvard
plan convinced the more progressive men on the Syracuse Faculty of
the need of a similar undertaking at Syracuse.

An initial move in that direction was made at a January, 1872, meeting of the Medical staff. At this gathering, and at a later one in June,
the Harvard program was discussed with much care and in great detail.
Bolstered by a timely word of encouragement from Dr. Peck those
favoring a systematic course gained control and in June carried a
motion, later made unanimous, endorsing the new curriculum. Not
wanting, however, to penalize those Hobart students who had matriculated in the lecture course and who had expressed a wish to complete their study at Syracuse, an exception was made in their favor.
In 1875, when the last of these privileged students were graduated, the
old lecture system was abolished. At the same time the college year,
which had been set at five months, was extended to nine. Generally
speaking the Faculty hailed the adoption of the new program, and
that in spite of severe outside criticism. The Faculty, it was charged,
was sacrificing growth and expansion by adhering to standards far in
excess of what was necessary.

    The action of the Faculty, no doubt, emptied some of the benches. The
matriculations increased in three years from 24 to 65 on the old plan. From
this increase we had a right to expect our classes would have ranged from 75 to
100 had we continued on the old plan. On the new plan of a three years graded

course of instruction the class dropped from 65 to 41, since then our classes have ranged from 40 to 60.

But to this and other criticisms the Faculty replied by placing in the *Annual*, "Those who expect to receive the degree of M.D. by a short and easy way, will not come here; or coming will not remain." And Dean Hyde allowed himself to be quoted in the *University Herald* in the following words: "I would rather see this school reduced to six students, to go down with its colors flying, than to return to the old way." Meanwhile "W.T.P." (Dr. Wm. T. Plant?) glossed the Faculty minutes of June 4, 1875, with "Full adoption of graded system with long term. The second school in the United States to adopt this plan fully."[3]

According to the first catalogue, issued by the College of Medicine during the summer of 1872, nothing was said of entrance examinations. Considerable emphasis, however, was placed upon the new curriculum which like the lecture course was divided into two terms. During the first semester of both programs there were to be lectures and recitations; clinical instruction was to feature the second term. Those who registered under the lecture system were to complete "three years' study in the office of a regular physician, and attend at least two full courses of lectures, the last of which must be at the Syracuse College of Medicine." More important were the comments relating to the new curriculum; these read as follows:[4]

Too frequently in the case of Medical students beginning their professional studies at our best Medical College, there have been no previous opportunities for the acquisition of even the elements of science, or any adequate mental discipline. To meet this demand something more is necessary than long continued courses of lectures from talented and accomplished lecturers. Practical knowledge and skill cannot be imparted in this way and under these circumstances. It is therefore designed, in the case of those students who are about beginning the study of Medicine, to organize a well proportioned and definite plan of study, which, beginning with the elementary branches of the science shall conduct the pupil through the whole course, with the same regard to order in requirement, mental discipline, and completeness of instruction as prevails in any other whole department of education.

3. Dean J. L. Heffron writing in the *Golden Jubilee* ranked Syracuse as the third American college to adopt a graded system. Possibly "W. T. P." was referring to the "long term" when he placed Harvard as the first and Syracuse as the second.
4. This quotation, modified slightly from time to time, reappeared in most of the catalogues between 1872 and 1893.

To gain these ends the new curriculum contained a number of requirements for graduation. In the first place each student was to complete a three year course and successfully pass examinations on course
work at the close of each year. Secondly, each candidate for a degree
was to present, and to defend if necessary, a dissertation "composed
and written by himself." Thirdly, he was to clear an oral test conducted by the Faculty in the presence of the State Board of Censors.
Finally, he was to be of "good moral character" and have reached the
age of twenty-one years. Special provisions existed for transfer students.[5] Nothing, it should be noted, was stated in the first catalogue
about women students; subsequent issues, however, state that women
had never been denied at any time.[6]

During the remaining years covered by this volume several important changes took place in the program as adopted in 1872. For example, in 1876 reference for the first time was made to entrance examinations. Students, not holding certificates of scholarship from a
college, academy, or high school, were required to pass examinations
in Arithmetic, Grammar, Geometry, and to show skill in spelling and
penmanship exercises. These requirements did not appear in the *Annuals* for 1877 and 1878; in their place the following was substituted:
"Students who join the School for the regular course are examined as
to their qualifications for the study of medicine, unless they present
evidence of scholarship from some creditable source." In 1880, the requirement became slightly more precise: candidates now were to be
tested in "branches of a common English education." Nine years later
the examinations were enlarged so as to include a portion of Caesar's
Commentaries, and in 1890 those not presenting certificates of scholarship were to be tested in Arithmetic, Algebra, Geometry, Natural
Philosophy, Composition, and Latin. Candidates who failed four of
these subjects were rejected; those who showed competency in but
four fields were admitted "conditionally," while those who did better
were admitted without "conditions." Evidently, the quality of these

5. Transfer students were required to spend the last year in residence at
Syracuse. In 1876 such candidates were asked to pass examinations in all courses
taken elsewhere; the following year this obligation was waived for those who
presented certificates of scholarship. Later, in 1879, the examinations were restored; in 1884 such students "may be examined" and in 1885 the procedure of
1877 was restored. In 1876 the requirement of a dissertation was abolished.

6. There were four women in session during 1872 and 1874.

examinations was not high; nor could it be otherwise so long as high school students were allowed to matriculate. More alarming, from a modern point of view, was the fact a student might be admitted without having had either an elementary course in Chemistry or Biology. Deficiencies of this type presumably were to be made up in college.

During the student's first year, between the years 1872 and 1893, instruction centered about the course work in Anatomy, General Chemistry, and Physiology. In 1877, Histology and Botany were added and at odd times there were offerings in Pathology, Microscopy, and Applied Anatomy. In the second year there were classes in Medical Chemistry, Materia Medica, Pathological Anatomy, and Didactic and Clinical Medicine and Surgery between 1872 and 1876. In the fall of 1876 and continuing through 1893 instruction was given in Medical Chemistry, Materia Medica, Anatomy, Physiology, Principles and Practice of Medicine, Surgery, and Clinical Medicine and Surgery. No other changes were made in the program except for the temporary addition of Pathology, Obstetrics, and Therapeutics. During the Senior year, from 1872 to 1876, students were required to take Pathological Anatomy, Didactic and Clinical Surgery and Medicine, Therapeutics, Obstetrics, and Medical Jurisprudence. During the next three years there were classes in Obstetrics, Gynecology, Dermatology, Ophthalmology, Materia Medica, Therapeutics, Principles and Practice of Medicine, and Surgical and Clinical Medicine and Surgery. In 1879, Materia Medica and Dermatology were dropped and Diseases of Children was added; the following year a course in Dental Surgery was offered. The latter was withdrawn in 1883; its place being taken by Pathology. State Medicine and Pediatrics were introduced in 1885 and 1887 respectively. Meanwhile, except for transfer students, graduation requirements remained much the same.

Closely paralleling this extension in curriculum was the growth of laboratory work, especially in the fields of chemistry and anatomy. Increased opportunities for clinical training was offered by the Good Shepherd and St. Joseph's Hospitals and by the University Free Dispensary. The latter was established in 1876, many of the drugs and supplies being generously provided by friends and "druggists" of the city. The scope and significance of the Dispensary became more evident as time progressed and in the fall of 1892 an Obstetrical Department was added by vote of the Board of Trustees.

Student interest in the Medical College was demonstrated, in part, by enrollment. According to the *Annuals*, the total number of students in attendance between the opening of the College in 1872 and the close of the academic year in 1893 was 866; of these 211 received degrees. Prominent among these graduates were Electa B. Whipple, '74; Augustus A. Young, '76; Albert L. Hall, '79, and Wheelock Rider, '85, who earned a name for themselves in medical circles of Buffalo, Newark, Fair Haven, and Rochester respectively. Mention also should be made of Arthur E. Mink, '87, later Professor of Mental and Nervous Diseases at the St. Louis College of Physicians and Surgeons, and Edmund L. Down, '92, who became a prominent member of the New York College of Physicians and Surgeons.

The success of these and other students was most gratifying to the Faculty of the College of Medicine of whom Drs. Mercer, Plant, Van Duyn, and Didama had been with the college since its inception. Born in England and educated at Genesee Wesleyan Seminary, Dr. Alfred Mercer was graduated from the Geneva College Medical Department in 1845. Later, he became a practitioner at Syracuse and in 1871 was appointed Professor of Clinical Surgery of the University College of Medicine; beginning in 1873 he also taught Minor Surgery. In 1884 he resigned these chairs to become Professor of State Medicine, a position he held until his retirement in 1895. Author of several significant articles and active in state and local medical associations, Dr. Mercer is best remembered as an exponent of medical education and public health. His colleague, Dr. William T. Plant received his medical degree at the University of Michigan in 1861. Shortly thereafter he became a navy surgeon and served with distinction during the Civil War. In 1871 he was appointed to the chair of Medical Jurisprudence of the College of Medicine; later, he was in charge of Clinical Medicine and Pediatrics. For a time he was Registrar. Although an author of some reputation, it was in the field of teaching that he excelled. Among his many friends was Dr. John Van Duyn, a graduate of the Kentucky School of Medicine and an army surgeon during the Civil War. In 1869 he opened a medical office in Syracuse and joined the staff of the Medical College in 1871. During his long service at the University, he held the chairs of Histology, Anatomy, Ophthalmology, Operative and Clinical Surgery, and Surgery; he was also Registrar, 1872 to 1874. Known to his many students as "our beloved, Dr. John," and described as "a fiery little man," Dr. Van Duyn was a remarkably fine and impressive teacher.

In his hands rested part of the responsibility for bringing about the integration of the Medical College and University in 1889. At that time, Dr. Henry Didama was Dean of the College, his predecessor being Dr. Frederick Hyde, a graduate of the Fairfield Medical College in 1836. For a time, Dr. Hyde practised at Virgil and Cortland, New York, and in 1854 became Professor of Obstetrics and later Surgery at the Geneva College Medical Department. After seventeen years of valuable service at Geneva, he was honored by his colleagues by being named Dean of the Syracuse University College of Medicine in 1872; his appointment as Professor of Surgery having been made the year before. During his Deanship, which was terminated by death in October, 1887, he guided the young college through its most trying years. He has been depicted as being a "tall, spare, angular man with rugged features and clear blue eyes, whose expression was ever earnest and serious." His enviable record at Syracuse was matched by untiring devotion to civic duties and responsibilities, chiefly at his old home at Cortland. Here, at various times, he was Trustee and President of the Cortland Academy, President of the Cortland Normal School, and President of the Cortland Savings Bank. In the field of medicine he rose rapidly, was one of the founders of the American Medical Association and twice represented the latter at international gatherings in 1876 and 1884. As an author, he produced a number of articles published in England and America.

His successor, the unanimous choice of his colleagues, was Dr. Henry D. Didama. Educated at historic Cazenovia Seminary, Dr. Didama was graduated from the Albany Medical College in 1846. After a few years of practice at Romulus, New York, he moved to Syracuse and in 1871 was appointed Professor of Clinical Medicine at the Medical College. Later, he was placed in charge of the Department of Principles and Practice of Medicine and Clinical Medicine, and still later of Science and Art of Medicine and Clinical Medicine. Throughout the state and nation, Dr. Didama was well known and became the distinguished President of the Syracuse Medical, Onondaga County Medical, New York Central Medical, and New York State Medical Societies. He also was a member of the British Medical Association. In 1893, he resigned from the Deanship of the Medical College and accepted the post of Chief of Staff at St. Joseph's Hospital in Syracuse. His associations with the University, however, were not severed. In 1893 he assumed the rank of Emeritus Professor of Clinical Medicine and in 1905 was made Dean Emeritus.

Among the other original members of the Medical Faculty reference should be made to Dr. John Towler, one-time Dean of the Geneva Medical Department. Dr. Towler was appointed Professor of Chemistry, Pharmacy, and Toxicology at Syracuse in December, 1871. However, when college opened in 1872 he held the chair in Anatomy. The following year he became Professor of Chemistry and in 1880, upon vote of the Medical Faculty, he was appointed Professor Emeritus, a rank he held until his death in 1886. Then there was Dr. Nelson Nivison who was Professor of Physiology until 1887 when he became Professor Emeritus; he died in July, 1893. His colleague, Dr. Hiram Eastman, a member of the Geneva Medical Department, served at Syracuse as Professor of the Principles and Practice of Medicine for but one year, after which he returned to private practice and died at Oswego, New York, in October, 1879. Dr. Edward B. Stevens came to Syracuse from the Miami Medical College of Cincinnati, Ohio. After what may have been an unhappy experience, he resigned in 1877 and presumably returned to Ohio where he died in 1896; while at the University, Dr. Stevens was Professor Materia Medica and Therapeutics. Dr. Charles E. Rider, Professor of Ophthalmology and Diseases of the Ear, 1872 to 1880, retired as Professor Emeritus in 1880 and returned to his home in Rochester, New York. Assisting him for the years 1872 to 1874 was Dr. John W. Lawton, who died at Syracuse in June, 1874.

Another charter member of the Medical Faculty was Dr. Hervey B. Wilbur, Superintendent of the New York State Asylum for Idiots, 1851 to 1883, and Professor of Diseases of the Mind and Nervous System, 1872 to 1876. In 1876, he became Lecturer on Insanity, a position he retained until his death in 1883. Among his friends was Dr. Joseph P. Dunlap, President of the Onondaga County Medical Society and prominent practitioner at Syracuse from 1845 to the time of his death in 1896; Dr. Dunlap was Professor of Clinical Medicine at the University, 1872 to 1873. His colleague, Dr. Roger W. Pease was Professor of Clinical Surgery, 1872 to 1876, and of Operative and Clinical Surgery from 1876 to his death in May, 1886. Reference should also be made to Dr. John O. Burt, Professor of Materia Medica, of Diseases of Children and Dermatology, of Therapeutics, and Medical Chemistry from 1872 to 1879, and to Dr. Wilfred W. Porter, Professor of Clinical Midwifery, Obstetrics, and Gynecology, 1872 until his death in June, 1885. Dr. Porter was a Trustee of the University, 1872 to 1885, one-time President of the Onondaga County Medical Society, and President of the Board of Trustees of the Geddes Union

Free Schools, 1856 to 1877.

In 1876 the Medical College was fortunate in obtaining Dr. William M. Smith, a graduate of the Medical College of the University of Pennsylvania in 1849. Later, he was Professor of Pharmacy, New York College of Pharmacy, and Physician at Sing Sing Prison. While at Syracuse he distinguished himself as Professor of Medical Chemistry and Botany. Equally well known was Dr. Gaylord P. Clark who came to the University in 1880 as Lecturer on Anatomy. Between 1881 and 1892 he was Professor of Anatomy, after which he became Professor of Physiology and, upon the death of Dr. Didama, Dean of the College of Medicine. Meanwhile, Drs. William H. Dunlap, John L. Heffron, Henry B. Allen, Alfred C. Mercer, Henry L. Elsner, David M. Totman, Frank W. Marlow, Nathan Jacobson, Aaron B. Miller, Scott Owen, James C. Carson, Frederick W. Sears, Gervas M. Wasse, and William H. May were added to the Faculty. All of these, including Drs. Smith and Clark were members of the teaching staff at the time of Chancellor Sims' retirement. Others who served for a time at Syracuse included Drs. George R. Metcalf, J. Gilbert Justin, Miles G. Hyde, Martin A. Knapp, Arthur B. Breese, Horace D. Babcock, and Ceylon H. Lewis. Finally, Professors Lucien M. Underwood, Charles W. Hargitt, and John J. Brown of the College of Liberal Arts offered special courses in the College of Medicine.

Athletics

10

Athletics, formal and informal, were none too prominent at either Genesee or Hobart. Here and there, as in the issues of the *Livingston Republican*, reference was made to baseball at Genesee but beyond that nothing of importance is known. In all probability, scrub games of various kinds were engaged in but of this we are left in the darkness of an academic age that not only frowned upon play as frivolity but actually condemned athletics as down-right injurious and dangerous. Nor, if one may judge from opinion as expressed in early issues of the *University Herald*, were conditions materially different when Syracuse University was established. Criticism, however, should be tempered with moderation and justice; and history, like athletics, believes in fair play. It should be noted, therefore, that students at Syracuse did not wholly reject and censure the views of their elders. On several occasions, for example, editorials in the *University Herald* voiced strong disapproval of football and completely endorsed faculty opinion that nothing should be tolerated on the campus that interfered with academic life and development.

At the same time the desire for physical relaxation asserted itself and the urge for the joy of competitive sport was demonstrated during the University's sojourn in the old Myers Block. Late in June, 1872, to illustrate, an editorial entitled "SHALL WE BOAT" appeared in the student paper. Syracuse, so it was argued, had a unique advantage in Onondaga Lake which "would be considered a gem of a sheet were it near one of our large boating colleges." Cornell University "has already formed several boat clubs and has erected a commodious boat house on the shores of the Cayuga" and Hobart College "is not without the pale of this boating mania, and neither ought we to be." Doubtless no one expected the impossible, particularly since classes were about finished for the year, but at least the way could be cleared for action in the fall. Syracuse, moreover, had a group of crew-minded students and "we expect at no distant period to record the fact of the organization of a Boating Association in the University."

Additional stimulus was generated during the summer by the College Regatta held at Springfield, Massachusetts, concerning which Syracuse students were informed in a September issue of the *University Herald*. Coupled with this item was an appeal for a crew at Syracuse—a crew that would raise the "rose tint and sky blue" of the University on high. An answer to this appeal was not slow in coming. Two enterprising students of the freshman class of 1877, Charles D. Holden, in whose honor the University Observatory was to be erected, at a later date, by his father, and George F. Hine, after having received financial assistance from friends in the city, journeyed to Rochester and returned with a four-oared shell. Later, a boat-house valued at seven hundred dollars was built at what was known as the Salina Landing. It is to be regretted no one of that generation saw fit to record the names of these friends and benefactors.

During the spring of 1873 rumor had it a regatta would be held in June on Onondaga Lake and that Cornell would send a crew to race against one representing Syracuse. Stimulated by these reports a group of Syracuse students trained under the most disheartening conditions. Although the *University Herald* sparked campus enthusiasm with news items and gave timely encouragement to the "pink and green," student cheers were not matched by gifts or contributions. At the same time faculty support was lacking and while no official veto came from the Chancellor's office it was common gossip Dr. Winchell frowned upon the proposed regatta and generally questioned the value and expediency of all "muscular sports." Athletics, he firmly believed, would interfere with the fundamental purposes of the University. Not wishing, however, to set his opinion above others, the

Chancellor wrote to some of his friends for advice and counsel; answers to these inquiries, if any, do not appear to have been preserved. Possibly, these friends softened the Administration's attitudes since no obstacles were placed in the way of the proposed regatta. On the other hand, no word of encouragement was heard.

Equally disconcerting to those who sponsored the crew was the physical labor involved in reaching the boat-house which was close to three miles from the campus. Streetcars or the Liverpool Stage provided transportation to what today is Hiawatha Boulevard but from that street one was forced to walk through the salt works, then Syracuse's chief industrial activity, to the boat-house which, according to the *University Herald* was on the "flat north of the city, at some distance from the lake, communicating with it by a little canal." The entire area, it was added, was under water during the spring and "boats were necessary to reach the boat-house." From other sources it is known that the land upon which the boat-house was built was low and had been reclaimed by the State of New York earlier in the century when the level of Onondaga Lake had been lowered. A more precise location is mentioned in the *Standard* for June 25, 1873. Here one reads the boat-house was opposite to the landing at the foot of North Salina. Presumably this must have been in the neighborhood of the old Iron Pier, a favorite amusement center for Syracusans at the turn of the century. A better description appeared in the *Syracusan*, December 10, 1885. According to this source the boat-house was to the right of the New York Central tracks and not far from those of the Northern Railroad. Moreover, the *Syracusan* places the house on the edge of Onondaga Creek a few rods from the lake by the same name. Added interest is given when the editor points out that the structure was then standing and adorned by what must have been a weather beaten sign bearing the inscription, "University Boat House."

In spite of these and other difficulties, Holden and Hine aided by a handful of loyal supporters, whose names are not recorded, continued their efforts, organized a "Syracuse University Boating Association" and successfully staged a regatta on Onondaga Lake, June 25, 1873. Scheduled to start shortly after two o'clock it was not until five o'clock that the first race got under way amid the cheers of several hundred spectators who crowded the barges and steamers that accompanied the boats over a three mile course. This contest was between single sculls representing the Union Springs Club of Union

Springs, New York, the Riverside Club of Rochester, and the Gramercy Club of New York City. Union Springs captured the event but did not have an entry in the four-oared race which was won by the New York shell. The presence of these out-of-town contestants may have been stimulated by the prizes, estimated to have a value close to four hundred dollars, offered by the University Association. Where Holden and Hine ever raised this sum is not stated. One thing, however, is established: the money must have come from friends in the city and not from the campus judging from the lack of student interest on the Hill. Again, if one may trust the local papers the regatta was not an intercollegiate affair—all of the races being between private or professional clubs. Disappointing as all this must have been to those who had dreamed of a student regatta, the fact remains something had been done to advance the cause of boating at the University. Why the rumored race between Cornell and Syracuse did not materialize is not known.

Appreciation, however, of the services rendered by Holden and Hine was shown shortly after college opened in the fall of 1873. Interested students, drawn chiefly from the class of 1875, took over the fortunes of the crew and agitated for the formation of a "Syracuse University Navy." And early in October a campus-wide meeting was held to discuss the proposal. At this gathering, Elwyn D. Plaisted, '77, offered in behalf of himself and Hine (no mention is made of Holden) to transfer to the proposed Navy the boat-house and shells, valued at nine hundred dollars, plus a debt of four hundred dollars. Enthusiasm ran high in spite of this indebtedness and on November 14, 1873, the "Syracuse University Navy" was organized. A. F. Berrian, '75, was elected President and Chester A. Congdon, '75 was chosen Commodore. All in all some eighteen students joined in the ambitious program. Expressed in terms of University enrollment this number represented a trifle more than ten per cent which by any comparison may be considered quite outstanding. It was not, however, enough and interest in the crew vanished almost as rapidly as it had arisen. Now and then in the years that followed one encounters an occasional reference to a Syracuse Crew. The *Syracusan* of December 10, 1885, for example, tried to revive the idea of a crew by calling its readers' attention to the 1873 regatta, the abandoned boat-house on Onondaga Lake, and the remains of a six-oared shell to the rear of that building. But in spite of this appeal which had been calculated to touch the student body to the quick no visible results followed. Nor was there any change in student attitude during the remainder of the period covered by this volume.

In attempting to appraise the factors that may explain the rise and fall of a Syracuse crew one is apt to think first of all in terms of faculty opposition. During the administrations of Chancellors Winchell and Haven official disapproval did dampen student interest and the impact of this negative attitude continued during part of the Chancellorship of Dr. Sims. One of the arguments used against athletics at the time was the complaint that college sports invited the use of "ringers." In the February 1885 issue of the *University Herald* there is reference to the hiring of local Irish boys at two dollars "to take a temporary course in 'analytical drafting'." The *Herald* did not state this took place at Syracuse nor does it refer to any particular form of athletics but it is difficult to escape the conclusion that the administration's condemnation of athletics was strengthened by such a story. On the other hand it is easy to exaggerate the significance of this opposition and thus overlook the absence of a real and abiding interest among the students. It should also be remembered that the maintenance of a crew even for that day was an expensive luxury, indulged in only by a favored few. Other activities, such as baseball, could be financed for much less and from the very nature of things would attract a larger student following. Finally, it should be recalled that the physical labor involved in journeying to and from a distant boat-house constituted a hurdle few tried to clear.

Most of these hardships were not met by those who promoted baseball; a sport, moreover, that did not in principle evoke serious disapproval from either faculty or administration. Bats, balls, and gloves were to be found in ample supply among the personal effects of the students and there were wide open spaces for a diamond both on and off the campus. Talk of baseball certainly must have taken place shortly after the opening of classes in the fall of 1871 and during the ensuing spring there may have been informal play between scrub teams. Logically, the next step would be to organize this activity and on April 20, 1872 the "Syracuse University Baseball Association" was formed with Heman W. Morris, '72, as its first president. The team, so we are told, consisted of James M. Gilbert, '75, catcher; John E. Weaver, '72, first base and captain; Edwin R. Redhead, '74, shortstop; Erastus W. Goodier, '75, left field; W. S. Kress, '75, center field; Charles D. Lathrop, '75, right field; and Judson B. Coit, '75, pitcher.

Several games were played that spring but between whom and where it is not known.

It seems likely that these matches may have taken place on the so-called University Grounds which tradition has placed on the flat land between Marshall and Waverly Streets in the general vicinity of University Avenue. This assumption is predicated in part upon the fact that the rough terrain of the campus was not suitable for play plus statements frequently made by older alumni that a "meadow" on University Avenue served as a diamond. Confirmation of this interpretation appeared in the *Syracusan* for October 22, 1886; here reference is made to the destruction of a diamond on the east side of University Avenue occasioned by the recent construction of several homes. Use of the University Grounds seems to have been made during the summer of 1872 when a picked team from Sing Sing played a local city nine which included James M. Gilbert, '75. Gilbert's interest also was shown by his election that fall to the Board of Directors of the University Baseball Association of which Judson B. Coit, '75, was President. In addition to promoting informal contests among the students, the Association should be credited with having agitated for the construction of a diamond on the campus proper.

During the course of the next seven years baseball continued to attract a number of students, the various games probably being played on the University Grounds. There is also a reference to a "Chestnut [Crouse] Street Grounds," the exact location of which has not been determined. Most of these encounters were with local city nines, such as the Syracuse Stars, Baltics, Bankers, and the Syracuse High School. Several matches were played with teams from Cazenovia Seminary and at odd times Syracuse was host to nines from Union, Hobart, Hamilton, Cornell, and Rochester; return games were played with these colleges. In most of these contests, Syracuse was the loser. In June, 1873, a game was lost to the Syracuse Stars by a score of thirty to fourteen. A year later Hobart defeated Syracuse in a nine inning game that lasted over three hours, the score being twenty-eight to twenty-seven. The following year, Cornell outplayed Syracuse in a seven inning game, twenty-five to twelve, though at a return match, a nine inning contest, Syracuse won twenty to fourteen. Later in 1879, Syracuse lost to Hamilton and Union in two hotly contested games by the score of five to four, and ten to nine respectively. However, at Newell Park in the city, June 28, 1879, Syracuse downed Rochester six to two; Syracuse making its runs on four hits and four errors, Rochester making one hit and thirteen errors. Finally, reference should be made to interclass games which were very popular among the students.

Student support, according to all available primary sources, was none too good. Financial assistance was far below what it might have been and most of the responsibility for expenses fell upon the handful of loyal members of the Baseball Association. As a result, the equipment was limited and often defective; in the spring of 1878 there was not a single bat on the campus fit for use. Now and then receipts warranted the spending of hard earned dollars for repair of the diamond and at one game the team trotted out to their positions attired in new uniforms that fitted "like amputated meal bags."

Nor was attendance anything to boast about. Time after time attempts were made to "pep" up local enthusiasm and on one occasion the "co-eds" were promised seats if they would grace the Varsity with their presence. The girls accepted the invitation only to find the Association had not been able to keep its word. At the last moment the University Registrar flatly refused to allow the boys to remove the Library Reading Chairs out to the field which, judging from the circumstances, may have been to the rear of the Hall of Languages. Generally speaking, the Faculty did not condemn baseball though tongues did wag at a meeting of that body in 1874 over those students who had absented themselves from classes so as to play Hobart at Geneva. Both Chancellors Winchell and Haven seemed kindly disposed to games played at home but in spite of this friendly attitude it was difficult to arouse too much interest among the majority of the students. All of which was highly discouraging to the players. Dilatory and half-hearted practices took place and more than one game was delayed because of the necessity of introducing the Syracuse players to one another. Nothing, it would seem, like an organized and prepared team ever went out onto the diamond. Among those whose names appear more frequently in the box scores, the reliability of which cannot be established, were William H. Dunlap, '75; William Nottingham, '76; and John F. Tallman, '79.

In spite of these and other hindrances, baseball had come to stay. Its promotion and development, however, were not dependent upon interclass games or those good natured contests often staged for the benefit of visiting alumni at graduation time. Important as this spade work was, and one should not forget that games were played in the fall as well as the spring, baseball became a major sport because of the stimulus it received from intercollegiate contests. Halting and uncertain steps in the direction of the latter may be seen in the games played with neighboring rivals during the late 1870's. More positive signs of growth appeared in the call, issued by Union College, for a meeting of these institutions that had taken part in the recent intercollegiate games. Such a gathering was held in March, 1880, with Syracuse being the host. At this meeting the New York State Intercollegiate Baseball Association was formed, Syracuse being one of its members.

Anticipating possible opposition from the Faculty, particularly because the schedule of games called for trips to other campuses, the local student publications did their best to justify intercollegiate baseball. Academic standing and interest in intellectual pursuits, it was argued, would not suffer, student health would be advanced, and only the misinformed talked about baseball being a dangerous sport. Moreover, it was added, only ten games were to be played, five at home and one each at Hamilton, Union, Madison, Cornell, and Rochester, and the entire schedule was to be completed between May 12th to May 24th. These and other arguments probably accompanied the petition submitted to the faculty praying for permission to participate in the Intercollegiate Baseball Association. After some deliberation, extending over two meetings, the faculty left the decision in the hands of the Chancellor who, it seems, sought advice from the heads of other institutions presumably within the league. Meanwhile, the University Club organized itself, arranged for practice games with local city nines, purchased new suits—white with red trimmings and adorned with an "S.U." on a shield worn over the breast—and engaged in several scrub matches on the University grounds. By late April, however, it became evident the Administration was going to adopt a negative attitude. Shortly thereafter, the faculty, so it was reported in the student papers, announced it would not grant excuses for absences occasioned by baseball; this decision blasted all hope of Syracuse participating in the Association. Three games, however, were played at Newell Park in the city of Syracuse with Union, Hamilton, and Rochester—each resulting in defeat for the Varsity. Charles S. Seager, '80, and Benjamin J. Shove, '80, were the Syracuse pitchers.

During the years, 1881 to 1883, baseball at Syracuse experienced a decided slump. Interclass contests and scrub games on the University grounds, sadly in need of repair, plus an occasional match with the Syracuse Stars, Cornell, Hobart, and Rochester tell the entire story. During 1884, there was talk of reviving Syracuse's membership in the State Intercollegiate Association, but in the end it was nothing more than talk. In part this was caused by faculty disapproval of out-of-city games and its announcement that it was not granting excuses for absences occasioned by baseball. On the other hand blame also rests with the students themselves who, so it was stated in the student papers, placed class rivalry and personal ambition above the needs of college baseball. The following spring a decided turn for the better took place and the University Nine, on its own initiative and responsibility, re-joined the State Association much to the dismay of the faculty who honestly questioned the wisdom and expediency of intercollegiate athletics. The entire matter was carefully reviewed by this body at a meeting, February 5, 1885 at which time the Dean was asked to write to the students concerned that the faculty did not sanction games necessitating absences from classes. Moreover, the Dean was to express the hope that no matches of that type would be scheduled. On the other hand, no criticism appears to have been raised about home-games and no objection was made to matches not entailing absences. To this extent, therefore, the University gave its approval of organized baseball; no change in this policy took place until 1890.

Acting on the assumption that half a loaf was better than none, the University Nine played games both at home and away without apparently violating the faculty ruling. Although the net result of these contests did little to flatter the Syracuse team—games being lost to Hobart, Cornell, and Hamilton, and one being taken from Union—local enthusiasm had never been higher. The team had been equipped with new uniforms, greater stress had been placed upon practice, and a total of four hundred and seventy-two dollars had been raised to meet the current expenses which ultimately reached five hundred and seven dollars. Unfortunately, much of this splendid effort and spirit were wasted so far as the year 1886 was concerned. In all probability—the sources are none too clear—Syracuse did not participate in the State Association and while it played several teams from neighboring institutions did not win a single game; the worst defeat being experienced in May when Cornell swamped the Varsity, twenty-seven to nothing. Local enthusiasm sagged but did not vanish and in the fall of 1886 the Athletic Association of the University promoted the construction

of a new diamond, the old University grounds having been appropriated by private dwellings. Precisely where the new diamond was located is uncertain. An alumnus, who was in college at the time, informed the author by letter in 1945: "The hill upon which Crouse
College was erected was then the only athletic field of the University."
Contemporary views of the campus sustain this assumption by showing a large cleared area on West Hill but none to the rear of the Hall
of Languages. Printed sources, however, refer to the field as being
"back" of the University which in the language of that day meant,
behind the Hall of Languages. And there is one view, probably of
1888, that shows baseball being played to the rear of that building. In
view of the physical difficulties imposed upon the players by a West
Hill diamond which would have a deep ravine on the east and a steep
hill to the north and west, it would seem wise to conclude that such a
field was used only for a brief period of time. Finally, it may be observed that when a cinder track was constructed to the rear of the
Hall of Languages a loud wail of protest arose from the baseball en-
thusiasts who deplored this encroachment upon the "diamond." It
seems likely, therefore, that the new baseball grounds were toward
the eastern end of the "old Oval."

Bolstered by a campus play-ground and encouraged by the friendly
comments from the new Chancellor, Dr. Sims, relative to the future
of athletics at Syracuse, student morale rose. It was the Chancellor's
hope that all college sports would center on the Oval. In the meantime,
the University Nine, behind the pitching of Hartman L. Oberlander,
Medicine, '87, won three games out of five played in the State Intercollegiate Association. The following year, 1888, the Varsity turned
in a better record, winning five of the six contests played in the Association; George W. Church, '89, being the leading pitcher. The next
year only four games were played—lack of funds forced the cancellation of the others—of which probably but one was won and that by
the close score of twelve runs for Syracuse and eleven for Union.
And of this victory there seems to be some dispute. The records for
all other contests appear to have been lost.

The year 1889, as will be shown in a subsequent chapter, was significant in the history of athletics at Syracuse. Among other things
football was recognized as a major sport for the first time. Heretofore
little interest had been shown in that branch of athletics. Occasionally,
interclass contests had been held, presumably on the University

grounds, and in 1884 there is reference to a game between a picked University Squad and a team representing the Medical College of Syracuse. Student enthusiasm, however, was relatively slight and campus opinion generally rated football as being a dangerous sport highly conducive to gambling. None of these arguments was raised against "polo" which during 1885 attracted some attention, several games being played with the local city teams and in one instance with a picked group representing the University of Rochester; William Sloan, '89, captained the team in 1885. It should be remembered, however, that "polo" as played in those days was more like hockey except for the very important feature that it was played on roller skates. The scene for these matches was the "Criterian," a public amusement center in down-town Syracuse.

Tennis also had its followers and no one seemed to think it dangerous or degrading. At the same time it never gathered unto itself the standing and reputation as did baseball and football. During the spring of 1888 several of the fraternities laid out a series of courts on the campus somewhat to the rear of the Hall of Languages. In the same year, Delta Kappa Epsilon, constructed a court on Walnut Park between Marshall and Adams Streets. This display of interest led to the formation of a Tennis Association in the spring of 1889, the officers being Will B. Crowley, '89, President; Horace E. Stout, '91, Vice-President; and Alice Dunn, F. A., '90, Secretary and Treasurer. Under their direction a local tennis tournament was held. Little enthusiasm was shown when college reconvened in the fall of 1889 though during the next year interest mounted rapidly. Evidence of the latter may be gleaned from the action taken by the faculty in ruling the campus courts as being University property and therefore open to all students fraternity and non-fraternity. More convincing testimony exists in the intercollegiate tennis matches held under the auspices of the New York State Intercollegiate Athletic Association. Tennis tournaments were held at Syracuse in 1890, at Geneva in 1891, and at Utica in 1892.

Meanwhile there were some who sought to promote interest in cricket, reference to which appears at odd times in the student publications. Moreover in the *Onondagan*, a yearly university book, students who played cricket are mentioned by name. But with the growth of baseball and the appearance of football, cricket gradually disappeared from the Hill. Mention also is made in these and other sources of an Archery Club, a Walking Club, and several other minor activities none of which aroused much enthusiasm and can hardly be classified as forms of organized athletics. Rather do they illustrate normal student desire for physical relaxation and entertainment. Mingled considerations of this type may explain why the boys of Delta Upsilon, perched high on Ostrom Avenue in Dr. Coddington's old home, formed a toboggan club and raced their sleds down Marshall Street to the "meadows" on University Avenue. Similar fun was enjoyed by groups from other fraternities and sororities, and on many a winter night sleigh ride parties took place.

A University Gymnasium

11 The general management and direction of athletics during the early life of the University was fairly well lodged in the hands of a student organization known as the Athletic Association of Syracuse University. Established in the spring of 1876 and preceded by the Syracuse University Boating and Baseball Associations, this society, after a slow and uncertain start, gradually gathered unto itself considerable strength and vitality. Naturally, it could not afford to ignore the Administration and Faculty who at all times possessed reserved powers and on occasion exercised the same. Out-of-town games, for example, were forbidden, seating accommodations for campus engagements were refused, and in one instance a request to alter the University Calendar so as to allow a match to be played under more favorable circumstances was flatly denied. If these and other restrictions seem severe it should be remembered they were more than balanced by the absence of what today are known as eligibility rules. Medical examinations were not required, scholastic standing was not maintained, and there was no audit or supervision over receipts and expenditures. Exceptions existed but in the main little control seems to have been exercised over such matters. Presumably, academic heads were not over-concerned about athletics which in educational circles

seemed relatively unimportant. And it should not be forgotten that the students themselves evidenced no keen interest in organized athletics even after the foundation of an association in 1876.

In that year those who believed in the future of Syracuse athletics challenged their fellow students by issuing a call for an athletic society. The response was most gratifying but like a spring freshet had little depth and several years were to pass before the founders of the Association were on certain ground. According to the organic law of that society anyone connected with the University might become a member of the Association upon payment of an annual fee of fifty cents. The officers and standing committees of the organization were entrusted with the direction of athletics on the Hill—baseball, football, and cricket being singled out for special mention—the purchase of supplies, the care of the grounds, and the recording and accounting of all monies received and disbursed. All officers were elected at annual meetings and only members in good standing might use the Association's property. Various changes were made in the constitution during the next decade and a half but little was done to alter the basic pattern established in 1876. Among those who distinguished themselves in the life of the Association were John S. Clark, '77; Charles O. Dewey, '85; William Y. Foote, '87; E. Vincent Aldridge, '81; Curtis E. Mogg, '78; and William D. Marsh, '79.

Outstanding among the accomplishments of the Association was the inception and promotion of "Field Day," the initial contest being staged in May, 1876, at the Syracuse Driving Park located east of Westcott Street in the general neighborhood of the present Nottingham High School. A glance at the program for this and other Field Days reflects considerable student support and interest. Much of the success of these events may be explained by their informality and by the fact that, being restricted to local student personnel, the door was open to all who might care to participate. There were the usual races— dash and long distance—hurdles, and a number of contests in jumping, walking, and weights. In addition there were "rope-pulls," egg races and on one occasion a football match between teams from the Colleges of Liberal Arts and Medicine.

Field Day became an annual event in the years that followed and while the full story of these track and field events has not been preserved, enough evidence remains to warrant the conclusion they served a most useful purpose. Few of the records made at Field Day merit attention today, but it should be remembered the participants had little training and preparation. The following records, gleaned from a score card of Field Day, 1886, illustrate the speed and prowess of local campus athletes. Frederick C. Esmond, '77, running broad jump eighteen feet and four inches; William Washburne, Medicine, '86, one hundred yard dash, eleven and three quarter seconds; J. Sidney Bovingdon, '87, hammer throw, fifty-two feet and nine inches; Benedict Hatmaker, '86, four hundred and forty yard dash, fifty-eight seconds; Preston K. Crowell, '86, standing broad jump, nine feet and two and a half inches; Edward White, '85, half mile, two minutes and five-eighths seconds; and Harry N. Marvin, '83, high jump, five feet. Bovingdon also held records of twenty-two and seven-eighths seconds in the one hundred and twenty yard hurdles and twenty-seven feet and nine inches in the shot put.

More specialized in nature was the work of the Association in promoting baseball, football, and, at a later date, tennis and track. Each of these sports at first was organized on a campus basis but as time went on teams were formed for the single purpose of competing with those of other colleges and universities. Intercollegiate contests led, as has been mentioned, to the formation of a New York State Intercollegiate Baseball Association, of which the Syracuse Athletic Association was an active member. Later, in the spring of 1885, the Syracuse society assisted in the establishment of the New York State Intercollegiate Athletic Association which immediately proceeded to institute the first of a series of intercollegiate track meets. Held at Geneva, with Hobart College as host, on May 30, 1885, teams from Cornell, Union, Hamilton, Hobart, and Syracuse vied for honor and supremacy. Quite a number of students followed their teams to Hobart and the peace of the village of Geneva was disturbed by college yells and songs from "noon until midnight." Cornell won the meet and Syracuse had to be content with but one first and four seconds: J. Sidney Bovingdon winning the one mile walk in the rather slow time of eight minutes and twenty-six seconds. Later in the evening a dinner was tendered to the various participants at the Kirkwood House.

The following year the track meet was held at Utica, Syracuse taking first in the mile walk and in the baseball throwing contest. In 1887, Syracuse was host and a cheer from the local supporters went up as Karl Swartz, '87, took first place in the pole vault, the bar being at seven feet and five and a half inches. The next year at Rochester, because of internal dissension within the State Association, Cornell was not represented and Syracuse captured nine out of fifteen firsts. All of which gladdened the hearts of the ninety Syracuse students who had followed their team to Rochester. Hamilton College stole the show in 1889 but from then on for the next four years it was Syracuse the winner each time. In 1891, for example, paced by Frank L. Mead, '91, who took first in the sixteen pound hammer throw with a mark of eighty-six feet and three inches, Syracuse garnered forty-three points to Hamilton's forty-one, Rochester's thirteen, Colgate's four and Union's none. Two years later, when the Syracuse group competed at Utica, C. Frank Ackerman of Syracuse won first place in the pole vault, the bar being at an even ten feet.

A comparison between these and other records established at the Intercollegiate contests and those of an earlier date made at "Field Day" clearly shows the improvements that had taken place in athletics. And for this advance, Syracuse was heavily indebted to the local University Athletic Association whose management and promotional work had been quite outstanding. Most conspicuous in this respect was the constant and oft repeated demand for a university gymnasium, the absence of which, some affirmed, was responsible for the humiliating defeat administered by Cornell in a dual meet held at Syracuse in the spring of 1887. How, it was asked, could Syracuse ever expect to win victories in any branch of athletics without an athletic field and a gymnasium? This was not the first time such a question had been raised, for hardly had classes convened in 1872 before the *University Herald* came out with a demand for a gymnasium. Physical education, it was declared, was as essential as academic instruction and the hope was expressed that a room in the basement of the Hall of Languages, then in process of construction, might be set aside as a temporary gymnasium. Other editorials and news items followed and every conceivable argument was advanced in favor of the enterprise. In one instance it was asserted that immorality among American college students was high because there was no "relief from fatigue incident to incessant brain work." Success in college could not be achieved without a "clear brain and an unwearied body," which in turn called for proper "gymnastic training." Finally, and in desperation, a threat was hurled at the faculty to the effect that if a gymnasium was not provided, the students would be forced to seek amusement and relaxation elsewhere with evident danger to soul and body.

Although soul-saving appealed to a faculty which consisted of several clergymen, the latter refused to be moved by a plea provocative of smiles and not of frowns. No one, least of all the students, honestly believed they were doomed to perdition merely because the authorities differed with them over the matter of a gymnasium. At the same time, the students knew what they wanted and were determined to force the issue. Campus opinion generally registered disgust over the faculty's position and rumor had it that some of the staff had actually styled gymnasiums as "man-killers." Year after year a constant running attack was maintained and the faculty were exposed to all types of remedial instruction. In some instances this amounted to a frontal assault upon the privileges and prerogatives of the teaching staff; in others, stress was placed upon the renting and equipping of a downtown building, such as the Myers Block, the "cast-off" shell of the University. Then there were those who talked in terms of student drives to raise funds for a gymnasium and the University Glee Club was named to lead this undertaking. Greater enthusiasm was engendered over the suggestion of individual class pledges. So confident were the promoters of the scheme that they went to the trouble of preparing subscription blanks. But when it came to affixing his signature many a student who before had argued for the plan turned his back upon the effort and the grand scheme vanished into thin air. It is interesting to note, in this respect, that Chancellor Sims, Dean French and Dr. Smalley are reported as having subscribed to this fund. Others of the faculty continued to oppose the demand for a gymnasium.

Possibly the presence of this opposition accounts for the appeal, made in the spring of 1883, by Hugh Parker, '84, to the Board of Trustees of the University asking for the speedy construction of a gymnasium. The Trustees recognized the sincerity of the petitioner. Of greater interest is the fact, the Board endorsed the request and voted to erect a gymnasium as soon as the necessary funds were available. No other answer was possible under the existing circumstances. The support and maintenance of the University was taxing every resource the Trustees possessed. To do more was out of the question and the construction of a gymnasium, however desirable, just had to be postponed. Such in brief was the position of the Trustees. All of which the students must have known and if they did not they should have since both the campus and city papers frequently carried news items relative to the University's financial standing. To the students, however, all this talk about a scarcity of money seemed meaningless and mysterious; financial considerations, it was stated, constituted a convenient smoke screen behind which the real reason, namely stubborn opposition to organized athletics was concealed. In clinging to this opinion a grave injustice was done to the Trustees and faculty. No group of administrators and teachers ever had done so much with so little—a fact the most cantankerous critic admitted when the heat of the controversy had subsided. For the moment, however, there were some who were so blind to the realities that they failed to note the Trustees had gone on record in favor of a gymnasium. The principle of organized athletics and physical training had been accepted.

The inability of the Trustees to implement the new policy may explain why student opinion ignored the acceptance by the Board of physical education at Syracuse University. Meanwhile and during the course of the next two years the cry for a gymnasium continued. Failing to gain immediate relief the suggestion was made, in the spring of 1885, that the old work-shop to the rear of the Hall of Languages be converted into a temporary gymnasium. The editors of the *Syracusan* seized upon the idea and issued a call for contributions in the form of boxing gloves, Indian clubs, and dumb-bells.

Located somewhat to the south and at the east end of the Hall of Languages was an old shed, twenty by sixty feet in dimensions, which probably had been built by the contractors of the Hall as a tool and work-shop. Had it been erected after the construction of the Hall it seems likely that some reference to the same would appear in the Minutes of the Board of Trustees. Be that as it may, a shed of some sort existed and for a number of years served as a "store house." Here the janitor—"Professor J. L. Sennett," the students good naturedly called him—kept mop-pail and broom; here the rakes, sickles and hand-mowers were stored; and here the students from neighboring villages are said to have stabled their horses. "Professor Sennett" retired in 1883 in favor of John H. Cunningham and it was the latter who reigned over the store house when some one suggested its use as a gymnasium. In spite of existing handicaps and satirical articles in the *University Herald,* the officers of the Athletic Association saw distinct possibilities in the shed. Janitor Cunningham's attitudes were explored and so were those of the faculty. No objection was raised and in a short time a punching bag was installed and appropriate places were assigned for the safe keeping of the few baseballs, cricket bats, gloves, and other equipment belonging to the Association. At the same time, Janitor Cunningham asserted his honored rights. Under that worthy gentleman, janitorial engineering reached a high level for not only did his latent genius narrow the space available for gymnastic training but the success of the latter was impaired by an adjoining hen coop whose feathered occupants vied with their honor in making life uncomfortable for the athletes. And those of the faculty whose class rooms looked out upon this rural scene probably raised their voices and nostrils in protest and disgust.

The combined and continued use of the "Gym" by Janitor Cunningham, the hens, and the students pleased no one. Moreover, the property of the Athletic Association frequently disappeared and there may well have been truth in the remark made by alumni at a later date about the dirt and filth that accumulated within the shed, especially if one accepts the tradition of Chancellor Sims' cow—or was it Dr. Coddington's—having been kept within the frame structure. In any event the students believed they had ample cause for complaint and being convinced the shed was both an eyesore and an insult plotted its destruction.

Who initiated the conflagration is not known but a wakeful resident of the Eighth Ward, noticing flames arising from the campus shortly after midnight on April 12, 1886, turned in an alarm from Box 72, located at the corner of Chestnut (South Crouse) and Harrison Streets. Soon the campus was crowded with students, jubilant and eager to witness the destruction of the "Gym." All along University Avenue heads were thrust out of windows and faltering voices asked "Where's the fire?" From this street rushed some of the faculty, one of whom, Dr. Comfort, ran head on into one of the instigators of the fire who was carrying a small kerosene can. Meanwhile, the bell in the west tower of the Hall of Languages, that had been silent ever since its clapper had been stolen by some one of the Class of 1885, suddenly came to life and pealed out an alarm. As might be expected the horse drawn engine and fire truck lost valuable time in climbing the steep grade—steeper than today—leading to the Hill and arrived too late to be of any help. Fortunately, the Hall was in no serious danger, though some adjacent trees were burned. Other details, highly colored and exaggerated, may be found in the local papers all of which do agree upon one simple fact—the "Gym" had become an ash heap.

During the next few days and while the conspirators basked in the glow of student applause the faculty assembled in solemn session. Not only had the one and only University building been exposed to fire, and it should be remembered there were neither city hydrants nor University wells on the Hill, but a situation had been created that forboded possible trouble with the City Fathers. Shortly after the alarm had been sounded and while Engine Number 1 was on the Hill another fire broke forth in the eating house of Louis Paris on East Genesee near Salina Street. Nothing of consequence developed from this second fire and the Common Council quietly and wisely ignored the escapade on the Hill. But had the second fire down town reached any proportions and had the Hall of Languages caught on fire, the burning of the "Gym" would not have been the laughing matter the students made it out to be. Moreover, there is some reason to believe that a local insurance company for a time was reluctant to consider the University's claims for damages.

Realizing the seriousness of the situation, the faculty lost no time in seeking out the culprits. How the guilty ones were discovered is not recorded. Faculty investigation and pressure plus possible information gained from some of the students brought desired results and on May 6, 1888, fourteen or fifteen freshmen appeared before the faculty. Here they were required to affix their signatures to a prepared statement which acknowledged their guilt, expressed deep sorrow for having caused so much trouble, and promised good behavior in the future. Whereupon, the faculty expelled the offenders for a year, but having done so straightway suspended the same and placed the students on probation for the remainder of their college life. A few days later public reprimand was administered before the student body at Chapel. And with this the faculty considered the matter closed. The students, however, continued to make light of the affair; those responsible for the fire becoming campus heroes.

Such in brief is the story of the "Old Gym" which never was a gymnasium in any sense of the word. Few students ever harbored any illusions about the "gym" and when using the term usually did so in a derisive manner. Another and not altogether different version of the fire, recently made by one of the "immortal" incendiaries deserves quotation. Writing in the summer of 1945 our informant states:

Thirteen of the Class of '89 were found guilty by the faculty; sentence being pronounced by Dean French. We were lined up in the Chapel and the Dean gave us a severe lecture and then told us that the only punishment fit to our crime was expulsion. After a long wait, he stated that as this was our first offense, sentence was suspended during our future good behavior. He also announced that none of the culprits would be eligible to any future honors to be conferred by the University, but when we came to graduation the majority of the Commencement speakers, which was the only honorable recognition then given, was given to those under suspension of expulsion. The fact is the Freshmen were prodded by the Sophomores to do the job and they had the sympathetic support of Professors Clark and Underwood who frequently remarked they hoped the old shed would catch fire and burn down. Therefore we could not resist doing the University a good turn in removing the eyesore. We were all told we would get no gymnasium so long as we attended the University.

During the course of the next three years there was little talk about a gymnasium. It seems odd the students would permit the matter to drop but though occasional comments did appear in the campus papers, particularly in respect to benefits for a gymnasium, the volume of such news items was less than before the fire. In marked contrast was the increased space given to formal athletics. During 1888, for example, the Varsity Nine, behind the pitching of George W. Church, '89, won the State Intercollegiate Baseball title. Similar distinction was won by the Track Team at a state meet held at the University of Rochester. Student support of the track team was shown by the chartering of a special car to carry some ninety Syracusans to Rochester.

Almost as good a record was maintained by the track and baseball teams of 1889. More significant, from the angle of future development, was the establishment of a Varsity Football Eleven. Stimulated and led by John B. Hillyer, '94, the Syracuse squad had little difficulty in defeating the local high school but a superior and better coached Rochester Varsity swept "Blake" Hillyer's boys by a score of thirty-six to nothing. Meanwhile the Athletic Association continued to promote athletic activities and kept alive the idea of a gymnasium. Unknown to many, the Association had a true friend in Chancellor Sims who, it is reported, had declared his sentiments in 1886 when he subscribed to a gymnasium drive. At that time and for the next few years, Dr. Sims could do no more, his hands being tied by a projected building program which ultimately led to the erection of the Administration, Crouse, and Holden Buildings. With the construction of these edifices behind him, the Chancellor informed the Trustees at their January, 1889, meeting that the time had come for Syracuse to have a gymnasium and an athletic instructor. In the meantime, if one may accept a reference in the *University Herald,* the attitude of the faculty had mellowed considerably. Thus after a period of nearly twenty years the Administration, faculty, and student body joined in a program that was to lead to the building of a gymnasium.

Needless to say the students of the University were delighted with the happy turn of events. Appreciative comments appeared in the campus publications and a round of applause greeted Dr. Sims when he announced a plan for the immediate improvement of the track and athletic grounds which were located south of the Hall of Languages. This track had been laid out during the fall of 1887 without proper regard for the baseball diamond which occupied some of the same space. Advocates of both sports read in the Chancellor's statement a definite promise of a rearrangement of the area and an improvement of facilities that would result in the abandonment of using public play grounds; in the future all campus athletics were to center on the Hill. Work on the new field and track, financed probably by Mr. John D. Archbold, was begun in the spring of 1890 and was far enough along to warrant its use that year for baseball. It was not, however, advanced to the point where the field and track could be used by the Intercollegiate Meet which, therefore, was held at Kirkwood Park—the honors going to Hobart. In baseball, the Varsity lost to Union and Rochester, defeated Hamilton and Hobart, and for good measure took both games from Colgate. Possibly one reason for the good record was the presence of a trainer on the campus, Joseph A. Wright who, though described as a student, received a small fee for his services from the Athletic Association. Among the other sums paid by this organization was ten dollars and fifty cents "for a catcher." Could this, by any interpretation, refer to professionalism at Syracuse?

Mr. Wright appears to have been a versatile fellow and in the fall of 1890 is listed as full-back on the Varsity. Early in that season the Athletic Association obtained the coaching talents of Robert Winston. Mr. Winston, so the *University Herald* records, came to America in 1883 after having won a name for himself as a "bantam boxer" and trainer at the Athletic Club of London, England. Since then he had coached at Rochester, Yale, Williams, and Princeton. His sojourn at Syracuse was exceedingly brief and in October, 1890, he left to assume a position at Williams. So pleased, however, were the Syracuse boys with Mr. Winston that they offered him a month's contract for the following year; the compensation for his services being thirty-five dollars plus expenses.

Captained by William M. Fanton, '92, the Varsity of 1890 played ten games of which two each were with Hamilton, Union, and Rochester; three with the Syracuse Athletic Club; and one with the St. John's Military Academy of Manlius, New York. The latter game, played before a "large" crowd on the University grounds—on a field said to be covered with several inches of mud—was won by Syracuse, twenty-eight to six. An interesting side light on the game was the presence of four Manlius teachers on the cadets' team, one of whom was the Commandant, Colonel Verbeck. The last game of the year was contested in a snow and sleet storm at Syracuse and to this day it is impossible to determine who won, each team claiming the victory. The occasion for this uncertainty arose out of a fight that developed between the players and the subsequent withdrawal of the Rochester Eleven by its coach. The referee, according to the *Standard*, awarded the game to Rochester. More satisfying to Syracusans was the report of the Treasurer of the Athletic Association for 1890 which showed receipts of over seven hundred dollars as against some six hundred dollars of expense.

Mr. Winston did not return to Syracuse in the fall of 1891, his place being taken by a Mr. Gailbraith, "noted" athlete and Y.M.C.A. leader at Cornell University. After the latter's return to Ithaca, Mr. Jordon C. Wells of Wesleyan took over and it was during his stay at Syracuse that a training table was introduced. Ten games were played that season and of these Syracuse won but four. This was the year Cornell defeated us by a score of sixty-eight to nothing, an earlier game with that rival having been lost, twelve to six. Student opinion explained the first defeat by the fact that Cornell's captain was none other than Syracuse's former coach, Gailbraith; the latter's name, however, does not appear in the lineup as given in the *University News*. No excuse of this nature can account for the crushing defeat administered by Union College, the final score being seventy-one to nothing. Hamilton also downed the Varsity, twenty-two to four, and even the cadets from Manlius won, four to nothing. In baseball, a schedule of eighteen games allowed a better record to be established, though defeats at the hands of Manlius, the local High School, Cortland, and Hobart as well as those by Colgate, Cornell, and Hamilton were far from pleasing. Much more agreeable to the injured feelings of those who witnessed the home games was the erection of a makeshift grandstand, possibly a hundred feet east of the present University

Library, capable of seating fifty or more persons. Information concerning this structure came to light in the summer of 1946 through a letter written by George F. Shepherd, '91, one time manager of the baseball team. "The grandstand," so Mr. Shepherd wrote, "you mention in your interesting letter . . . that I had a little connection with was hardly worthy of that name . . . I was manager of the baseball team in 1890 or 1891. I graduated in 1891. To give place for a few to sit, I bought some lumber and built a few seats accommodating perhaps 50. It was located not far from home plate and some 100 ft. e. of the present library." This grandstand should not be confused with the larger and more pretentious one pictured in the *Alumni Record, 1835-1899.*

Meanwhile the Varsity Track Team covered itself with glory. In part this was due to the coaching of Mr. F. G. Fiddler, formerly of London, England, and a personal friend of Mr. Winston. Mr. Fiddler's success was materially aided by a team consisting of men like Frank L. Mead, '91; Gordon Hoyt, Med., '94; and Frank L. Purdy, '91. Led by these men Syracuse won the State Intercollegiate Meet, held at Geneva in May, 1891. Mead won the sixteen pound hammer throw with a mark of eighty-six feet and three inches; Purdy took the one hundred and twenty yard hurdle in eighteen seconds, and Hoyt captured the two hundred and twenty-yard dash in twenty-three and one-fifth seconds.

Purdy and Hoyt again were prominent during 1892 and together with others clinched Syracuse's triumph at Utica in the State Intercollegiate Track Meet. Less impressive was the record of the University Baseball Team, captained by George O. Redington. The season opened with an easy win over the Syracuse High School but was followed by an overwhelming defeat at the hands of the Athletic Stars of Syracuse. Union then took the Varsity into camp, and at Burlington, the Vermont Nine won both games of a double header. Later, a return match with Union was lost and the Syracuse rooters had to be content with an even break in twin matches with Hamilton and Rochester. Disappointing as this was to the friends of Syracuse it was nothing by comparison with the showing made by the Varsity Football Team. Coached for two weeks at the start of the season by one Ray Hermandez, formerly a member of the Cornell Squad, the Syracuse Eleven won none of its nine games. It did tie the Syracuse Athletics in a scoreless game but this empty honor was erased by two subsequent defeats by the same opponent. Cornell, Hamilton, Union, Rochester, and St. John's Military Academy also won over the Varsity.

Offsetting the dismal record was the promise of better days ahead. It will be recalled that in January, 1890, the Chancellor had asked the Trustees to provide for the erection of a gymnasium. The Board, apparently without hesitation, endorsed the proposal and voted to house within the projected building both the Athletic Department and the Student's Christian Association. All, however, was dependent upon an advance subscription of ten thousand dollars. Immediately thereafter, Dr. Sims initiated a drive for this sum and in a short time informed the Trustees that the required funds had been raised. Professor Arthur B. Clark, of the College of Fine Arts, was then engaged to act as architect. Professor Clark's plans were accepted and during the spring of 1891 the contractors and masons were at work on the structure which, facing the athletic grounds, occupied in a general way the site of the present Hendricks Chapel. By December the building was completed and in January, 1892, classes were held in the Gymnasium for the first time.

Meanwhile the Board of Trustees had adopted a series of regulations as to the use and control of the new edifice. According to these rules, the Young Men's and Young Women's Christian Associations were to nominate a "General Secretary and Director who shall have personal charge of the work in the said associations and gymnasium." Subject to the approval of the faculty and Trustees this officer was to have general supervision over both athletics and Christian work. All expenses incident to that office were to be borne by the two Associations though from a study of the Trustees' Minutes it would appear that maintenance costs were met by the University. Mr. Otis C. Skeele of Boston was appointed as the first director; he was followed in January, 1893, by John Alexander R. Scott. All students were required to take medical examinations and, unless excused, were to attend classes in physical training.

According to the architect's drawings, the basement of the "Gymnasium and Y.M.C.A. Building" was divided into two sections, the smaller part being allotted to the women students of the University. In addition, provision was made for a bowling alley, fifty-one feet by fourteen in dimensions, a boiler room, fifteen by twenty-four, and a tank or swimming pool, approximately fifteen feet square. Appropri-

Campus view in 1887, facing north, Holden Observatory at left, Hall of Languages at right

Holden Observatory, Mr. G. M. Maxwell in foreground, 1887

Liberal Arts Faculty, 1891. Center: Dr. C. N. Sims; clockwise, starting at upper left-hand corner: L. G. Underwood, W. P. Coddington, J. S. Clark, C. J. Little, J. R. French, F. Smalley, O. F. Cook, E. N. Pattee, J. T. Fisher, H. A. Peck, E. Haanel, J. J. Brown

Crouse College Building, 1889

Myers Block, location of University 1871-1873

Class of 1876 with Dr. Winchell (standing) and Dr. Bennett (seated), in front of Hall of Languages

D.K.E. tennis court on Walnut Park near Marshall Street, 1887

University Band, in front of Hall of Languages, 1888

ate locker rooms, bath, and toilet stalls were allotted to each section, access to either being closed depending upon whether the men or the women were using the gymnasium floor. The first floor consisted of a Director's room plus two large parlors and a gymnasium floor, sixty-nine by fifty. Above the latter, on the second floor, was a "running gallery," to the right of which and over the parlors was a large "audience room." The entire structure was to be of brick and stone. Most of these specifications were completed even to the extent of including the pool; nothing, however, seems to have been done about the bowling alley. Many generations of Syracuse students used this building which, after the construction of Archbold Gymnasium, became known as the "Old Gym" and was used only by women students. Later, in 1928, the "Women's Gymnasium" was moved from its old site, now occupied by Hendricks Chapel, to its present location, somewhat to the south of Steele Hall.

Syracuse at Play

12 Clio, devoted patron of history, marks March 30, 1870, as the date of the University's foundation. For it was on that day an unknown clerk in the office of the Secretary of State, Albany, New York, filed a certificate of incorporation signifying the birth and existence of Syracuse University. Such meticulous accuracy, essential as it may be for lawyers and historians, meant little to the forty-one students who gathered, September 4, 1871, in the Chapel of the Myers Block for last minute instructions prior to the opening of classes the next day. Theirs was the promise of being charter members of an institution whose future seemed bright and promising, and to them the Chapel service forever was reckoned as the moment of Syracuse's birth. Here they bowed their heads in prayer as Dr. Daniel Steele, Vice-President of the University, invoked God's blessing upon Methodism's most recent educational effort. Here they sang those soul-inspiring hymns peculiar to that age and a great Christian Church, and here they received general information as to the conduct and procedure of class study and instruction. Following these simple, but impressive exercises, they were dismissed for the day. But as they broke, they paused on the stairs and in a spirit of comradeship joined the faculty in singing "*Quod Libet.*" Student life at Syracuse had begun.

In respect to college life, leadership quite naturally fell to those few students who formerly had been at Genesee. Through this human channel, that forever has related Syracuse to Lima, a rich and varied assortment of college traditions was translated to the new campus. References to these student practices appear in the early issues of the *University Herald*. The story of class rivalries, the feeble but determined effort for formal athletics, the rise of Greek letter societies, and the songs the students sang unfolded themselves in a most interesting manner. Most of the earlier tunes heard at Syracuse were the common property of other educational institutions. In this category stood *"Quod Libet,"* which for almost a half century echoed through the corridors of the Hall of Languages. Less emotional in nature was the pleasing jingle of "Ten Little Indians," the catching air of "Bingo," the swing of "I've got a Sixpence," the folk song of "Go Down Moses," and the tearful tale of "Peter Gray," whose death at the hands of the "bloody Indians" brought final disaster to his fair "Lucy." Then there was a group of airs peculiar to life at Lima, one of which, "The Song of the Bolt," so the author of *Carmina Collegensia*, published in 1876, stated was taken from a recitation once delivered at Genesee and which so aroused the ire of the faculty of that college as to cause the suspension of an entire class.

There was little that was original in these songs so far as Syracuse was concerned. A notable attempt to endow Syracuse with a song of its own, however, was made in August, 1871. Then it was Rev. George Lansing Taylor, prominent in the founding of the University, penned what he called the "Syracuse University Hymn." Set to the revolutionary air of the *Marseillaise*, Syracusans blessed Onondaga's lakes, invoked the "nymphs, fawns, hours, graces," paid homage to Gelon, Theocritus, and other classic celebrities, and closed each of the five stanzas with the chorus:

> *All hail the glorious day*
> *Of Syracuse's birth*
> *We'll sound her name! We'll hymn her fame!*
> *And peal her anthem forth.*

Sung for the first time at the laying of the corner stone of the Hall of Languages, this heroic verse, generally known as the "Syracuse Hymn," was used on formal occasions throughout the next two decades. At no time, however, did it ever capture the imagination of either student body or alumni, and an examination of commencement programs, concerts by the Glee Club, and other public events reveals its absence a number of times. Such neglect casts no reflection upon its author who most appropriately had provided Syracuse with an Alma Mater at a time when little existed upon which a more enduring tune might be built. The complete absence of anything like a Syracuse tradition and the lack of a body of Syracuse graduates furnished no basis for a real college song. An Alma Mater, in other words, could not be composed until the University had become *the* Alma Mater to its own graduates.

Each year, however, that followed stimulated growth and student life took on a deeper and local meaning. Accordingly, musical compositions gradually made their appearance. Melville J. Wells, '75, was the author of a song entitled "Waiting" which was adapted to the tune of "Key Note" by one W. B. Bradbury. George E. Smith, '76, rendered a tune rich in reference to Syracuse. Known as "All Hail," the first verse ran as follows:

> *O loved Syracuse, our most excellent mother*
> *Now loudly, with joy to thy Honor we sing*
> *And raise to the clouds the sweet praise of thy virtue*
> *Inspired by the motive affection doth bring.*
> *Though youthful indeed, not a whit is thy merit*
> *Diminished by that, for thy youth only gives*
> *A charm to thy person, and sweetly it crowneth*
> *Thy worth with a freshness and beauty that lives.*

Another song that attracted some attention was one contributed by Professor John S. Clark, a graduate of Syracuse and a member of the Faculty of the College of Liberal Arts. Written in Latin, this song was known as "Alma Mater, Syracuse," and was set to the tune of "Araby's Daughter." Six years later, the commencement exercises were graced by the composition of Miss Alice E. Clark, '82, arranged to the tune of "America." The opening lines of this song read as follows:

> *Alma Mater, leal and true,*
> *Come we to bid adieu*
> *To thy Honored Walls*

Later, in February, 1886, the Glee Club presented a "Syracuse Medley" at Smyrna, New York. Whether the medley as well as other songs that appeared from time to time, such as one called "Snow Fall," should be recognized as Syracuse songs is a matter of opinion. It is, however, common knowledge that the students of these years realized they had no Alma Mater song and on several occasions earnest attempts were made to fill this pressing need. The editor of the *University News*, for example, in May, 1890, deplored the dearth of Syracuse airs. Students at New Haven might thrill to "Dear Old Yale" and those at nearby Ithaca might carol "Far Above Cayuga's Waters," but so far as Syracuse was concerned, the editor declared, the campus at Syracuse was strangely silent. George W. Elliott, '73, was of the same opinion and prevailed upon the *University News* to print a composition of his arranged to the Finnish National Hymn. Elliott's contribution was well received. Of special interest are the first two lines:

Majestic swells the graceful Hill
From Onondaga's Vale

The song reappeared in a subsequent issue of the *University News* and was featured by the Glee Club during the spring of 1891, but that, in all probability, was its last recorded use. In the meantime the editors of the *Onondagan* had offered a ten dollar prize for a new college song, both alumni and students being invited to compete. The contest closed in February, 1891. Shortly thereafter the *University News* published the prize composition whose author, an alumnus, elected to keep his name a secret. In commenting upon the song, entitled "Salt," a critic cautiously remarked that it fell "far short for a college song," a conclusion generally endorsed on the campus. Another product of the same year was one offered by the University Librarian, H. O. Sibley. Following the well known melody, "Old Oaken Bucket," Sibley's "Syracuse University Song" opened with the line: "Hail, Hail Alma Mater, how nobly thou standest." The following year renewed interest prompted Frank W. Noxon, '92, to present a three verse composition, "Singing in the Halls" set to the hymn, "Chapel Steps."

No other comparable effort was made until the spring of 1893 when the Glee Club stressed the need of a new and more suitable Alma Mater. Being somewhat musically inclined, Junius W. Stevens, '95, a fraternity brother of Frank W. Noxon, gave the matter some thought and on March 15, 1893 at the Wieting Opera House the Glee Club concluded a successful concert with the premiere rendition of the present Alma Mater. The program for that evening's entertainment, fortunately preserved at the University Library, carried the words of the first three verses and chorus, and adds the musical score of the former. More information may be found in the campus and city papers none of which seemed over impressed with Stevens' efforts. Nor does one meet the song again until the fall of the same year when a group of co-eds, assembled in front of Dean French's home, greeted a new Chancellor, Dr. Day, with the song now dear to all Syracusans. The next year, the Ladies Glee Club presented the song at a benefit concert given at the Bastable Theatre. During the remainder of the century the popularity of the tune increased though on several significant occasions it was not used. It is of interest to note that present research shows its title to have been "Song of Syracuse," though at times it was called, "Flag We Love." It might also be added that as originally drafted the closing verse began, "When the shades of life are falling," and not as is now sung, "When the shades of night are falling." Finally, it should be mentioned that the flag eulogized by Stevens was "Orange."

An earlier reference to the University color appeared in Noxon's tune where one verse contains the line, "Orange, float on High." But Orange has not always been the color of Syracuse. Student interest in a University color showed itself in June, 1872, when a meeting was held in the Myers Block. At this gathering a majority, "after an uproarious time," voted for Rose Pink and Pea Green. The minority, who had advocated Sky Blue in lieu of Pea Green were not easily silenced and at another college meeting the year following were able to effect a compromise—Rose Pink and Pea Green becoming Rose Tint and Azure. Colloquially, however, it was Pink and Blue, a combination most appropriate for teas, concerts, commencements and all formal occasions. On the other hand, Pink and Blue did not fit into the spirit engendered on a gridiron or diamond; it lacked vitality. Student managers invariably complained about the lifeless and tame effects produced when these colors were displayed upon a baseball or football uniform—a criticism that echoed through the *University News*.

Little, however, was accomplished though in the spring of 1890 both the alumni and student body brought the issue forcibly to the front. Considerable discussion followed and in June of that year the

Pink and Blue banners were furled forever; in their place was raised the "Flag We Love, Orange." Precisely why the color orange was adopted remains somewhat of a mystery to this day. The *Syracusan* for June 16, 1890, suggested the decision was predicated upon the historical affinity once existing between the Colony of New York and the House of Orange. Another explanation was offered a few years ago by Mr. Frank J. Marion, a Trustee of the University and a member of the Class of 1890. According to Mr. Marion, his class had urged the adoption of their class colors, orange and green. When it became apparent that this could not be realized, the class voted for and was instrumental in securing the acceptance of orange. Orange, Mr. Marion added, was seized upon after a remark by Professor John S. Clark, '77, to the effect that to his knowledge not a single American university or college had orange as its color. In support of Mr. Marion's views reference may be made to the records of the Alumni Association. Interest in the question of the University's colors was shown at the 1889 gathering of the society when a committee composed of Dr. Clark and William Nottingham was appointed to consult with the faculty and students as to a change in colors. Dr. Clark rendered a report in June, 1890, recommending that the college colors be changed and that the new color be orange. A motion favoring orange and white being lost, the Association voted in favor of orange. It would appear, therefore, orange was accepted by general consent of the students, faculty, and alumni; no formal vote, however, is recorded in the Minute Book of the College of Liberal Arts. Present research, moreover, fails to show that either the Trustees or the faculty ever officially adopted orange as the University color.

During the course of the next two years the use of "Orange" became well established. Both Noxon and Stevens, as has been mentioned, used it in their songs and in 1893, according to the *University News*, a railroad coach carrying students to an Intercollegiate Field Day at Utica had on one side of a car a dark "blue banner, bearing the word 'Syracuse' in orange letters, the whole being draped with streamers of orange." Adopted at a student meeting in February, 1891, an "Orange button" appeared on the campus. This may well have been the name given to the small skull cap Freshmen were supposed to wear. The idea of a skull cap was first suggested in February, 1874. Later, in the same year, after several college meetings, it was voted that both

Freshmen and Sophomores might wear such a cap; nothing more has been unearthed about this subject.

More complete is the story about a college yell. Cheers of some type must have been heard early in the life of the University, though it is not until the winter of 1879 that any reference to a yell appeared in print. Then it was the editor of the *University Herald* in an article about college yells referred to "Syra–Syra–Syra–SY–RA–CUSE." Evidently this cheer did not echo much beyond the vale of Onondaga since it was not included in a publication, *Acta Columbiana*, which contained the cheers of many colleges and universities. All of which touched the editors of the *Syracusan* to the quick. Syracuse, according to these students, possessed a cheer "far superior" to certain other institutions. "The familiar 'Syr-ah! Syr-ah! Syr-ah! Syr-a-cuse' when given with a sharp accent on the syllable *ah* of the final part, is an exceedingly effective whoop." And it was this "whoop" that greeted Dr. Sims in 1881 when he was formally inaugurated as Chancellor of the University at the University Avenue Methodist Church.

Without doubt this cheer must have boomed forth on other occasions during the year that immediately followed. Variations, however, are known to have appeared, such as:

> *Syra, Syra, Syra, Syracuse*
> *Syra, Syra, Syra, Syracuse*
> *Syra, Syra, Syra, Syracuse*

In this particular version, introduced for the first time in the spring of 1888, nothing is said about accenting the vowel "a" in "Syra" or of dividing "Syracuse" into a hyphenated word as is the present custom. Emphasis was placed upon maintaining the voice at the same strength throughout the cheer except toward the end when a lower and softer tone was suggested. From the same source one gleans information of a rival yell which is heard as late as 1893 and which ran as follows:

> *Hip Hoo Rah*
> *Hip Hoo Rah*
> *Sy-ra-cuse! Sy-ra-cuse!*
> *Rah Rah Rah*

Finally, it should be noted there was nothing *sacra sancta* about these and other college cheers as may be seen from the privileges taken by a

Sophomore class when it perpetrated the following parody of a Freshman yell:

> Syra- Syra- Syra-
> Wah- Who- Wah
> Ninety-one, Ninety-one
> I want my ma

Freshmen, however, were by no means as infantile as this cheer
might indicate. Bubbling if not bursting with an inexhaustible source
of energy and determined not to yield an inch to their superiors in
loyalty to Alma Mater, they were in the forefront of most student
undertakings. Commendable as many of these activities were there
must have been times when the Administration wished these students
did not exist. Worried looks, it is known, swept over the faces of the
faculty on Christmas Day, 1871, as they viewed the mutilated and
decorated signs of the University on the Myers Block. Nor was this
concern lessened by the humble apologies of the contrite sinners, for
hardly had peace been restored before the halls of the block echoed
with the din of freshmen-sophomore battles egged on by sophisticated
upper classmen. Disturbances of this type continued throughout the
decades that followed, many of them being carried into the sacred
precincts of the University Chapel.

Equally disconcerting to the authorities were the escapades and
pranks perpetrated during the Chapel services. Viewed from the perspective of today many of these antics may seem highly entertaining
and harmless but one may be sure they were far from being amusing
to the Administration of that age. A classic illustration may be gleaned
from the local papers of 1886. Chapel, it seems, had begun. Appropriate selections from the Bible had been read and a hymn had been
sung with an enthusiasm that foreboded little good. Deep silence followed as Chancellor Sims, head bowed and eyes closed, fervently
prayed "for the college, the nation, President Cleveland and the Senate, the cause of Christianity and good government throughout the
world, and the parents of the students who in distant homes were
watching with anxious eyes the struggles of their loved ones." Suddenly the stillness, which the rich and even voice of the Chancellor
always obtained, was broken by a rustling sound which seemed to
come from above the chapel organ. Every eye save that of the Chancellor turned in that direction for there suspended over Dr. Sims'

head was a life-sized crayon drawing of his head, the body being sketched in miniature. His hands were in his side pockets and under his feet was a prostrate student whose cheeks were wet with tears and by whose outstretched arm was a beer bottle and a corn-cob pipe. Stifled laughter greeted the appearance of the portrait and as Dr. Sims closed his prayer with a loud amen, his opened eyes beheld the burlesque. Startled but clinging to his dignity, the Chancellor skipped his usual morning talk and nodded to the Seniors which was the accustomed signal for the dismissal of the students.

But no one wanted to leave. The show had only started and as it progressed pandemonium followed. Laughing co-eds pulled the Chancellor's portrait from its high perch and, within a few moments, tore it to pieces, each portion becoming a treasured souvenir. Meanwhile the hall rang with Sophomore cheers for the Freshmen of 1889, the acknowledged authors of the affair. And what of the faculty? A sadder and more disconsolate staff never filed from the Chapel, in the wake of which gradually drifted the students. After the last straggler had left, Dr. Sims, who had remained behind, closed the door from the outside and proceeded to address the student body. With apparent seriousness he labored them for their misconduct, announced his determination to bring the guilty ones to justice, and called upon the upper classmen to vocally protest against such disturbances, especially a "desecration" of the chapel. Additional light on this episode is lacking but preceding as it did, by a few weeks, the burning of the old gymnasium, one may be sure the affair was not forgotten when punishment was meted out to those who had fired the old store-house.

Earlier in the fall of the same year, 1885-1886, many sidewalks in the vicinity of the University had been ripped from their foundations and placed against adjacent trees. Benches, from Professor Clark's room in the Hall of Languages, crowded the middle of one of the streets, and his desk stood alone in front of the home of Rev. Dr. Wilbor. This was not the first time the wooden sidewalks had been lifted by Syracuse students. Way back in 1878 and on other occasions the walks leading to the Hall of Languages had been torn up. And rumor had it that a group of students, in their own inimitable way, had dedicated that building several months prior to the formal ceremonies in the spring of 1873. Sophomores, we are told, were responsible for the affair, but who stole the clapper from the college bell is unknown to this day. In commenting about the latter episode the

University Herald wonderingly asked why the bell had "its mouth turned toward the roof of the tower, its tongue gone," and why within its "spacious interior" there were several quarts of frozen water.

Most of these escapades, including the painting of the signs of a local cigar store, involved daring but no great ingenuity. There were occasions, however, when some intelligence was actually shown. To illustrate, certain freshmen managed to obtain possession of a supply of the printed cards used by the Administration to summon students who were delinquent in their work to the Dean's office for friendly advice. These stolen cards were then sent to a number of credulous sophomores who, in accordance with instructions written on the notices, called at the Chancellor's home. More significant was the practice, common at old Genesee, of perpetrating "mock schemes" at Sophomore literary exercises. These exhibitions caused no end of entertainment though they seriously disrupted and lessened the value of these literary activities. In 1885, for example, hundreds of small sheets of papers on each of which was printed a barb relative to the speakers, floated down from the balcony following the conclusion of an opening prayer by Dr. Sims. Mention should also be made of the Valentine Party staged by the Class of 1875. On this occasion the sidewalks leading to the Hall of Languages and the entrances to the same were plastered with cheap and somewhat questionable valentines.

The spirit of love hardly could be said to have been present at the commotion prompted by the sophomores in the fall of 1885. The genesis of this episode may be found in certain practices once existing at Genesee College. Student activities at Lima in respect to freshmen were strangely modern in many ways. A freshman, in brief, might be seen on the campus but he decidedly was not to be heard. His mannerisms and opinions clashed violently with the traditions and views of his superiors who perforce, therefore, felt called upon to put all newcomers in their proper places. Thus it happened at Genesee that a custom known as "salting" developed, the avowed purpose of which was to take the freshness out of the first year men. To gain this end, freshmen benches in the chapel were sprinkled with salt. This harmless but symbolic practice was brought to Syracuse but hardly had classes convened on the Hill before the self-contained sophomores began throwing salt at their rivals. Soon this was improved upon by the device of rubbing salt into the hair of the yearlings. All of which caused the latter to fight back, much to the evident delight of juniors and seniors whose hands in promoting these class conflicts were only partially concealed. No one ever was seriously hurt in these scuffles, though no "salting" passed without a number of torn shirts, smashed hats, scratched faces, and occasionally a red nose or a black eye.

Mild as these injuries were, "salting" was condemned by the faculty as a "barbarism" not wanted at Syracuse. Administrative pressure had its influence and in 1883, after a rather boisterous "salting," the lower division students buried their hatchets and forgot all ancient enmities. "Each incoming Freshman class has been greeted with the firm grip of fellowship by their natural enemies, the sophomores, and Chancellor Sims thought the strain of brotherly love was driving from his little garden all the weeds of savagery that had grown rank in colleges for hundreds of years;" so ran an article in one of the city papers.

The peace that settled over the campus did not pass without some misunderstanding. And in the fall of 1885, the sophomores led by H. H. Hawkins and E. C. Mason broke the short-lived truce. Premonitions of impending strife had been felt when college opened in mid-September. Nor were these expectations idle for early on the morning of September 17th, while the Hill was asleep, a band of hustling sophomores invaded the campus. In a short time the sidewalks, trees, and buildings were covered with small proclamations on which was printed:

```
                    '89
        ROWDYISM! RUST! RIND!
```

The gauntlet had been thrown down. Surely the freshmen would accept the challenge, so reasoned all as they gathered in the halls preparatory to ascending the long stairs that led to the Chapel. Once seated within this spacious room, services began. Hymns, prayers, and psalms followed in proper order and with unusual reverence. But hardly had the grand amen been sounded before the air, in the underclassmen corner, was full of flying salt. Hastily classes were dismissed and as the freshmen reached the lower floor they were greeted with the refrain:

> *The Fresh are prancing down the stair*
> *Good-bye, my lover, good-bye,*
> *Clawing the salt out of their hair*
> *Good-bye, my lover, good-bye.*

The freshmen bore their humiliation with good grace and humor, allowing their rivals to shower them with more salt, and receiving the cat-calls and parodies in silence. Once the initial hubbub had ended, the first year men showed their feelings by singing, "Here's to '89, Drink her down." By this time Dean French had arrived and on seeing him the crowd disappeared convinced that bigger and better class rivalries were in store.

Signs of impending strife showed themselves as flashing canes, some tipped with silver heads, appeared on the campus in the hands of the freshmen. Now the carrying of canes was by tradition reserved for others than yearlings. The conduct of the latter, therefore, was high impudence and the upper classmen and sophomores determined to stop the irregularity at once. In years past similar disputes had been ended by a cane rush but this practice, like that of "salting" had been abolished in 1883. The increase of "unsalted freshmen" plus the burning desire of the sophomores to show their authority resulted in an agreement between the lower classes to revive the cane rush. Accordingly, a day or two after the "salting" and following the close of another Chapel service, '88 and '89 thundered down the stairs and poured out upon the campus where a respectable body of alumni with high collars, tall hats, and much dignity had gathered to witness a rush. On the heels of the contestants came the remainder of the student body—men and women—all joining with the lower classmen in yelling various class cheers.

Meanwhile the contestants, minus hats, coats, and vests, had drawn themselves up on the campus some twenty feet apart. When all was ready, the referee tossed in a cane and the fun began. Such pulling and pushing the campus had never witnessed and the arena was soon dotted with small mounds of squirming warriors trying their utmost to keep one another from rushing to the aid of those who were battling for possession of the cane. Brawn and numbers counted heavily in favor of the freshmen; skill and strategy, however, were on the side of the sophomores. At an opportune moment, the latter spotted their key man, one Sackett, who had managed somehow to keep himself free from the melee. Suddenly the cane was tossed to Sackett whose fleet feet soon outdistanced those of his pursuers and on passing the western limits of the campus was judged to have won the contest for the Class of 1888.

Rushes and salting had nothing in common with the underground activity of hazing. Instances of the latter took place early in the University's history. Chancellor Winchell, so his diary shows, experienced "care and anxiety" over the problem. Generally, few freshmen suffered much indignity or injury but no matter how small the humiliation the offense was viewed with great concern by Administration and faculty alike. Of particular significance was the attack upon two first year men on October 16, 1873. Certain members of the Sophomore class, it seems, assaulted these students and violently tore from them their "silk hats." Later, the hats were returned with a sharp warning that further violence would follow in the event they were worn again. Straightway the offended freshmen reported the affair together with the name of one of the sophomores to the faculty which lost no time in summoning the latter before it. The student in question appeared but to the consternation of the faculty publicly announced his determination to persist in such behavior on like occasions in the future. Touched to the quick the faculty required him to give a written pledge to refrain from "hazing in all its forms" and that in case he declined to conform to these requirements his name would "be removed from the roll of this institution." Brought to his senses by this decision, the guilty sophomore quickly repented, made peace with his superiors; the affair was forgiven but not forgotten.

Late in March, 1881 the peace of the campus was rudely disturbed by the "hazing" of Ezra S. Tipple who was seized on East Genesee Street in the vicinity of Forman Park, blinded, gagged, and thrust into a hack and conveyed some four miles to the east. From here he was led to the edge of a wood forty or more rods away from the road and bound with ropes. His hair was then cropped on the crown and on the left side and an attempt was made to force some liquid, supposed to be linseed oil, down his throat. And with that his four "persecutors" withdrew leaving him to find his way home as best he could. The evening, we are told, "was stormy, it was snowing." Five days later the four offending students were arrested on a charge of assault and battery. A jury trial followed but contrary "to the general expectation" a verdict of "not guilty" was returned. Meanwhile the press throughout Central New York had given the event and incidentally the University considerable publicity and notoriety. Even the *Northern Christian Advocate* called for the immediate suppression of rowdyism. And this is precisely what the faculty determined to do.

Two of the alleged attackers had the good sense to appear before
the faculty in response to a summons but upon being questioned refused to admit their guilt. One stood firmly by his statement given
to the Police Justice that he was at the "Block" (meaning his society
room) at the time the assault had taken place; the other declined to
say where he had been that evening. In the face of these answers the
faculty voted to "indefinitely" suspend them from the college. Ultimately both of them probably yielding to pressure from home, admitted having played a role in the hazing of Mr. Tipple. In return for
this confession the faculty agreed to rescind its decision provided an
application was made for a letter of dismissal from the University
"which letter will be silent as to his being in good standing and will
omit the word 'honorable'." The third and fourth members, having
declined a second summons, were suspended from the college. One of
these, however, did send in a written statement which is interesting
enough to be quoted in full: "I beg leave to say that I am one of the
parties who have been arrested at the instance of Mr. Tipple, *tried* and
acquitted by the verdict of a jury of any connection with that affair
whatever. This is the only explanation I have to make."

Several other cases of hazing occurred during the administration of
Dr. Sims. In each instance, according to the minutes of the Liberal
Arts faculty, the accused received a fair hearing, no other conclusion
seems possible. Student opinion differed at times but when all was said
and done the action of the faculty, tempered as it was with moderation and kindness, was ultimately accepted as final. Similar attitudes
were expressed relative to the discipline imposed by the faculty for
violation of rules concerning conduct at classes and in the halls. In
1888, for example, a male student who persisted in singing in the halls
while classes were in session was in and out of the Dean's office and
before the faculty for several weeks before being placed on probation
for the remainder of the term. And surely the young men who broke
into the Hall of Languages and Crouse College Building probably
never forgot their experiences with the Dean and faculty.

A happier side of student life did exist at Syracuse and it is to this
one turns with a certain sense of relief. One of the more interesting
traditions instituted in the early years on the Hill was the "Pipe Ceremony," established by the graduating class of 1875. Conceived as a
farewell gesture on the part of the seniors, the event captured the
imagination of the student body and for nearly a decade constituted

an outstanding feature at graduation.[1] Grouped around the steps leading to the Hall of Languages—sometimes around a class tree—and surrounded by visiting alumni and friends, the seniors gathered to pay honor to their Alma Mater. College and class songs as well as dignified speeches and orations fittingly prepared the scene for the ceremony proper. At this juncture one of the seniors, chosen by his classmates for the occasion, solemnly filled the historic pipe, lighted the same and passed it to each member of his class. After the last senior had completed his part of the rite, the pipe was handed to a representative of the junior class to whom now descended the responsibility of keeping the spirit and tradition of Syracuse intact. Following this came the "presentations" which in the spirit of class day included gifts to the various members of the graduating class.

Each senior class, moreover, signalized its departure from the campus by making a gift to the University. The Class of 1873, for example, presented a sun dial, said to be worth a hundred dollars and reported to have been placed at the northwest corner of the Hall of Languages. The Class of 1875 adorned the campus with an elm tree and expressed the hope succeeding classes would follow the example until the main walk to the Hall of Languages was flanked by parallel rows of trees. In 1884 a marble tablet was placed in the Chapel in honor of Chancellor Haven and the Class of 1885 provided the funds for the installation of the present clock in the center tower of the Hall of Languages.

Also featured at Commencement and attracting far more attention was the burial of Calculus by the sophomores. Calculus, it will be remembered, was a requirement for graduation in the College of Liberal Arts. As such it may have been as much a burden as Citizenship I is reported to be today. Once the dreadful hurdle had been cleared in the sophomore year there was much rejoicing and in 1873 the sophomores evidenced their feelings by introducing the practice of burying their hated tyrant and enemy. And for good measure they also interred another arch foe, General Geometry; later classes added Analytical Geometry. Prior to 1876 these burials took place on Science Hill, the site of the present Crouse Building. Typical of these interments, which annually attracted large crowds of spectators, was the burial of 1875, the program of which read as follows:

---

1. There is a hint in the *University Herald*, February 1866, that the ceremony was abolished because it was "too immoral for a co-educational institution."

'76 HER SHOW
Grand Nocturnal Celebration
of the
Recapture of General Geo.
Metry A. Calculus
By the Satanlights of Pluto

The denounced procession will proceed from the starboard perforation of
the coup of the classics after the little fowels have ceased to pray and peram-
bulating will bring up at the terratical depression aloft the Bloody Green.
There his mortal remains will suffer differentiation and entire consummation
to the cremation theory.

The entire scene was punctuated with dismal howls and groans while
flashing torches revealed the mourners arrayed in ghastly regalia. A
tearful oration reminded all that Calculus' escape from Hades had
burdened the sophomores with the torments of hell, but now recap-
tured he would pursue his victims no more.

Later, an enterprising sophomore class inaugurated the idea of burial of Calculus at sea. Frenchman's Island in Oneida Lake was selected
as the site for the launching of the funeral ship, *Boscovich.* From the
deck of this ship willing hands consigned the mortal remains of "John
R. Calculus and wife, Mary Anna Lytics" to the sea. Onondaga, Cazenovia, and Skaneateles Lakes witnessed similar celebrations in the
years that followed, each burial becoming the occasion for greater
display and show. Care, of course, was always exercised lest some
bothersome freshman might spoil the spectacle and in one instance,
when cremation was practiced, the sophomores brought the ashes
back home with them in an urn. Burials from the campus furnished an
opportunity for much merry-making, often to the annoyance of the
faculty who expected more dignity and decorum than the students
wanted to show on these joyful excursions.

Student Activities

13 Syracuse University celebrated its Fiftieth Baccalaureate on Sunday, June 13, 1920. At this Golden Jubilee, Chancellor Day presented a timely review of the University's history. During the course of well chosen remarks, he told of an interesting and lively conversation that once took place between two loyal and devoted friends of the University, Dr. Benoni Ives of Auburn, New York, and the Honorable George F. Comstock of Syracuse. Ives and Comstock, it appears, were discussing the projected establishment of the University. Perfect agreement and accord existed between the two until Rev. Ives slanted his comments toward the moot question of co-education. Judge Comstock immediately questioned the wisdom of admitting women and stoutly affirmed "he would not consent to co-education" at Syracuse. Whereupon Dr. Ives firmly replied: "That ends the whole matter. We will never consent to a single-sex university." Additional argument ensued, the outcome of which was Comstock judiciously beat a retreat stating "While it was not his judgment he would rather have a university with women than to defeat the university without them."

Although the details of the conversation may be questioned, the existence of a body of opinion hostile to co-education cannot be

doubted. Few institutions at that time had opened their doors to women and for Syracuse, dogged as it was by many other pressing problems, to allow women to matriculate seemed to some as endangering
the very life of the new college. The impact of the Genesee tradition,
where co-education had existed since its inception, plus the liberalism
of the founders of Syracuse, however, could not be denied. And on
August 31, 1870, in delivering an inaugural charge to the Faculty,
Dr. Jesse T. Peck reminded the members of the organic law of the
University which stipulated that the conditions "of admission shall be
equal to all persons." "This pregnant clause," Dr. Peck continued,
"is no accident." "It represents the clear and well defined purpose of
the Trustees that there shall be no invidious discrimination here
against women . . . ." And with that Syracuse University embarked
upon its course pledged to the principle and ideals of co-education.

An undercurrent of dissent, however, continued to evidence itself
among the male members of the student body. Their arguments
against the presence of women on the campus may be found in the
early issues of the *University Herald*. Here one reads of woman's
place being in the home, that her feminine charm was spoiled by campus activity, and that woman's inability to learn was an established fact.
To what extent the authors of these clichés believed in them can not
be determined. Probably some of them did, particularly those who
came from homes where Victorian notions about women prevailed.
Others may have harbored a sense of inferiority when they contrasted
conditions at Syracuse with those at Yale or Cornell where only
men were admitted. Syracuse, so it was said, must do likewise if it
wishes to be a great institution. All of the traditions such as the mock
schemes and salting were endangered by women at Syracuse. Nor
were they convinced when the co-eds flatly denied these allegations;
no not even when the women students endorsed the rough and ready
traditions by standing on the side lines and cheering their men on to
greater efforts.

The controversy provoked rejoinders from quarters other than
the women members of the University. The Syracuse *Daily Standard*,
for example, had this to say: "Before the University was opened, the
trustees stated it would be opened to all and the young editors persist
in discussing the matter as though the policy of the University would
be changed for them. It is strange that these students do not go to some
other University where it is not present, because there is no law which

says they must stay. But perhaps they could find no place where they would be happy. The paper should build up and not tear down the reputation of the University." And Professor Brown publicly remarked at a college reception, "Ladies have a wonderful means of quickening perception. Ladies startle my sense of propriety by their mental quickness. As a well educated man will make a good husband so will a well educated woman make a good wife."

Gradually the din subsided. Women won their rights and in time earned the respect of the men though for a time they were kept off the editorial boards of certain student publications. Lags of this type persisted long after the limits covered by this volume but it is safe to assume that by 1884 co-education had been accepted at Syracuse. A telling statement to this effect was made by the Chancellor in his address to the Trustees in June of that year.

> The experiment of co-education had been tried in Syracuse University and its immediate predecessor, Genesee College since 1830—long enough to enable us to speak intelligently and confidently concerning its practicability and value. The unanimous opinion of our several faculties is that those dangers which many suppose attend the system, such as overtaxing the strength of young ladies, their constitutional unfitness for the course of study pursued by young men, undue familiarity between the sexes, loss of refinement, etc., are imaginary, not real: and that co-education, by following the evident providential order of society does in fact secure the best instruction, is refining, and elevating and secures the best preparation for practical life.

Although the Chancellor should be pardoned for not having said Genesee Seminary instead of Genesee College, his views and conclusions were warmly endorsed by the Trustees.

The presence of women, however, at Syracuse did give rise to certain problems that amused and sometimes annoyed both the college authorities and the students. Take for example, the case of the young man whose ardor for a certain young woman became so pronounced that the two were subjected to ridicule in the *University Herald*. Then there was the girl whose love-notes fell into the hands of a student reporter who, sensing what he thought was news, published the story in his paper. Devoted couples who loitered in the halls often were greeted unceremoniously by an unappreciative onlooker. On occasion, love-making was carried on in the reading room of the Library. Hoping to scotch the practice, Dean French in one of his chapel talks commented on what was known as "snuggling" and expressed the wish it might stop. Probably, he added, the women were more to blame than the men because the latter would hardly dare to meet their lady friends in the Library without first having been invited. There is nothing to show "snuggling" ceased as a result of the Dean's talk. Equally unmoved were those Freshmen who not only violated college mores by missing chapel but, taking advantage of the Chancellor's presence at Chapel or class sneaked their "dates" into his office.

Attendance at classes was strictly enjoined upon all students one of whom, for a small fee, had the chore of ringing the college bell. Absences, of course, did take place especially when the faculty were lax about enforcing rules. And it must be admitted the record of the teaching staff in respect to their presence at classes could have been better. As an illustration, reference might be made to a news item in the *Herald*, February, 1885. Here complaint is registered against a recent faculty decision that three tardinesses equalled an absence. To which, an editor replied, "How many times and how long may a Professor be tardy before a class can be cut?" On several occasions classes were dismissed because the room assigned had been appropriated by a professor without first having requested the use of the room. Eudelmer F. Cuykendall, '76, records in his diary of Chancellor Haven's class in English literature being cancelled so as to allow Professor Richardson's class in public speaking to meet. Moreover, examinations were carelessly scheduled with the result they often coincided both as to time and place with some regularly assigned class. Cuykendall also tells of an incident that once happened in Dr. Coddington's class in Philosophy. An examination, it seems, was to end at one o'clock but when the hour came, "Professor Coddington said, 'Hand in your papers tomorrow!' "

Another interesting bit of student life may be gleaned from scattered references to class conduct which, generally speaking, ran according to approved standards. In vivid contrast stands the behavior of students in Professor Brown's chemistry class who offended the senses of their instructor by spitting tobacco juice upon an already abused floor. Nor should one forget the startling and provocative interruptions that often disturbed the peace of chapel and elocution exercises. As to the latter, reference may be made to "cheesing." When a student faltered in the delivery of a speech or showed signs of not having prepared an assignment, his classmates demonstrated displeasure by stamping their feet. "Cheesing," as this stamping was called, also took place in the halls following the exercises though by what methods is not known.

Student vitality and enthusiasm were more happily evidenced in the College Association. Information relative to the latter is limited, partly because its activities were spasmodic and partly because it lacked a program that enlisted campus wide support. Presumably, the College Association was to relate matters having a general interest and appeal to all students. It was first, therefore, in advancing every phase of athletic development from a local Field Day or an intercollegiate football game, to the erection of a university gymnasium. Thanks to its efforts hymnals were placed in the Chapel; it also joined with other groups in presenting an all-campus lecture series. And when General Grant visited Syracuse in the fall of 1880 the College Association put a student section in the city parade that honored the President of the United States. But it did not have enough work to keep itself busy. Campus wags declared its meetings were set so as to avoid attendance at chapel and class; others insisted its gatherings were devoted to song and story. Charles N. Cobb, '77, was its first president in the fall of 1876. Others to hold this office were Frank L. Mead '91; Frederick A. Cook, '81; and Edgar S. Maclay, '85. College Associations also existed for the Colleges of Medicine and Fine Arts though little is known of their activities.

Equally vague is the story of Syracuse's membership in the Intercollegiate Literary Society, which as the name indicates was an organization devoted to promotion of literary efforts among American institutions of higher learning. Once a year, it seems, aspirants for honor and award gathered at a designated eastern city and engaged in a number of varied contests. Those interested in declamation competed in the oratorical contests; others strove for distinction in writing, translations of the Classics, and skill in foreign language. Syracuse was represented at many of these meetings, especially in the late 1870's, but at no time was local enthusiasm great. Outdistanced by older and better endowed institutions, Syracuse fared none too well. Basically, according to the *University Herald*, the Society's purpose was to stimulate development of individual talent without regard to the colleges represented. Inevitably, however, the argument continued, emphasis was placed more and more upon the college and less and less upon the student with the unfortunate result that it was Yale versus Princeton, Syracuse versus Harvard, and not Jones against Smith. Once this aspect or procedure became prominent, individual contestants were tutored and drilled by the faculties, excused from classes,

and allowed other privileges that seemed to defeat the primary purpose of the society. And as might be expected, the participants became
more interested in the prizes than their efforts. To what extent these
views constitute a true and valid criticism of the society need not concern us. On the other hand they do throw some light upon another
student activity at Syracuse.

Recruits for these contests must have been gained in part from those
who participated in the various elocution exercises, known as Exhibitions, that featured Chapel and Commencement ceremonies. Long a
standard feature at Genesee College these exhibitions continued to
attract attention at Syracuse for some time. The importance of elocution in the curriculum of the College of Liberal Arts has already
been noted. Evidently the faculty believed that skill in the spoken
word was as important as in the written word. And when one remem-
bers that a goodly proportion of the graduates of that early day were
preparing for the ministry, the requirement in elocution was more
than justified. Formal class work was supplemented by speaking at
Chapel and different student gatherings. Greater emphasis, however,
was placed upon the Elocution Exhibitions presented by selected
students from each of the four college classes. The Senior Exhibitions
constituted the supreme test and those who asked to participate in
these exercises, which were timed to coincide with alumni reunions
at graduation, were carefully picked and trained. To win a place on
these exhibitions at the hand of the faculty was a prize zealously
sought after—no greater or higher honor could be given to any student. Each speaker, and sometimes there may have been too many,
declaimed to the utmost of his ability upon some subject of current or
general interest. Political and religious questions predominated though
generous attention was given to historical and social matters. Interest
in these exhibitions was, for a long time, wide and genuine as may be
seen from an examination of both the student and city papers. Frequently the editors printed copious extracts or lengthy summaries of
the orations. However, by the early 1890's discontent was registered
by the students. In 1892 the seniors sought to have the exhibitions
abolished, a petition that received careful consideration by the faculty.
In February of the next year five members of the faculty—Drs. Coddington, Smalley, Haanel, Mace, and Hargitt voted in favor of the
petition; an equal number, Drs. Sims, French, Hedden, Peck, and
Emens were opposed. The chair then ruled the request lost, where-

upon the matter was reconsidered and after some debate was postponed. Shortly thereafter, and presumably with the knowledge of the faculty, a committee rendered a report relative to similar practices on other campuses. Investigation, it was stated, revealed that out of nineteen colleges in New England and the Middle States only Northwestern and Columbia had abolished the senior orations. Evidently this information settled the issue as orations were still being delivered at Syracuse in 1894.

Forensic skill also was fostered by the literary exercises of the Greek letter fraternities, the campus debating clubs, and by a number of societies which from time to time made their appearance. A study of the *Onondagan* will amply repay the curious who may seek additional information. Here one will note student groups such as an English Club, a Shakespearean Society, a History Club—all of which required formal presentations of a prepared address or talk. Practically every department of Liberal Arts, as well as those of Medicine and Fine Arts, had its own club. Of these mention should be made of the Agassiz Club founded in 1884 under the inspiration of the splendid teacher, Dr. Lucius Underwood. Professor Underwood also was active in the Microscopic Club. In the College of Fine Arts, Dean Comfort aided in the development of the Aesthetic Society in 1874, an organization that had a long and respectable history. Equally prominent was the musical club—Euterpe. Then there was the Ictinus Society, founded in 1881 for students in architecture, and the Cecilia Club, established in 1886 as a Women's Glee Club.

A University Glee Club, probably in the form of a double quartet, appeared in the spring of 1875 and gave several concerts in the city and nearby villages. Creditable as the effort was, little real enthusiasm existed and few bemoaned its absence the next year. Various attempts to revive the society were made during the next decade. Sometimes, as in 1876, considerable vitality was shown but the crescendo powers of the club never carried over to the next year. Another effort was made in 1880 though to quote the *University Herald,* "A glee club perished at Syracuse University in the gentle spring of 1880 after long months of lingering pain." Two years later this paper hailed with evident delight the record of a new club which during the winter of 1885 gave concerts at Lima, Buffalo, Tonawanda, Hornellsville, Hamburg, Manlius, and Cazenovia. At first absences from classes were not excused though in 1892 three cuts were allowed. In 1886 the club, directed by Benedict R. Hatmaker, '86, journeyed to Florida for what was reported to have been a most successful venture. Meanwhile in 1881 a Brass Band had been formed, and in 1892 a Banjo, Mandolin, and Guitar Club was established.

More complete information of these musical societies may be found in the student publications of which the *Herald* was the oldest. A college meeting to discuss the idea of a student paper was held in the Myers Block, April 12, 1872, a preliminary canvass having been launched two days before. At this later meeting, presided over by Francis J. Cheyney, '72, a committee was appointed to obtain subscriptions which before the month had passed exceeded two hundred. Encouraged by this demonstration of good will another meeting was held April 30th at which a committee was appointed to draft a constitution and a set of by-laws; a second committee was to arrange for publication. On May 13th, these committees submitted reports which were accepted and the title of the paper was adopted. A week later it was voted that two persons from each class be "appointed" to act as editors and publishers of the first issue which was slated to appear late in June. These gentlemen, so appointed—by whom the *Herald* in its initial issue of June 22nd does not state—subsequently met and chose George W. Elliott, '73, as Editor-in-Chief. The others drew lots. Francis J. Cheyney, '72; Edwin R. Redhead, '74; and Judson S. Coit, '75, became editors; John M. Dolph, '72; Delos Cronk, '74; William H. Shuart, '76; and E. K. Creed, '75, publishers. On motion the printing contract was awarded to the Syracuse *Journal*.

In its inception the *Herald* was to be published monthly throughout the College year by an Association composed of four members elected from each class and four others chosen by each of the two secret societies. It would appear, therefore, that the fortunes of the paper were to rest in the hands of twenty-four students, eight of whom made up the editorial and publishing boards. Of these eight, Cronk, Cheyney, and Coit were members of Delta Kappa Epsilon, Shuart and Elliott belonged to Upsilon Kappa, in time to be known as Psi Upsilon, Redhead was an Alpha Delta Theta transferred from Wesleyan, while Dolph and Creed in all probability were non-fraternity men; who the remainder were the *University Herald* did not state. These names appeared in the masthead of the first issue together with information as to advertising and subscription rates. Single copies were to sell for twenty-five cents; a yearly subscription, payable in advance, was to be two dollars. In the editorial column that followed, a humble but sincere statement of aims and objectives was presented. No glittering promises were made though a hope was expressed that a paper would be produced "that shall by no means be a discredit to the University" and to the city of Syracuse. "Our aim," it continued, "shall be to conserve all educational interests . . . and to reflect accurately the sentiment of the community of which we form a part." Judging from the format and content of the initial number, the editors established a high standard of performance. Following existing convention, advertising adorned both sides of the first and last sheets. As for the articles, these covered twelve pages and presented a wide range of interest. Poetry and prose appeared and through these opinion was expressed as to the physical appearance of the University, the need for dormitories, a possible school of journalism, a university crew, and local news relating to fraternities, athletics, social events and personals. In size the issue, which had no cover, measured approximately nine and a half inches by twelve.

Indicative of the caliber of the Association in its early days, mention should be made of certain changes in management that occurred. Beginning with the December, 1872, issue, the Association was altered so as to include two members elected from each class, four each from Delta Kappa Epsilon and Upsilon Kappa, and four from the Atticaeum, a literary society that became Delta Upsilon. Early in the next year the constitution of the Association was revised so as to provide an editorial board consisting of twelve members elected in equal number from the Senior and Junior classes. Five years passed and the *University Herald* became a useful and permanent feature of campus life. The faculty recognized its value to the University by allotting a room for its editorial board in the Hall of Languages. But within the Association itself discord developed. In part this must have sprung from the cleavage that existed between the fraternity and non-fraternity elements. Evidences of this crop out in the issues of the paper during 1877 and 1878; they also may be found in the columns of a rival paper, the *Syracusan*, and later in the *University News* for December, 1887. Again, bitterness usually characterized the college elections to the Board and the dregs of these contests were carried over into the management of the paper. In April, 1876, the editors of the *Herald* frankly admitted conditions were unsatisfactory—both the spirit and letter of the constitution, they charged, were being openly violated. Bias crept in and while "we theoretically choose men to represent classes we in reality choose them to represent societies." Moreover, it was alleged that individuals voted who were not members of either the Senior or Junior classes. Financial difficulties likewise dogged the efforts of the editors. Subscriptions kept at a low level and there were some who refused to meet their obligations. In such instances it was the fraternity element that seems to have assumed the losses. Finally, it should be noted that dissension developed over the absence on the Board of members from the Fine Arts and Medical Colleges and against the provision in the constitution that excluded "the ladies of the University from a direct representation." Attempts to correct these conditions generally failed. All were convinced that more orderly methods should be employed but when it came to implement any proposal existing tensions made a solution impossible.

An acute illustration of these difficulties occurred in 1878 when an incoming board found itself saddled with debts and quarrels. Determined to rid itself of these handicaps, the Board decided to cut the Gordian knots and established a new paper free from these difficulties. Most of this was unknown to the student body and when in October, 1878, no issue of the *Herald* appeared, the campus was visibly concerned; it also realized how valuable the paper had been in university affairs. At the same time it witnessed the appearance of the *Syracusan*, the avowed organ of Delta Kappa Epsilon and Psi Upsilon. Now in the last previous issue of the *University Herald* not a single member of Delta Upsilon is mentioned as being on the editorial board—a fact that possibly throws light upon the unfortunate situation that had developed. Delta Upsilon, it should be remembered, though a Greek letter fraternity, was a non-secret society and rather naturally might have thrown its influence in favor of the non-fraternity element that occasionally appeared on the Board. Be that as it may it is difficult to believe that Delta Upsilon, whose connection with the *Herald* had been intimate, was entirely in the dark as to the intentions of their rivals, Delta Kappa Epsilon and Psi Upsilon. In any event it was the Delta Upsilon Fraternity that now spearheaded the movement for a continuation of the *Herald* and in November issued the first number of volume seven of the paper. The new Association was managed by a board of seven editors and from the language in the issue all were to be from Delta Upsilon. Indeed of the five mentioned, J. W. A. Dodge, '79; Frederick H. Howard, '81; Eugene G. Mateson, '79; and Wilbur

S. Smithers, '80, were members of that society.

During most of the period covered by this volume the *Herald* retained the same general size and appearance it had in 1872 and continued to cater to the literary and news wants of the campus. Succeeding editorial boards enriched its offerings in these fields, allotted space in its columns to the various schools and colleges as they appeared in the growing life of the University; issued special editions from time to time, introduced cuts and pictures, added an illustrated cover, lowered the price, and sought in every way possible to advance the well-being of the University. The *Herald* most certainly was not a newspaper; on the other hand it was not a literary magazine. Rather did it combine the two in a manner and style that did credit to its sponsors and which stimulates the reader of the present age. Although its editors somewhat favored the fraternal background of the paper it would be unfair to conclude they abused their opportunities.

Equally sound was the conduct of the editors of the *Syracusan* which made its appearance, October 14, 1878. In this issue the reasons prompting the establishment of the paper were briefly presented together with a statement as to the aims and purposes of its Board. In general the *Syracusan*, which was to appear every three weeks, was to follow the pattern set by the "old Herald" but was to be managed by a board consisting of representatives of Delta Kappa Epsilon, Psi Upsilon, and Zeta Psi. In size, it was somewhat smaller than the *Herald*. Single copies were to sell for fifteen cents which was also the price of the *Herald*. Unlike the latter, however, there was no advertising which may explain why the yearly subscription was a dollar and a half, fifty cents more than what Delta Upsilon charged for its paper. Bryon N. Shoecraft, '79, a member of Psi Upsilon was editor-in-chief; David H. Hotchkiss, '80, on the business staff, was also of the same fraternity. Delta Kappa Epsilon was represented by Frank N. Westcott, '79, William H. Stevens, '80, and Henry T. Dawson, '80. Zeta Psi's interests were protected by Frank W. Talbot, '80, and Benjamin J. Shove, '80. Edward M. Curtis, registered in the College of Fine Arts, probably was not a member of any society.

During the years that followed the editorial board broadened the coverage of the *Syracusan*, introduced advertisements, issued special editions, and generally served its public in much the same way as did the *Herald*. In the fall of 1884 internal strife developed among the editors and at the beginning of 1885 Zeta Psi was "excluded;" its place being taken by Phi Kappa Psi. In March, Zeta Psi requested its return to the Board. Psi Upsilon was ready to let "by-gones be by-gones" and when the other members demurred, tried to intimidate the latter by refusing to do her "share of the work until the demand is allowed." It was not allowed and Psi Upsilon, after some hesitation, elected to remain in the Association. A decade later, however, Psi Upsilon parted company with the paper as did Phi Kappa Psi and the "Syracusan Association" seems to have become the property of Delta Kappa Epsilon. Not until these secret societies unlock their records will the cause for the "feeling of enmity manifested by the chapters of the several fraternities" be known. In reference to this episode it was the opinion of William P. Westfall, '88, a member of Psi Upsilon that both the *Herald* and *Syracusan* in 1885 seemed to be in a period of stagnation. If true, this attitude of indifference did not last long because in 1887 Mr. Westfall publicly complimented these papers on the quality of their services.

Mr. Westfall published these views in the first issue of the *University News* which appeared December 13, 1887. In addition to Mr. Westfall, who was editor-in-chief of the paper, the following were members of the board: Lyman P. Hitchcock, '89; Seymour C. Ferris, '90; John C. Culligan, '91; John A. Hamilton, '91; John C. Shoudy, '90; William E. Palmer, '91; Olin S. Twist, '91; William H. Rowe, '89; and Miss Florence M. Farnham, F.A. '88. Of these all were members of Psi Upsilon except John Shoudy, a non-fraternity member of the College of Medicine, and Miss Farnham who belonged to Gamma Phi Beta. Probably this array of Psi Upsilon men explains what the *University News* had in mind when it announced the paper was not going to be published by the Psi Upsilon Fraternity but rather by the "University News Association of whomsoever this association is composed." There was room for a third paper and the *News* aimed at fulfilling that need. Those interested in a yearly subscription for forty weeks might obtain the same upon payment of fifty cents; single copies were to sell for five cents. An examination of the introductory issue reveals a paper of eight pages with advertisements scattered throughout; in size it was somewhat larger than either the *Herald* or *Syracusan*. In June, 1888, the *News* became a weekly publication appearing on Monday morning and sold for one dollar a year; individual copies remained at five cents. A survey of the editorial boards of 1892 and 1893 shows the *News* was still in the hands of the Psi Upsilon Fraternity.

The *University News* came to an end in June, 1895, as did the *Syracusan*. The occasion for their discontinuance came as the direct result
of faculty action stimulated by the new Chancellor, Dr. James R.
Day. It was the Chancellor's opinion, and the faculty endorsed his
position, that the *News, Syracusan*, and *Herald* should be replaced by
a publication sponsored and directed by the University. The initial
step in this direction was taken in June, 1894, when a special committee
of the faculty was created to investigate the entire matter. After considerable exploration and discussion the faculty in June, 1895, adopted
the report which provided for the establishment of a University paper.
Meanwhile, the special committee had waited upon the several student
editorial boards and made known the decision of the Administration
to issue, in the fall of the year, the *Syracuse University Forum*. Believing it was the duty as well as the privilege of all students to support
a university enterprise, the *News* and *Syracusan* announced their papers would be discontinued with the Commencement issues of 1895.
The editors of the *Herald*, however, decided to continue their effort,
stating that as a monthly publication it would furnish an outlet for
literary effort on the campus. At the same time, an attempt would be
made to quicken alumni interest in the University by serving as an
alumni news sheet. No opposition to these declared aims came from
the Administration and the *Herald*, in an abbreviated size, continued
to appear until 1906. To what extent Delta Upsilon succeeded in
gaining its objectives is a matter that transcends the scope and purpose
of this volume. It is, however, a significant fact in the history of the
University that for over a quarter of a century all campus journalistic
activities were in the hands of existing fraternities and that of these
Delta Upsilon played, perhaps, the leading role.

Meanwhile there appeared in January, 1877, a publication known as
the *Syracusan* sponsored by the Delta Kappa Epsilon and Psi Upsilon
Fraternities. The editors, all members of the Junior class of the College of Liberal Arts, included Clarence N. Blowers, George W.
Weaver, Shirley E. Brown, and Rhoderick P. Hollett. The *Syracusan*
measured five and a half inches by nine and consisted of eighty-three
pages of content material plus a section devoted to advertisements.
Most of the latter referred to local clothiers, printers, stationers and
other shops, business houses or firms. There was one, however, that
may have shocked and possibly irritated Administration and faculty;
it ran as follows: "Loos, Kaufman & Co., Cor. Washington, Warren,

and Genesee Streets, Syracuse, New York, Importers of Wines and Liquors. First Class Restaurant Attached."

The volume had paper covers and was illustrated with fraternity crests and a number of cartoons generally slanted in a humorous vein toward some alleged shortcoming or irregularity on the part of some individual, society, or member of the faculty. One section of the *Syracusan* was given entirely to affairs of the University. Here appeared the college calendars, the names of the Trustees, Administration, and faculty, the various degrees granted during the previous year, reference to the Alumni Association, and a directory of students attending the University. Next in order came material concerning the secret fraternities arranged in order of establishment. No mention was made of the Delta Upsilon Fraternity though in the copy preserved at the University Library there is a tipped insert containing pertinent information followed by a comment that reference to the society in the annual was omitted "by request." After the fraternities appeared the "Ladies Societies"—for so the sororities were then known. The various clubs and societies were then allotted space and here it is interesting to note that several of the fraternities had quartets, octets, and orchestras. Athletic, musical, and literary organizations received attention and there was an historical sketch of the University. A page of the *Syracusan* was devoted to student obituaries.

In commenting upon this and the *Syracusan* of 1879 the Syracuse Daily *Standard* had this to say:

> One year ago the secret societies of our University issued an annual and called it the *Syracusan*. It was a right spicy publication full of dry humor, wit and satire, with a sprinkling of common sense and news. The venture was a grand success. It emboldened the Tory men to try again. They did so and yesterday turned out a bright, sparkling number even fuller than its predecessor with the rich annals of college fun and nonsense. The cuts are fine ones and very abundant. The number is decidedly creditable and over it one who has been there can while away half an hour very pleasantly.

All of which was somewhat more complimentary than certain references that appeared in the *University Herald* edited by the secret fraternities' rival, Delta Upsilon. In justice, however, to the latter it should be added that the *Herald* for February 1, 1878, printed the story as it appeared in the *Standard*.

The *Syracusan* for 1879 and the three subsequent years was published by the Delta Kappa Epsilon, Zeta Psi, and Psi Upsilon fraterni-

ties. Its editors continued to be members of the Junior class and together with their respective societies assumed entire responsibility,
financial and otherwise, for the publication. What the costs were and
at what price individual copies were sold is not known. Probably
some profit attended these efforts though a reason assigned for the
absence of the *Syracusan* of 1883 was the loss sustained by the sponsors
of the previous year. During this period, 1879 to 1882 inclusive, the
annual remained much the same as to size, binding, appearance and
general content. The sting or barb that characterized the humor seems
to have been softened and each succeeding issue tended to become
more ornate in style and more profuse with illustrations. Advertisements also increased in number—mute testimony to rising costs resulting from improved production.

Although the Juniors of 1882 "disheartened by the financial losses
involved in the publication of the previous books made no attempt to
produce an annual" the Juniors of 1883 revived the custom. "Elected
by our tribe," so ran the title page, "we have built and filled the wig-
wam, Onondagan we call it." Published in March, 1883, under the
protecting hand of the Delta Kappa Epsilon and Psi Upsilon Fraternities, the *Onondagan* of 1884 was slightly larger and more elaborate
than the *Syracusan's*. Subsequent issues followed these standards and
in 1893 the *Onondagan* appeared bound in stiff boards and measured
seven by nine and a half inches in size. In a general way each year witnessed less of the former spice and ridicule and introduced more and
better illustrations and feature articles. The appearance of an alumni
directory, serious articles in prose and poetry, and a dignified treat-
ment of fraternities, sororities, and social clubs were outstanding
characteristics.

College custom and tradition required publication of the *Onondagan* by the Junior class. Actually, as has been indicated, this responsibility was met by the fraternities without whose support the annual
could not have been a success from either a financial or literary point
of view. And each *Onondagan* seems to have been well received. Behind the scenes, however, a certain amount of inter-fraternity rivalry
existed. At times this jealousy came to the surface. Certain editors,
we are told, willfully altered "fraternity matter in order to gain a mean
partisan advantage." Conduct of this type brought its own reward in
the form of fewer student subscriptions. Possibly it was the absence
of adequate financial support that dampened the enthusiasm of the

editors in 1890 and led ultimately to the abandonment of the *Onondagan* for 1891. On the other hand there is good evidence to believe the editors failed to bring out an annual because a fire destroyed their type and plates. The *University Herald*, not altogether a friendly critic of the *Onondagan*, admits the existence of this disaster. At the same time it points attention to the fact that had the editors not been guilty of gross negligence the *Onondagan* could have been published before the fire.

The campus, however, was not without an annual that year. Members of the freshman society, Beta Delta Beta, produced the *Doggonon*, a volume full of foolishness and jest. Even the advertisements were silly if not meaningless. And various members of the faculty, the derelict editors of the *Onondagan*, and the Delta Upsilon society were ribbed in a most determined manner. *Onondagan's*, however, did appear for the remaining years covered by this volume and the traditional contributions rendered by this annual to student and university life were continued.

Graduate Work and Degrees

14 E arlier in this volume mention was made of graduate work at Genesee College. Here, it will be recalled, higher degrees were conferred either as the result of professional experience gained in a particular field following graduation or in honorary recognition of one's services to the College, the Methodist Church, the State, or the Nation. Graduate work in the modern sense did not exist. But what of Syracuse University? Would it follow where Genesee had led or would it temper its inheritance by incorporating within its curriculum some of the more recent trends evidenced elsewhere in American institutions of higher learning? For the time being the Faculty and Trustees, busy as they were with more pressing matters, gave little thought to graduate programs and degrees and it was not until November, 1871, that the following preamble and resolution was adopted:[1]

WHEREAS,—The Alumni of Genesee College feel a lively interest in the welfare of Syracuse University, and many of them have expressed a desire to adopt it as their 'Alma Mater', therefore,

1. The primary objective of re-conferring the degree already received was to meet a possible legal question that might arise as to the relation enjoyed by the Alumni of Old Genesee to Syracuse University.

206

RESOLVED,—That all Alumni of Genesee College who shall make application therefore, will be admitted by the Syracuse University to the same degrees to which they have heretofore been admitted by Genesee College, and will thereupon be deemed to all intents and purposes to be Alumni of the Syracuse University.

In accordance with this proposition and upon the recommendation of the faculty of the College of the University, the Board of Trustees generously bestowed graduate degrees—Master of Arts or Master of Science as the case might be—to some one hundred former students of Genesee most of whom, it would appear, had been out of college for three years or more. In addition a Master of Arts *ad eundem* was granted to Mr. Julius C. Hitchcock, Genesee '61. More significant was the awarding of an honorary degree of Doctor of Philosophy upon Mr. James H. Hoose, Genesee '61. At the time Mr. Hoose was Principal of the Normal College at Cortland, New York, a position he held until 1891. Later, he became Professor of Pedagogy at the University of Southern California, Los Angeles, and an Alumni Trustee of Syracuse University, 1872-1879. He was also the author of *First Year Text Book in Numbers, Pestalozzian System* and *On the Province of Methods of Teaching;* in addition he contributed articles to several educational journals.

The conferring of these degrees high-lighted the first annual commencement of the University which was held in Wieting Hall, Thursday, June 27, 1872. It is interesting to note, however, that the *University Herald* five days before had published a rather sharp criticism on existing practices relative to the granting of such degrees. "We predict," so the editorial ran, "that in all our real first class colleges the time will be when to obtain a master's degree a severe examination on a post graduate course will be necessary." At present, so the argument continued, degrees were granted to persons "utterly devoid of the least qualification for such a title." "We do not know that there is any remedy for this prodigality, except an appeal to the good sense of our educational institutions. Be sparing of these titles. Many, very many, whom some college has dubbed an M.A. or D.D., are no more worthy to bear such a title than 'Asinus pelle leonis' is to be called the 'king of beasts'." Perhaps it is just as well our primary sources do not disclose the reactions of either faculty or the recipients of the degrees to this editorial.

Evidently the former did not take these comments seriously as the events of the next year were to show. This is partly evidenced by the publication in the summer of 1872 of the University's first *Annual*. In this catalogue of seventy-two pages no comment is made of graduate work though reference appears to advanced degrees. The degrees of Master of Arts, Master of Philosophy, and Master of Sciences, so it was stated, would be conferred upon graduates of three years' standing in the Classical, Latin-Scientific, and Scientific courses respectively who have been engaged during that period in professional, literary, or scientific studies. Applications for these honors were to be submitted to the Secretary of the Faculty at least two weeks prior to Commencement. As a result of this announcement five Master of Arts and two Master of Science degrees in *cursu* were conferred in June, 1873. A Master of Science *per adoptionem*, a Master of Arts *per adoptionem*, and four Masters of Science *quasi per adoptionem*—all graduates of Genesee College—were granted. Rev. J. Chapman Jones of Trinity College, Dublin, received a Master of Arts degree *ad eundem* and Rev. M. C. Cramer, United States Minister to Denmark, the degree of Doctor of Divinity. Rev. Jason N. Fradenburgh, alumnus of Genesee College and Principal of the State Normal School at Mansfield, Pennsylvania, received a Doctor of Philosophy degree.

The distinctions conferred upon Drs. Jones and Cramer were honorary in nature and accorded completely with the intent of the University to award this degree in deserving cases. Dr. Fradenburgh, however, received neither an honorary nor an earned degree. The former, insofar as present day standards are concerned, most certainly would not necessitate the passing of an examination and were such to be required it seems likely that many of our institutions of learning would have smaller endowments and fewer buildings. But by the same token an earned degree today would entail a program of graduate study as well as residence and thesis requirements. And not one of these hurdles was placed in Dr. Fradenburgh's path though he was required to take an examination, the nature of which is not known, which he successfully cleared. To have demanded more would have been contrary to accepted practices then being generally followed throughout the American academic world. By insisting, however, upon an examination Syracuse was pioneering in graduate work.

At the same time it should be admitted there was confusion and uncertainty in the minds of the Faculty and Administration as to what degrees ought to be granted and what in the way of graduate work might be required. Nor was the situation materially improved by a statement that appeared in the *Annual* for 1873-1874 which was issued sometime after the 1873 Commencement. Here one reads:

Advanced degrees are conferred upon 'Bachelors' of the College of Liberal Arts who have devoted three subsequent years to professional, literary, or scientific studies and make due application therefor, (enclosing five dollars for diploma) and furnish satisfactory evidence of compliance with the literary traditions of the degree. It is intended that every parchment issued by the University shall represent adequate labor and results produced. The advanced degrees are as follows: 'Artium Magister' (A.M.), 'Philosophiae Magister' (Ph.M.), 'Master of Science' (M.S.) upon candidates who have received respectively the degrees of A.B., Ph.S., and B.S. Applications for Masters' degrees should be made to the Secretary of the Faculty at least two weeks before the Commencement.

The University is not committed against the policy of conferred honorary degrees; but it is firmly determined to restrict them to cases which will clearly command the general approval of the world of letters and science. This restriction implies that the approved candidate is one whose own works, commends him to the title, and will confer honor upon it. Testimonials are evidence, *prima facie,* that the candidate has not attained the proposed standard of eminence.

Meanwhile, and particularly during the spring of 1874, the faculty devoted much thought to the twin problems of graduate work and advanced degrees. In part, this demonstration of interest may have been quickened by the appearance on the campus of Thomas Hooker, A.B., Williams College, as a resident graduate student in Physics and Analytical Chemistry. More significant was the guiding hand and mind of Chancellor Winchell whose deep devotion to science and scholarly research had already marked him as one of America's foremost students and educators. His reputation and attainments in these respects, it will be recalled, had made a strong impression upon the Board of Trustees and faculty when the former was casting about for its first chief executive. Nor should it be forgotten that Dr. Winchell accepted the invitation to come to Syracuse on the understanding he was to continue his research and productivity and direct the academic and intellectual life of the University. It was, therefore, quite natural for Chancellor Winchell to undertake a program calculated to stimulate graduate work at Syracuse. Individually and collectively, it would seem, he approached the faculty and urged them to investigate conditions carefully. Meanwhile, according to his diary, Dr. Winchell spent considerable time on the matter himself.

After several protracted meetings, at which the Chancellor was present, the faculty accepted a report recommending the establishment of post-graduate courses for advanced degrees. This report was adopted by the Board of Trustees subject to such detail modifications the faculty might care to make. By this time the faculty, for reasons that are not clear, voted not to print the proposed scheme of courses until the entire program might be made more complete. Possibly the answer may be found in the annual report of the University Treasurer which in this instance followed the Panic of 1873 by one year. The University, in substance, could hardly make ends meet as it was without embarking upon some new venture that would entail additional expense.

Interestingly enough neither the Minutes of the Faculty nor those of the Board of Trustees provide any description or clue as to what kind of a graduate program the faculty had in mind. On the other hand the *University Herald* for June 30, 1874, carried a statement that throws some light on the matter. Equally significant is the fact that the statement appeared as an announcement by the Chancellor. "The time has arrived," so Dr. Winchell is reported to have said, "when Post-graduate courses ought to be organized and announced." Such a step, he declared, would enhance the usefulness of the University and arouse the keen interest of professional and other educated individuals. Residence at Syracuse, though highly desirable, was not to be imperative; nor did the candidate have to be a graduate of Syracuse University. Any person having completed a course of study usually prescribed for baccalaureate degrees whether at Syracuse or any other institution was to be admitted to candidacy.

For each degree there was to be a definite amount of continuous study equal in value to what was to be required of resident students. Nothing, it is to be noted, was stated as to number of courses or hours that had to be taken. Possibly, following the practice in respect to baccalaureate degrees, the intent was to expect thirty hours each year. Be that as it may the particular essential conditions for the doctorate of philosophy were to hold the first place and its attainment necessitated the heaviest requirements. The minimum term of study was placed at two years except for those who already possessed a master's degree in which case one year was viewed as being sufficient. All examinations for the doctor's degree, however, covered both years. Finally, the candidate was to submit a thesis "embodying the results of original investigations." Masters' degrees of Arts, Science, or Philosophy were to be conferred upon any one who held a baccalaureate degree and who had completed one year of post-graduate work plus an approved "original thesis." All graduate work was to center about the departments of Philosophy, Mathematics, Philology, Natural Science, History, and Literature; each discipline being authorized to arrange a course of study suitable for the general candidate but adaptable to individual needs.

Nothing, however, was said as to the details of the proposed program of graduate work; these being left for future action by the faculty. But the latter, burdened with other matters and conscious of the need of harboring every penny, were slow to act and the *Annual* for 1874-1875, which appeared in 1875 contained little that was new and generally ignored Dr. Winchell's statement of June, 1874. Actually, a comparison of the two reveals several significant differences. According to the *Annual*, for example, no mention was made of either a masters' or doctors' degree; in every instance the reference was merely to "advanced" degrees. On the other hand the evident intent of the announcement was to encourage graduate study at the masters' level. And while no particular course or courses of study were mentioned "any one who wishes to devote a year to such study" was requested to consult personally with the faculty. Incidentally this statement in the *Annual* continued to be printed without alteration for the next six years though in the issue of 1881-1882 an abbreviated description appeared; in this same *Annual* reference was made to the masters' degree. In the *Annuals* that followed, however, nothing was said about course work though the repeated statement, since the issue of 1877-1878, of the granting of advanced degrees must be interpreted as signifying that course work was essential. Finally, in respect to the *Annual*, all reference to graduate work prior to 1877-1878 was limited to the College of Liberal Arts though beginning with that year advanced degrees were first offered by the College of Fine Arts.

A graduate school at Syracuse, therefore did not exist; nor was there to be one during the years covered by this volume. The colleges of Liberal and Fine Arts, however, encouraged graduate study and made reference to the same in their respective bulletins, information concerning which reappeared in the *Annual*. Of the two the work undertaken by the College of Liberal Arts was the more important; evidence of this fact may be seen by a study of the several special bulletins issued by that College relating solely to graduate work. The first of these bulletins appeared early in 1876 and bore the title *Syracuse University—Post-Graduate-Courses of Study*. After quoting the general statement about graduate work as it appeared in the *Annual*, the bulletin read: "In addition to the above should any alumnus of this University, or of any other, wish to spend two years at the University, pursuing such studies as might be recommended, the degree of Ph.D. will be conferred upon such as shall pass the requisite examinations." Thus the University through its College of Liberal Arts was prepared to offer resident graduate study leading to the doctors' degree.

Having made this announcement, which clearly reflected the sentiments expressed by the Chancellor in 1874, provision also was made for the granting of a master's degree in Arts, Science, or Philosophy, and a doctor's degree to "Non-residents." Candidates for these degrees, all of whom were to have a baccalaureate degree, were required to undertake a systematic study of materials and readings which were carefully listed and explained in the bulletin itself. These requirements, referred to as "courses of study," were arrranged under the following heads: (1) Greek, (2) Latin, (3) French, (4) German, (5) Mathematics, (6) Hebrew, (7) Esthetics and the History of Fine Arts, (8) Chemistry, (9) Physics, (10) Anglo-Saxon and English, (11) Geology, (12) Zoology and (13) History. Each of these fields was broken down into several groups, study in three of which constituted a year's work. A second year's work gained the doctors' degree. One did not have to possess a masters' degree in order to win the doctorate, but the latter in no event would be awarded for less than two years of study. In addition, the departments of Latin, Zoology, Geology, and History required a paper or thesis the length of which varied, that in History was not to exceed five thousand words. The fee for all examinations was placed at twenty dollars and there was a diploma charge of five dollars. All candidates for these degrees were to make known their desires at least six weeks prior to the time of examination which in 1876 was set for June 10th.

During the course of the years that immediately followed the appearance of this graduate bulletin few changes were made in the program outline. In 1883, it should be noted, each of the several fields required a thesis of not less than four thousand words and in 1884 an additional fee of five dollars was charged for matriculation. Six years later it was resolved not to accept masters' degrees from other institutions and that examinations for all advanced degrees must be taken at Syracuse. About the same time all candidates for the doctors' degree were advised to concentrate their two years' work in the same department. Again, in 1891 the *Annual* carried a statement informing all candidates for the doctoral degree, who had not reported to the Dean of the College of Liberal Arts for three years, that their names would be dropped from the list of post-graduate students. Finally in 1893 the graduate bulletin announced that after October 5th of that year all candidates for the degree of Doctor of Philosophy were required to be in residence at Syracuse for two years. This action, somewhat revolutionary in nature but thoroughly in keeping with modern requirements for that degree, had been voted by the faculty early in the same month. At that time it also was resolved that all degrees *in cursu* were to be discontinued after June, 1897, and that the masters' degree would be granted upon the completion of an advanced course of study embracing a year in residence or of two years in non-resident study. Masters' degrees, moreover, were to be dependent upon the passing of an examination and the presentation of a thesis that demonstrated evidence of ability to prosecute independent investigation. Candidates for the doctorate were also required to pass examinations and submit such thesis as might thereafter be prescribed. Meanwhile and in keeping with the changes made by Liberal Arts, the College of Fine Arts had required all candidates for higher degrees having bachelors' degrees in architecture, painting, or music and who had pursued professional work for three years after graduation (changed to five years in 1893) to present to that college an approved piece of original work, pass an examination on a course of reading in esthetics and in the history of his department of art, and the payment of a graduation fee of twenty-five dollars.

The enthusiasm engendered by the inception of the new graduate program, initiated in the early 1880's, stimulated the faculty of the College of Liberal Arts to review its attitude toward honorary degrees, particularly the D.D. and L.L.D. In June, 1881, it was resolved that the faculty would not recommend more than three candidates for the degree of D.D. and that the Chancellor be requested to ascertain the sense of the Board of Trustees as to the propriety of recommending any of their number for honorary degrees. Three years later, when an applicant for the D.D. degree requested a recommended course of study it was voted that such a procedure was not desirable. And later when a holder of a doctors' degree from Syracuse asked to be examined over courses for the D.D. degree, the faculty replied that while they would be glad to examine him (he had offered a sum of money for the same) and if passed they would give him a certificate, they would not, however, assure him of a D.D. Honorary degrees, in brief, were not to be bought at Syracuse. It is instructive to note in this respect that when in June, 1882, the Faculty of the College of Liberal Arts received a communication from the American Philological Association and the American Association for the Advancement of Science voicing protest against conferring honorary doctors' degrees, an answer was made stating that Syracuse since 1876 had conferred this degree only upon examination.

Between the opening of college in the fall of 1873 and the Commencement of 1893 a total of eight hundred and ninety-four registrations on the graduate level took place at Syracuse University. Of these forty-three were resident students in the College of Fine Arts as opposed to six resident post-graduates in the College of Liberal Arts; the remainder, namely eight hundred and forty-three were non-resident and were all in the latter college. No particular profit would be attained by listing or counting those who matriculated in non-resident courses but did not complete them as they were in no proper sense students at the University. Their names in most cases, especially after 1883, may be found in the *Annual* and since many of them reappear in subsequent issues and are annually counted in the combined registrations of all students it is patent that many of the eight hundred and ninety-four are counted more than once. Far more accurate as an appraisal of graduate study at Syracuse is an analysis of those who earned graduate degrees, master's or doctor's, either as resident or non-resident students. An earned degree, it should be remembered, does not include an honorary award or a degree *ad eundem* or *in cursu*. As already explained an earned degree at Syracuse constituted one that included among other things an examination over a systematic study of certain recommended subjects the rigidity and standard of which was higher for the doctorate than the master's.

The first master's degree earned on examination at Syracuse was granted in 1876 to none other than Frank Smalley of the Class of 1874, whose association with his Alma Mater extended from the time of his registration in the fall of 1871 to his death in 1931. Mr. Smalley received his degree in Geology. In the brittle language of the minute book the citation reads as follows: "On recommendation of Dr. Winchell it was *Voted* that the work done by Professor Smalley [he was at the time an instructor in the University] during the past year in Geology, Zoology, & Botany, be deemed equivalent to one year's work in the Post-Graduate Course—without examination." In Mr. Smalley's case it was thought unnecessary to require a formal examination; his high performance as a teacher and student being viewed as sufficient. Other masters' degrees in Arts were conferred upon examination in the years that followed; there being a total of ninety by June, 1893. Meanwhile seven students received a master's degree in science upon examination; seventeen others won the degree of Master of Philosophy. All in all a grand total of one hundred and fourteen persons earned their masters' degrees by examination during the years covered by this volume. In contrast it is of interest to note that three hundred and ninety-eight masters' degrees were granted without examination in Arts, Science, Philosophy, Music, and the Fine Arts. Of the latter over ninety were granted to graduates of Genesee College.

Quite an opposite picture is met when one examines the degree of Doctor of Philosophy. Here one finds one hundred and twenty-seven persons earned this degree by examination between the years 1873 and 1893 as opposed to but three honorary awards. The recipients of the latter were Professor James H. Hoose of Cortland Normal School, Winfield Scott Smyth, Principal of the Cazenovia Seminary, and Henry Randall Waite, prominent public lecturer, author, and editor of the *International Review*. No honorary doctorate was granted after 1876.

Looking at doctoral degress earned by examination, twenty-five were granted in Christian Evidences. English Literature was next with seventeen; History followed with thirteen and Philosophy was fourth with ten. Latin and Geology had eight and seven respectively, and Greek had seven. Chemistry, Mathematics, and German had five each while Physical Science (Physics) had four. Zoology, Botany, Art, and Modern Languages each had three. Biology had one and there was one combination doctorate in Latin and Greek. There were six others, all granted before 1879, with no designated field and in 1892 one doctorate, *ad eundem*, contrary it would seem to practice, was given.

It is difficult, from a study of available sources, to determine or evaluate the scope and nature of the examinations required for earned

degrees at the masters' and doctors' level. In the case of Mr. Fradenburgh (1873) the examination covered modern and ancient languages,
Chinese and Japanese, a study of the American Indian, and the field
of Botany. For one who was both pastor and teacher the coverage
might be viewed as being sufficiently broad and it is interesting to
note that he received the highest grade in Botany. Unfortunately, the
Faculty Minutes make no similar or comparable statement as to any
other examination but with the improvement in standards we have
witnessed it seems reasonable to assume that the examiners became
more thorough and circumspect as the time moved on. Surely those
few who were resident students may have been submitted to a more
rigorous examination than the others. But it must be admitted, in the
face of available evidence that examinations in general could not have
been too searching according to modern standards. Probably in respect to those seeking the doctor's degree the record was better and
it should be noted that there were applicants who were denied ad-
mittance to candidacy. The picture is also brightened by a sampling of
the theses required for the doctorate. Although the University Library
has no thesis prior to 1880 those that are preserved for the next thirteen years do afford a basis for a tentative conclusion. Many of them
are approximately 27 x 21 centimeters in size and range in length
from fifteen to a hundred pages. In some instances the theses resemble
an essay; in others, they are more like a summary or digest of materials
used. Although the author of this volume is not qualified to pass upon
the content or merit of each thesis examined it should be stated that in
those cases where a judgment could be formed the impressions were
favorable. In 1883, to illustrate, there was submitted by Franklin
N. Thorpe a thesis in history entitled, "The Federal Principle in History, 1765-1865." Written in long hand, this thesis of seventy-two
pages bears testimony to the impact of the new historical methods
then being introduced throughout the country and practiced at Syracuse. Mr. Thorpe cites his sources and seems to be critical in their use,
and while they are uniformly secondary in nature the candidate did
well in digesting and interpreting the same. Granted that today the
effort would be rated a brilliant term paper and no more, the fact remains Mr. Thorpe's contribution gave ample promise of future productive scholarship.

Mr. Franklin N. Thorpe became a teacher, lawyer, and author of
national importance. For a number of years he was a Professor of

American Constitutional History at the University of Pennsylvania and in 1889 he was admitted to the Supreme Court of the State of Pennsylvania. In 1898 he published at London and New York a two volume study, *Constitutional History of the American People* and in 1901 there appeared his *Constitutional History of the United States, 1765-1895,* in three volumes. Both of these constitute a review of the genesis and evolution of federal and state constitutions and preceded his monumental study, *Federal and state constitutions, colonial charters and other organic laws of the states, territories, and colonies now or heretofore forming the United States of America.* Compiled and published under authority of the Congress of the United States, this work appeared in seven volumes in 1909. All of Thorpe's writings are mentioned in a *Guide to Historical Literature,* long recognized as a reputable bibliographical index to historical writing.

In the field of Zoology, distinction was won by David S. Kellicott who received his doctor's degree in 1881. Dr. Kellicott was Professor of Zoology at the University of Buffalo for seventeen years; later he moved to Ohio State University where his work was rewarded by a University grant that placed him in charge of the Lake Laboratory at Sandusky, Ohio. He was the author of numerous learned articles and several books, notably his *Catalogue of the Odonata* of Ohio, and the *Dissection of the Ophidan.* Thomas B. Stowell received his degree in 1881, the subject of his thesis being "Nervus Vagus" in the department of Biology. During this stay at the State Normal Schools at Potsdam and Cortland, Dr. Stowell contributed many articles on the nervous system of the domestic cat. His interest in this field never lessened though as time went on he devoted more and more attention to professional education. In 1909 he became Chairman of the Department of Education of the University of Southern California in Los Angeles, and in 1918 Dr. Stowell became Dean of the School of Education of the same institution.

Mrs. Martha E. Foote Crow was awarded the doctors' degree in English Literature in 1885. After teaching for a short time at Wellesley College, she became Lady Principal of Iowa College, now known as Grinnell College. In 1891 she became Dean of Women at Northwestern University. Also recommended for the degree of doctor of philosophy in English Literature was Rev. Ezra Tipple who for several decades was recognized as one of the outstanding clergymen in metropolitan New York. He was the author of several books among which reference might be made to the *Drew Sermons* and the *Life of Freeborn Garretson*. Mr. Tipple became an Alumni Trustee of Syracuse University which also honored him with the degrees of D.D. and L.L.D.

Clearly, graduate work at Syracuse did not exist as is understood today. At the same time the several faculties of the University were alert to current educational trends and were striving, amid patent limitations, to raise academic standards on the Hill. In part this was evidenced by some undertaking intensive graduate instruction abroad, notably in Germany; others sought to enrich themselves and their courses by travel and general study in Europe and the United States. Probably the most conspicuous illustration of faculty will and determination to improve conditions on the campus was demonstrated by the labor devoted to the devising of ways and means for improved graduate work. Efforts of these types were encouraged by the Administration which also sought, when the occasion warranted, to add men to the teaching staff who had shown skill in research and who gave promise for the future. Valuable and constructive spade work, therefore, characterized the graduate work at Syracuse during the first twenty-five years of the University's life. Visible and tangible fruits were none too conspicuous but preparation for future harvesting was much in evidence.

The Alumni Association

15 In the minds and hearts of those who established Syracuse University, Genesee College was ever held dear. Naturally there had been keen disappointment over the failure of the College Committee of the Methodist Conferences of Central and Western New York to effect the removal of Genesee College from Lima to Syracuse. But there is no evidence that points to the presence of ill will or hostility on the part of the founders of Syracuse toward Genesee College. Both had the vision of a great Methodist University at Syracuse and both had given generously of time and effort to achieve that end through the removal of Genesee College. And it was due to no fault on the part of either that carefully prepared plans had been for naught. Speaking to this effect before a large gathering that witnessed the laying of the corner stone of the Hall of Languages, August 31, 1871, Rev. Arza J. Phelps aptly stated: "From the first the Trustees of Genesee College have been true to the faith and have done all in their power to consummate this noble work. . . . The removal was opposed by the citizens of Lima." Additional testimony of the cordial relations that existed between Genesee and Syracuse is to be found in the well-known fact that the majority of the original faculty of the University had been on the staff at Lima. Moreover, several who had served as Trustees of Genesee accepted similar responsibilities at Syracuse. Nor should one overlook the presence of students from Genesee in the graduating classes of Syracuse between 1872 and 1875.

More significant, however, was the step taken by the faculty and Trustees of Syracuse which led to the granting of alumni status to those graduates of Genesee who wished to become identified with Syracuse. The initiation of this happy idea stemmed from a meeting of the faculty on November 14, 1871, at which a resolution recommending such action was enthusiastically passed and referred to the Trustees.[1] The latter heartily endorsed the proposal early in December of the same year. Whereupon Vice-President Steele in an address before an alumni gathering of Genesee graduates held at Syracuse in the same month stated: "The University would, without expense, confer upon all. . .who wished it the same degree received from Genesee College."

In extending the right hand of fellowship to the graduates of Genesee, the University was motivated in part by the need of implementing a provision within the bylaws for alumni representation upon the Board of Trustees. According to these regulations:

> Three members of the Board shall be members of and represent the Alumni of the University; they shall be elected by the Alumni Association . . . it being provided that until the Alumni shall number twenty-one the election of the three Trustees provided for in this section shall be made by the Board of Trustees.

But not wishing to wait until the University had graduated at least twenty-one students and anxious to cement the existing friendship between the alumni of Genesee and the new institution, the Trustees waived the privilege accorded them of naming the initial alumni trustees and notified the Genesee graduates that upon receipt of alumni status they might elect their representatives "at Commencement." A formal announcement of this proposal was made May 16, 1872, accompanied by a letter to the Genesee Alumni signed by John Alabaster and Henry R. Sanford, Chairman and Secretary respectively of the Alumni Association of Genesee College. In this letter the following appeared:

> Commencement will occur at Syracuse, Thursday, June 27. The trustees will meet Tuesday afternoon, June 25, at which time the degrees will be conferred

1. See p. 207 for a copy of this resolution.

upon all of us who have signified our desire for them, and in accordance with
the action of the meeting held [at Syracuse in December] . . . the graduates
of Genesee College are requested to meet at the Syracuse University on Wed-
nesday, June 26, at 10 o'clock a.m., for the purpose of organizing the Alumni
Association, the election of . . . trustees and for a Reunion.

It is hoped that the attendance will be large and that the ties that clustered
around 'Lima Hill' may thus be perpetuated.

The response to these invitations was most pleasing and on June 25,
1872 the Board of Trustees voted the necessary degrees and conferred
Syracuse University Alumni status upon a hundred graduates of
Genesee College. The next day formal notification of these actions
was made to these graduates then in session at Syracuse. Straightway
the latter organized themselves into the "Alumni Association of Syracuse University." In all probability, as will be noted presently, no permanent organic law or constitution was adopted at the time. Precisely
why is not known. Were we in possession of the minutes of this meeting our knowledge might be more complete. Light, however, may be
gleaned from the Syracuse *Journal* and *Courier* for June 27 and June
28, 1872 respectively. Here one reads of a large gathering of Genesee
graduates who met and effected a "temporary organization." Surely,
therefore, it was not the lack of numbers that prevented a permanent
establishment. Nor may an explanation be found in the absence of spirit and enthusiasm. Both the business and social sessions of the gathering
echoed with intense expressions of loyalty and interest. Probably the
answer to the problem may be found in a desire to build an alumni association upon a sure and certain foundation. Barely six weeks had
elapsed since the idea of such an association had been broached and
there may have been some who sensing certain difficulties preferred a
temporary organization upon which in a year or two a permanent society could be founded. Be that as it may the sentiment of the gathering clearly favored a loose rather than a rigid organic law for the time
being.

In the absence of a copy of the temporary constitution that was
adopted conclusions as to its content and nature should not be too
sharply drawn. From the *Courier* and *Journal* it may be established
that the objectives of the association were threefold: to advance the
fortunes of "Alma Mater," to perpetuate the friendly ties formed at
Genesee and to be knit at Syracuse, and to promote a diffusion of

liberal culture. Again, from the announcement of May 16, 1872, it seems safe to assert that membership in the association must have been defined in the terms outlined by the Board of Trustees and that one of the powers of the organization was that of electing alumni trustees. The city papers would also support the suggestion that the constitution contained a clause which extended honorary membership to the wives and husbands of all members. Finally, in view of the election of officers that took place at this gathering the fundamental law of the association must have made provision for the same, and it is difficult to believe that a clause respecting dues was not added.

In accordance with this temporary constitution the following officers were chosen: Rev. Otis L. Gibson of Towanda, Pennsylvania, President; Rev. Sidney O. Barnes of Adams, New York; Mr. Francis J. Cheney of Antwerp, New York; and Miss Celia A. Hard of Syracuse, Vice-Presidents; Professor Henry Sanford of Fredonia, New York, Recording Secretary; Mr. Joseph Jones of Ilion, New York, Corresponding Secretary; Rev. Manley S. Hard of Syracuse, Treasurer; and Mr. R. D. Munger of Bloomfield, New York, Historian. The alumni members of the Board of Trustees elected at this meeting consisted of the Hon. Edward C. Walker of Batavia, New York, Rev. J. Dorman Steele of Elmira, New York, and Professor James H. Hoose of Cortland, New York. Suitable resolutions were also passed expressing the joy of those present in becoming alumni of the University. "We take pride and satisfaction in the thought that *we* are to have some part in shaping the future career of this institution," and "we heartily and unreservedly pledge ourselves to the support of our new Alma Mater by every means in our power." And in this respect let it be added that subsequent events were to increase and not diminish the intensity of this loyalty and devotion. Other resolutions were passed, speeches made, and letters read from absent Genesee graduates all of which expressed similar pleasure in their new relationship. In the evening a literary and social gathering was held.

During the course of the college year, 1872-1873, the Alumni Association continued to manifest an interest in the University. Rev. Otis L. Gibson, representing the organization, delivered a most appropriate address at the installation of Chancellor Winchell. And through the columns of the *University Herald* a request was made of each graduate for vital and personal statistics which in time, it was promised, would appear in an *Alumnate Register*. Again, in June, 1873, a goodly number of the association attended the first annual meeting at which officers for the ensuing year were elected. All of the officers with the exception of the Recording Secretary were graduates of Genesee College though even in this instance, Mr. Roland S. Keyser of the Class of 1872 had completed all but his senior year at Lima. The preponderance, if not unanimity, of Genesee graduates is quite understandable. Actually, Syracuse University had only a handful of graduates and few of these measured up to the standards required for holding alumni office. Recognition of this fact appeared in an editorial in the *University Herald* for January 31, 1873. At the same time the editor, without expressing any ill will, hoped that as soon as Syracuse graduates had acquired the necessary qualifications "there will be no hesitancy on the part of the Genesee graduates to give them the trusteeships and as many honors as they deserve." The 1873 meeting also seems to have discussed the need for a more permanent constitution and a committee was appointed to submit the draft of such a document and a set of bylaws at the 1874 gathering. Finally, it should be noted that the business sessions of the Association from 1873 to 1893 were held in the Hall of Languages, usually in the Chancellor's Class Room which was the large assembly room on the first floor. The evening sessions assembled generally either at the Parlors of the Hall of Languages or at one of the city hotels such as the Temperance House.

Some forty alumni, most of whom had attended Genesee College, were present at the 1874 gathering of the association. The most outstanding achievement of this meeting was the adoption of a constitution and bylaws which probably were placed in the minute book by the secretary, W. A. Brownell, following the 1876 meeting. Minutes of gatherings previous to 1875 have not been located though excerpts and comments do appear in the local city papers and the *University Herald*. An examination of Brownell's entry and the records of meetings as reported by the press indicate, except for one or two items, that the documents of 1876 were the same as those of 1874. Probably the most important amendment to the earlier constitution concerned the status of the alumni of the Syracuse Medical College. Less significant was the change in the amount of dues. Originally placed at fifty cents a year they appear in Brownell's copy as one dollar.

According to the constitution as adopted in 1874 the object and purpose of the "Alumni Association of Syracuse University" was "to foster in all proper ways every interest of the University," to retain the friendships formed at college, to keep a record of all alumni activities, to unite in annual literary and social exercises, and to provide memorial services for the deceased. Membership in the organization was probably limited to the graduates of the Colleges of Liberal and Fine Arts; those of the Medical College being excluded doubtless because they had their own alumni association and also because of the peculiar relations then existing between the Medical College and the University. The absence of the Medical Alumni at the 1876 gathering of the University Alumni Association was the subject of much discussion the burden of which was that all medical graduates should be classified as members of the University Association. Whereupon the constitution was amended (and as such it appears in the Brownell copy) to read, "Graduates from each of the colleges of the Syracuse University, including the graduating class of each current year, and all receiving degrees from the same shall be members of this Association, and all shall be recognized as legal voters who have received or have been recommended by the Board of Trustees to receive diplomas." Now it will be recalled that in the chapter dealing with the early history of the Medical College the point was made that the graduates of the Medical Department of Geneva College do not appear to have accepted the Trustees' offer to receive degrees and alumni status as had those of Genesee. It would seem, therefore, somewhat irregular to consider the Geneva graduates as alumni of the University. It should not, however, be assumed that the University Alumni Association consciously exceeded its authority. What was done was probably effected without intent and in ignorance of the real situation.

A word also should be added about honorary members who in the "temporary" constitution of 1872 consisted of the wives and husbands of active members. It may be that the 1874 document contained some provision for honorary members though no reference to such appears in the Brownell copy. It is of interest to note that in 1875 the Association voted honorary membership to Dr. and Mrs. Samuel A. Lattimore, Dr. and Mrs. (William) Wells, and a Judge Dusenbury. Dr. Lattimore at one time had been Professor of Chemistry at Genesee and in 1875 held a similar position at the University of Rochester. Dr. Wells had taught modern languages at Genesee between 1852 and 1865, and in 1875 was on the faculty of Union College. Neither of these gentlemen nor their wives were graduates of either Genesee or Syracuse.

Judge Dusenbury probably was the Joseph Dusenbury who was graduated from the Geneva Medical Department in 1844. Again, in 1877 Rev. John B. Foote "honorary member of the Alumni Association of Genesee College was recorded as a member of this association." By this time certain conflicting notions seem to have arisen as to honorary members and at the 1878 meeting the topic was widely discussed the result of which was the passage of a resolution that any person by a two-thirds vote might be made an honorary member of the association and be entitled to all its rights and privileges "except that of voting and holding office."

Returning, however, to the content and scope of the 1874 constitution one notes that provision was made for the annual election of a president, three vice-presidents, a recording secretary, a corresponding secretary, a necrologist, a treasurer, and an executive committee of seven. Annual meetings were to be held on the day preceding commencement and the constitution might be amended at any annual meeting by a two-thirds vote of the members present and voting. The bylaws defined more precisely the duties of the officers, created the additional positions of Historian and Poet, specified what constituted a quorum, set the dues, and provided for the election of the alumni trustees.

The organic law of 1874 continued to serve the Association for a decade. The only alteration of significance came in 1878 when the article defining membership was by resolution interpreted to mean "all persons who have received or who have been recommended by the trustees to receive degrees from Syracuse University, and such other persons as have been duly elected members of this Association." And all of these were to be "entitled to the same and equal privileges." Precisely what did this resolution seek to establish? Was its intent to enroll as active members those who may have attended Syracuse but were never graduated? Did it convey the right of voting and holding office, such as alumni trustee, to individuals who were not graduates of the University or holders of honorary degrees but who might be elected to membership in the Association by the vote of its members? Could the Association elect to membership an individual who never had attended Syracuse or who had not received an honorary degree from the University? And how did this interpretation concern the graduates of the Medical College? In other words what was an alumnus of the University and by whose authority could alumni status be defined? The evidence upon which an answer must rest is by no means conclusive. On the other hand there is abundant proof that constitutional issues were not matters that greatly concerned the alumni of that generation and there seems to have been a willingness on the part of many to make things easy and pleasing for all within the association. It is true that time was spent on the membership problem, upon what the Historian was to do, and whether absentee balloting might be used. But viewed in their relations to the major objectives of the organization they most certainly were held much less important.

None the less by 1882 the sentiment was expressed in several quarters that the constitution needed drastic revision particularly in view of the association's recent efforts to establish an alumni endowment fund. Early in that year a meeting of the Executive Committee was held at which time a committee composed of James M. Gilbert, '75, William Nottingham, '76, and Edwin Nottingham, '76, was appointed to take steps leading to the incorporation of the society. Chancellor Sims and Dean Comfort were present at this meeting and expressed themselves as favoring the undertaking. But when the committee began to implement their assignment they discovered there was no state law under which the alumni of the colleges and university could be incorporated for the purpose thought desirable. To obviate this difficulty it was suggested that the committee obtain the enactment of a special measure incorporating the University Alumni. This scheme, however, was dropped in view of the general objections that were raised against all special legislation. The committee, therefore drafted an act to provide for the incorporation of the alumni of colleges and universities throughout the State of New York. The form of the proposed measure was then sent to Albany where in June, 1882, it was passed by the State Legislature.

These facts were made known by the committee at the annual meeting of the association in June, 1882. It was an unusual compliment that was then paid to the committee. So well had its members executed their commission that the association accepted, with but one amendment, a resolution introduced by Mr. Edwin Nottingham that a select committee be appointed by the chair to file a certificate of incorporation, adopt a constitution and bylaws and "take such other steps as may be necessary to incorporate the Alumni of the College of Liberal Arts and Fine Arts of Syracuse University" as might be required by the state law. As may readily be seen Mr. Nottingham's resolution made no reference to the Medical College and it was this omission that caused the passage of an amendment providing for the elimination of the words "College of Liberal Arts and Fine Arts." As a result the incorporated society was to include the alumni of the University. It was also resolved that the select committee having finished its task they were to have the constitution and bylaws published in the college paper.

A year later, Mr. Edwin Nottingham, in behalf of the select committee on incorporation reported that a certificate of incorporation "had been filed and a constitution adopted." After a lengthy discussion, most of which seems to have centered about what constituted membership and the amount of dues, the report and constitution were adopted. Whereupon and in accordance with the constitution fifty-six persons signified their membership in the incorporation by signing their names. In looking over these signatures one reads the names of such well-known persons as William, Edwin, and Eloise Nottingham, Lucien M. Underwood, John S. Clark, Benjamin J. Shove, George W. Peck, M. W. Dean, W. A. Brownell, M. S. Hard, J. H. Zartman, and Celia A. Hard all of whom played an important role in the annals of the Association.

A printed copy of the constitution and bylaws of 1884 may be found in the Minute Book of the Association as well as in the *Alumni Record* of 1887.[2] The constitution and bylaws consisted of seven articles each. The name of the corporation was the "Alumni Association of Syracuse University," the object of which was to secure the benefits granted to alumni societies of a state act of 1882 and amendments to the same. Briefly these may be stated as the advancement of learning, culture, the well-being and prosperity of an academic institution, the handling of funds, the administration of literary exercises and ceremonies, and the direction of all matters usually pertaining to alumni associations.

Membership in the local Syracuse association was defined as consisting of any "graduate of or person who has received a degree from Syracuse University or any college thereof or what was formerly known as Genesee College" provided such person signed or caused to be signed for him both constitution and bylaws and paid an annual

2. The copy appearing in the April 22, 1884 issue of the *University Herald* was a preliminary draft of the organic act of 1884.

fee of one dollar. According to these provisions individuals who matriculated at Syracuse but who were not graduated were not eligible for membership though holders of honorary degrees might join the society upon signing the documents and paying the necessary fee. It should also be noted that no provision was made for graduates of the Geneva Medical Department; on the other hand there was nothing to prevent graduates of Syracuse Medical College from applying for membership. Finally, it should be observed that graduates of the various colleges and recipients of honorary degrees did not automatically become members of the association. Membership, in other words, entailed responsibilities and duties and the acceptance of these obligations was implied in the requirements of signing the constitution and of paying the fee. If a graduate did not wish to assume these conditions he did not have to and, it is believed, he was in no sense less an alumnus for not having joined the association. But he was not a member of the Alumni Association and could not, therefore, enjoy any of the rights and privileges of membership such as voting for alumni trustees. It should be added no provision existed for honorary members.

The governing body of the society rested in a Board of Directors, thirteen in number, elected annually at the regular meeting of the corporation; directors held office until their successors had been elected. At each annual gathering and from the Board of Directors a president, vice-president, and a secretary and treasurer were to be elected and these so chosen served in these capacities both for the Association and the Board of Directors. Within ten days after their election the Directors were to elect an Executive Committee of seven of whom the president, vice-president, and secretary and treasurer were to be three. To the directors and executive committee were assigned the duties and responsibilities necessary for the conduct and life of the society. Each member of the association was to pay an annual fee of one dollar non-payment of which debarred an individual from membership. And no person who was not a member in good standing could be chosen an alumni trustee. Alumni trustees were chosen by majority vote at an annual meeting of the association. The bylaws of the society provided for annual meetings of the society, the board of directors, and executive committee, defined the duties of all officers, and provided for the filling of vacancies in either board or committee. A majority of the members of each group constituted a quorum; for the annual meeting, however, twenty persons were needed to conduct business. Finally provision was made for the amendment at annual meetings of either constitution or bylaws by a two-thirds vote of those present.

The organic law of 1884 went into effect at the annual meeting of that year. During a morning session the old association completed its work, arranged for the transfer of all records, and in the afternoon the society formally organized under the new constitution. William Nottingham was chosen president, Carlton C. Wilbor, vice-president, and James M. Gilbert, secretary and treasurer; Professor J. H. Hoose was elected alumni trustee. Succeeding officers included such well-known alumni as Dr. E. O. Kinne, Med. '76; Willis A. Holden, '80; Dr. Frank Smalley, '74; Miss Carrie E. Sawyer, '87; Rev. Joseph H. Zartman, '78; and Rev. Charles E. Hamilton, '86. Meanwhile a few minor changes were made in the constitution one of which provided for a recording secretary; the organic law of 1884, therefore, continued to function throughout the remaining years covered by this volume. Equally important was the resolution adopted at the 1892 meeting providing for the establishment of alumni associations in other cities. The first of these societies was the Syracuse University Alumni Association of New York City founded in the fall of 1891. Rev. Ezra S. Tipple, '84, was its first president; Mrs. Nettie M. Walsworth, '90, recording secretary; and Miss Jennie L. Whitbread, '87, corresponding secretary. Prior to that date Francis E. Trowbridge, '82, a member of the New York Stock Exchange, Director of the American Exchange Bank, and on the editorial staff of the New York *Sun*, had stimulated a reunion dinner at the Windsor Hotel in New York City, December 17, 1886. Approximately a year later, Richard E. Day, '77, was instrumental in organizing a "resident alumni association" at Syracuse. The effort though enthusiastically greeted lasted scarcely a month. Mr. Day was editor of the *Northern Christian Advocate*, 1879-1880, and on the editorial staff of the Syracuse *Daily Standard*, 1880-1899.

Among the objectives ever held high in the annals of the association was the establishment of an alumni endowment drive. The first recorded notice of a projected drive may be found in the minutes of the society for June, 1875. At this gathering a committee headed by Rev. J. Dorman Steele, whose memory is preserved in the chair of physics that bears his name, seems to have been appointed to confer with the Chancellor as to how the association might materially aid the University. Moreover, the Association through its president, George W. Elliott, addressed a printed letter to the "Graduates, Patrons and Friends of Syracuse" inviting their support in a drive to raise $25,000 for an Alumni Professorship. What followed is not known though according to the *University Herald* of July 3 and October 11, 1876, the subject was discussed at the annual meeting of that year. Debate was followed by action and a definite plan for raising funds was submitted by a committee appointed for that purpose. The target set was $50,000 which, when raised through subscriptions of twenty-five dollars each, was to provide an endowment for an Alumni Professorship. Little if anything seems to have been accomplished and in 1877 a reorganized committee was empowered to "take charge of, push and solicit" funds for an alumni endowment. In spite of this energetic commission the committee probably did nothing which may explain why none of the same were present at the 1878 meeting of the society. The idea of an endowment, however, was made quite prominent at this gathering and a new committee headed by Rev. Charles H. Fowler, '59, presented a report that was enthusiastically adopted. The report is to be found in the minutes of the society and is significant enough to be quoted in full.

Resolved—that we will raise $40,000 as an endowment for an alumni professorship. The following are the conditions:

(1) The subscriptions shall be on interest at seven percent from the time made.

(2) No part of the principal to become due until the $40,000 is raised.

(3) That none of the principal in any event can be called for within less than two years from the date of the subscription.

(4) That not less than six months notice be given before any of the capital can be called in.

(5) That not more than one fifth of the principal can be called for in any one year.

(6) That the annual interest be paid to the trustees to be used for current expense.

(7) That principal as collected shall be paid into the Treasury of the trustees.

Having accepted this plan of action the following were named the Committee on Alumni Fund, Rev. C. H. Fowler, Rev. M. S. Hard, Charles W. Elliot, Rev. John Alabaster, and Professor James H. Hoose, Chairman. At the afternoon and evening sessions the committee went back and forth among those present soliciting subscriptions. As a result of their efforts the sum of $4,800 was raised. Probably the amount was increased to an even $5,000 as an item to that effect appears in the report of the General Agent of the University for the fiscal year ending June, 1879. It makes little difference which figure is correct as the sum in question was in the form of subscriptions and not cash received. In the Agent's report it appears as an asset of the University.

Interest in an endowment fund reached greater heights at the 1879 meeting. Hardly had the session been called to order and the minutes of the previous meeting read and accepted than the order of business was suspended so as to hear the report of the endowment committee. The report, a complete copy of which is not available, consisted of two parts: first a new plan for raising the sum of $40,000; and second, a series of resolutions endorsing and implementing the new scheme. The proposed plan, which was adopted, represented considerable improvement over the design accepted the year before, at least one is led to this conclusion from an article that appeared in the *Journal* for June 25, 1879. The previous proposal, it will be recalled, was little more than an arrangement entered into by the members of the association themselves; moreover, nothing but the interest was to be transferred to the University Trustees until the entire sum of $40,000 had been raised and then only under several conditions. According to the scheme adopted in 1879 each alumnus was to enter into a contract with the Trustees to pay a sum prior to a specified date regardless as to whether $40,000 had been subscribed or not. Other details are lacking but the merit of the new proposal took the fancy of those present and was adopted without change. The cordial reception accorded the plan was not evidenced in respect to the resolutions which after prolonged debate were laid on the table. The *Journal* reports that contention arose over the suggestion an alumnus should be appointed to correspond and travel at the association's expense, subject to certain restrictions, for the purpose of soliciting funds. It was the sentiment of at least one alumnus present that graduates in distant parts could render this chore without expense to the society.

In contrast to what may have been a sour note at the meeting it is pleasing to record that the editorial staff and managers of the *University Herald* offered the society a cash subscription of fifty dollars. A motion to accept the same was unanimously adopted. Later a new endowment committee was appointed. On this body was Mr. Edwin Nottingham whose interest in the University is known to all. And it was Mr. Nottingham who presented the report on the endowment fund at the meeting of 1880. The report, which was adopted, recommended a new plan for raising this fund. According to this scheme each alumnus was to enter into an agreement with the Trustees to pay the latter annually, between the date of the contract and the close of the year 1890, a specified amount toward an endowment of $40,000. In return the Trustees were to promise that upon receipt of the total sum they would establish an Alumni Professorship and to apply to the maintenance of the same the income from the fund. In the meantime, all monies paid were to be invested either in government securities or real estate loans secured by bonds and mortgages or to be placed on deposit at interest in a savings bank; all interest accruing from either method was to be applied to the Alumni fund. The Trustees, moreover, were to render an annual statement of their administration of all alumni funds. Provision also was made so that alumni who already had subscribed to the drive of 1878 might convert their obligations into the form of a new contract. Finally, the report provided that in the event the whole sum of $40,000 had not been secured by December 31, 1890, each person contributing to the drive was to receive back "his pro rata share of the monies so paid in together with the increase of the same."

Having accepted the report and after having drafted a new form of contract both report and contract were taken in person to the Board of Trustees by the Alumni Trustee, Dr. J. Dorman Steele. The reaction of the Trustees to the scheme while not negative in nature was none the less cool. Precisely what they disliked about the plan is not known. The Minutes of the Association are of no help while those of the Trustees are not much better. From the latter, however, as well as from certain references to be found in the *Alumni Record* of 1899, edited by Dr. Smalley, it would appear the Trustees disapproved of the notion of a contract that was burdened with conditions unfavorable to the University. Thus while the University authorities welcomed and approved of an endowment fund they intimated that a new scheme of raising and administering the same might be considered by the Association. And with that the entire matter rested until the next meeting of the society in 1881.

At this gathering Chancellor Sims, who was inaugurated as chancellor on June 28th of that year, appeared and addressed the alumni on the general financial status of the University and also offered "valuable suggestions as to the best methods to be pursued in raising an Endowment Fund." He did not, however, welcome the suggestion that his office should handle the drive; in his opinion the Association was better qualified to assume the chore. Whereupon it was agreed to adopt the form of pledge outlined by the Chancellor. The pledge read as follows:

> We, the undersigned, agree together in consideration of each other's subscriptions to pay to the Syracuse University for an alumni endowment drive, the sums set opposite our names. The conditions of these subscriptions are that the principal shall be paid in five annual installments, beginning with the 25th of June, 1882, and annually thereafter with interest from date. The interest may be used for current expenses of the University, but the principal shall be held for endowment exclusively.

It is to be noted, therefore, that a pledge rather than a formal contract was to be used by the Alumni Committee in raising the desired funds. All interest, moreover, accruing from these pledges might be used for current university expenses and not necessarily to be added to the endowment as had been proposed in the scheme of 1880. In all probability this difference in the two plans came as a result of the Chancellor's remarks about the existing financial needs of the University. The willingness of the Association to coordinate its program with the wishes of the Administration also was shown by its assuming the task of collecting all funds and the responsibility for other matters incident to the drive. And then as an additional demonstration of good-will the alumni elected Professor Frank Smalley, in whom all including the Chancellor had the utmost confidence, to become chairman of a special committee to solicit funds particularly from the members of the outgoing senior class and other recent graduates. The seniors responded with a pledge of $1,500. So pleased were the alumni attending the 1881 meeting that they "re-resolved to raise $40,000 and to secure $10,000 at once."

The raising of this fund was necessarily a slow and tedious affair. Syracuse University as yet had few alumni of large means and it may well be doubted if more could have been secured in any way other than the persistent annual soliciting that was "as sure to confront an outgoing class as were the final examinations." But like so many final examinations, pledges were quickly forgotten and the amount actually paid between 1881 and 1885 was quite small. According to Dr. Smalley and the records of the society, the total amount paid between

1878 and 1885 was $945, out of a subscription of $62,000. Most of this in all probability had been received since 1881 and was handed over to the Trustees. Moreover, since the sums transferred were too small to be advantageously invested the Chancellor directed them to be held as a "loan . . . bearing interest at 6 per cent" and subject to the call of the society.

Impressed by this relative poor showing the alumni at their 1885 meeting listened attentively to the Chancellor's report on finances and his suggestions as to how the alumni drive might be articulated in an all-university effort for an endowment of a hundred thousand dollars. In particular Dr. Sims suggested that the Association agree to raise ten thousand dollars of the larger amount and to provide an annual interest payment of six hundred dollars until the principal had been paid. And when paid the amount was to be ear-marked by the Trustees for the projected Alumni Professorship. The Chancellor, it will be recalled, already had obtained pledges amounting to nearly sixty thousand dollars payment of which, however, was dependent upon the endowment project being totally subscribed. Thus a ten thousand dollar pledge from the Association would be of material advantage.

In response to this plea the alumni increased the target from forty thousand dollars to forty-two thousand. Moreover, they agreed to the Chancellor's request that ten thousand of this amount should constitute a part of the University's endowment drive. But when it came to making a promise to pay six percent interest on this amount each year until the total sum had been paid the society found itself forced to compromise. The task of meeting an interest charge of six hundred dollars was far beyond the resources of the Association. The spirit was strong but the flesh was weak. In lieu the society promised to remit to the Trustees whatever interest might accrue upon funds received and invested by the Association. Thus while the Chancellor might direct the treasurer to make an entry in his books of an Association pledge of ten thousand dollars toward the University endowment fund, the control over the sums raised and the interest thereon remained in the hands of the society. Thus an explanation is offered for the entry in the treasurer's annual reports for the next few years—"Alumni Association Pledge $10,000."

Entries in these fiscal statements are not always so easily solved. There is, for example, no single item showing receipt of interest on this pledge; in all probability it is concealed within the entry of "interest" which seems to cover income from many sources. The treasurer's reports, however, do list separately the receipt of money from pledges paid and in the statement submitted on June 27, 1893, all but $3,183.51 of the $10,000 had been paid. Meanwhile, the amount of the subscriptions increased and at Commencement 1893, the fund stood at $20,406. The subsequent story of the drive extends beyond the administration of Chancellor Sims and need not for the present be told.[3] A word or two, however, might be added concerning the $10,000 pledge. By Commencement 1898, the total alumni subscriptions, estimated to be good, amounted to $28,556 of which $10,535.75 had been paid and turned over to the treasurer of the University. In addition, $3,086.70 had been paid to the same officer in the form of interest. Thus by 1898 the University had received in full the $10,000 pledged in 1885.

The story of the alumni drive to endow a professorship is most interesting and instructive. It speaks volumes for men like Dr. Smalley, William Nottingham and his brother Edwin, Dr. M. S. Hard, N. A. Wells, Francis E. Trowbridge and many others whose loyalty to the University has been told over and over again. Nor should it be forgotten that the pioneers in this undertaking, the fruit of which a present generation enjoys, were graduates of Genesee College. The devotion of the latter to their new Alma Mater also was evidenced by their spade work for the *Alumni Record* of 1887. According to the editors of this volume the first attempt to compile an alumni record took place at a meeting of the Alumni Association of Genesee College held at the Vanderbilt Hotel in Syracuse—a gathering timed to coincide with the Methodist State Convention of February, 1870, which laid the foundations for Syracuse University. What transpired is not clear and it may be the reference should have been to the meeting of Genesee alumni which met at the same hotel in December, 1871. At this gathering, it will be recalled, Vice-President Steele invited them to become almuni of Syracuse University. Six months later appropriate degrees were conferred upon a large number of Genesee graduates who demonstrated their pleasure by forming a Syracuse University

3. In the Minute Book of the Association the figures submitted by Dr. Smalley do not precisely tally with those given by the treasurer. The evident discrepancy between the two may well be explained by the shortcomings of the accounting system then used by the Administration; or it may be the treasurer's reports include sums paid prior to the inception of the $10,000 pledge.

Alumni Association and by undertaking the project of obtaining information concerning all alumni.

Beginning in the summer of 1872 and continuing throughout the life of the "Old Association," as Dean Smalley was wont to style the society during the first decade of its history, constant attention and effort were focused upon the matter. At first the response to the letters sent out by the association and to similar requests that appeared in the student papers was generally unsatisfactory. In the "Personal Column" of the *Herald* for November 20, 1877, which always was begging for alumni news the following appeared: "If some of the alumni will only die or marry they will confer a favor on the 'Personal Ed.' and be immortalized by a note in our column. If the latter prove no inducement we propose to offer chrones to all who will immolate themselves on the altar of patriotism." Judging by the absence of alumni news in the *Herald* few seemed willing to die or marry for Alma Mater.

Nor did matters improve during the course of the next two years and the *Herald* regretfully announced that the long expected "Alumni Record" had as yet neither shape nor form. At the June meeting of the Association in 1880, however, the subject was debated at length and a special committee headed by Rev. Joseph H. Zartman, '78, and assisted by representatives of the College of Liberal Arts, Medicine, and Fine Arts was appointed to initiate a special drive to gather desired information. Assisted by a preliminary canvass that had been made by his fraternity brother, Philip I. Moule, '78, Mr. Zartman sent out a call for information through the "churches and selected papers." In spite of this concerted effort the response was disappointing; Mr. Zartman reporting in 1881 that only forty replies had been received. Hoping to stimulate greater interest the society authorized the printing of a special questionnaire which the committee distributed in March, 1882. Considerable information was obtained but for reasons not stated no attempt was made to publish the same. Maybe the fact the *Onondagan*, published by the Classes of 1883 and 1884, contained a brief directory of alumni argued against publication especially in view of the condition of the society's treasury. Added support to this conclusion is to be found in the passage of a motion in 1884 to appoint a committee to work with the editors of the *Onondagan*. Nothing however, materialized due to printing costs and the absence of sufficient alumni money to meet a share of these costs. Nothing daunted the

Association in 1885 determined to go forward under its own resources and a special committee composed of J. H. Zartman, '78, Lucien M. Underwood, '77, and Charles W. Winchester, Genesee '67, was appointed to publish an alumni record under the direction of the Board of Directors.

The special committee appears to have done a splendid job and the Association in 1886 ordered the record to be published. The *Alumni Record*, covering the years 1872 to 1886 inclusive, appeared in January, 1887. It consisted of 380 pages, chiefly devoted to vital statistics and biographical information of the graduates of Genesee College, the Geneva Medical Department, and Syracuse University. In addition, it contained several sketches and an introductory note of historical value. The editors frankly admitted the record was not complete particularly in respect to the alumni of Genesee College and the Geneva Medical Department. They were, however, proud of their efforts and no greater compliment was paid them than the acknowledgment made by Dean Smalley in his *Alumni Record* of 1899. Much that appeared in the latter volume was taken from the *Record* of 1887. Six hundred copies were printed at a cost of $486.05. By June of the same year $378.10 had been realized from sales, the price being $1.10 a copy, with 155 copies unsold. Additional copies were sold as time went on and it is likely the Association suffered little if any loss on the venture. Of greater interest was the determination of the alumni to prepare for a second volume and in 1892 a small sum of money was pledged to assist Dr. Smalley to whom the task of editing the second record was assigned.

The life of the Alumni Association did not center entirely around the business sessions, important as they were, in respect to such matters as an alumni record and endowment fund. The satisfaction and joy gained by revisiting a campus already burdened with traditions and pleasant memories of the past plus the human touch of renewing old acquaintances must have gone far toward making the annual meetings a success. Evidences to this effect abound in the college and city papers; more impressive are the minute books of the society and the gaily colored or decorated programs of literary exercise and banquet. Here the Alumni Historian, Poet, and Necrologist vied with the officers and guest speakers for honor, distinction, and applause. The modern age will never cease to wonder at the patience and endurance borne by Syracusans of that day in listening to what were long epic poems punctuated with classical references or to the six, seven, and sometimes ten toasts that inevitably characterized a dinner. Trustee, Chancellor, Professor, Alumnus, or Friend rose at every gathering to say a kindly word or deliver an address of some importance. Witness, for example, the Alumni Reunion of June 22, 1875—the year Genesee College finally closed its doors. Heartfelt and unstinted praise for the University's spiritual and intellectual ancestor was key-noted time after time. And the constant reading of letters and telegrams from Genesee graduates unable to be present brought forth rounds of applause. Small wonder that Chancellor Haven after having listened to spirited talks by Dr. John M. Reid, President of Genesee College, 1858-1860, and by Mrs. Belva A. Lockwood, Genesee, '57, must have felt assured as to the future of Syracuse. Since the devotion of her adopted children was as large as that of her own, the destiny of the University was in safe hands—the hands of the Syracuse Alumni Association.

Gifts from the Greeks

16 Earlier in this narrative, reference was made to the presence of secret societies at Genesee College. One of these, and probably the most outstanding, was the Mystical Seven which, according to *Baird's Manual* was organized at Wesleyan University in 1837. Twenty years later, unknown to the Administration at Genesee College which forbade fraternities and "closed" literary societies at Lima, a Genesee Chapter, known as "Scroll and Pen," was founded. Two of its charter members, so it is recorded in the *Alumni Record*, 1872-1899, of Syracuse University, included Alden G. Wilcox and Thomas D. Tooker of the classes of 1855 and 1856 respectively. Of the class of 1857 the seven-pointed star badge of the fraternity was worn by Peter B. Bradley, John A. Brodhead, Micajah C. Dean, Harmon S. Hogoboom, and Henry H. Hutton. Louis Kistler, Melville M. Merrell, of the class of 1858, Charles H. Fowler and Isaac Gibbard of the class of 1859, and John Slee, Joseph W. Snow, and Charles W. Underhill of the class of 1860 also were members. Additional names appear for the years that followed. Of the eighteen male students who were graduated from Syracuse University in 1872 nine had been members of the Mystical Seven at Genesee College. Delos Cronk, Syracuse '74, was a Mystic and is listed as a freshman in the *Genesee College*

Catalogue, 1868-1869. The latter source for 1870-1871 mentions Dallas D. Lore who is credited by Mr. Dexter Wilson, '12, as having been a Mystic in his informative and interesting account of the Phi Gamma Chapter of Delta Kappa Epsilon. Mr. Lore did not graduate from Syracuse and his name does not appear in any Annual of Syracuse University.

Cronk, Lore and the other Mystics of Genesee College constituted in a general way the original members of a Syracuse Chapter of the Mystical Seven which in September, 1871, appeared for the first time on the campus of the University. Of these probably only Weaver, Mann, Morris, Cronk, and Lore were actually enrolled as students, the others merely biding their time until they were graduated from Syracuse in June, 1872. The latter could have received degrees from Genesee in either 1871 or 1872 had they wished but since that institution had all but disappeared after the establishment of Syracuse they elected to be graduated from their new Alma Mater. In the hands of five active Mystics, therefore, rested the life and future of the society at Syracuse. Their first step was to obtain a meeting room and after some search space was found on the top floor of the old Clinton Block overlooking the Canal Basin. Then with an enthusiasm that has ever characterized fraternity men—an enthusiasm parents never cease to marvel at—the dirt and debris of a former occupant were removed and the way was cleared for prospective pledges. An "unusually brief" rushing period followed the outcome of which resulted in the pledging of Charles A. Fowler, a sophomore, and William A. Wood, Judson B. Coit, Erastus W. Goodier, Levi Jennison, Charles D. Lathrop, Samuel W. Kress, Appolos F. Berrian, and Melvile J. Wells, freshmen. These gentlemen were initiated in early October and together with the actives constituted the Mystical Seven which in November, 1871, received a charter from the Delta Kappa Epsilon Fraternity. Aiding these men in their quest for a charter had been John H. Durston, a member of the Yale Chapter of Delta Kappa Epsilon and at the time an instructor in Modern Languages at Syracuse. Early in December, 1871, the local chapter petitioned the Trustees of the University for the use of a room in the proposed Hall of Languages. Though styling themselves as the Delta Kappa Epsilon Fraternity they described the group as a "College Literary Society." The Trustees granted the request and referred the matter to the Executive Committee of the Board and the faculty with power. With that, however, the matter dropped possibly because the demand for space exceeded the available number of rooms or because it was realized that if the privilege was granted to one society it would have to be granted to others. Neither the Minute Book of the Executive Committee nor of the Faculty contains any reference to the affair.

Among the early members of the local chapter tradition credits William Nottingham, '76, as having been the chief spirit and promoter. Thanks to his efforts the 1874 Convention of the Fraternity voted to gather the following year at Syracuse. The Vanderbilt House on West Washington became the headquarters of the fraternity as delegates from other chapters assembled in October, 1875. After the business sessions had ended the members led by the Gloversville Band marched to the Wieting Opera House where a large and select audience listened to the public exercises. Dr. Alexander Winchell acted as master of ceremonies which when finished were followed by a "sumptious banquet" at the Vanderbilt. "The next morning," so the *University Herald* reported, "the delegates left . . . much pleased with the Syracuse University and a goodly number confessing conversion to co-education."

At the time of this gathering the society may still have had its "rooms" in the Clinton Block though by June, 1879, one reads of the "old" quarters in the Wieting Block. And here the fraternity remained until a disastrous fire in the early summer of 1881 completely destroyed the Block. The financial loss to the society was considerable but severe as it was it was nothing in comparison to the loss of records and memorabilia. Later, when the new Wieting arose, the lodge rooms were "rebuilt better than before." Meanwhile the society appears to have established an "eating club" on Irving Street. Later in 1878 the club gathered on Genesee Street and in the next year it was at the corner of University and East Fayette Streets. Two years later the society rented a house at 1005 East Genesee, shortly thereafter renumbered 1019, though it was not until the spring of 1892 that the chapter rooms in the Wieting Block were given up in favor of a more improved "cathedral" on the third floor of the "Deke" house on East Genesee. Members of the chapter of that period will also recall the annual encampments that took place at Tully Lake.

Approximately the same time the Mystical Seven was founded at Syracuse the Upsilon Kappa Fraternity was established on the same campus. The antecedents of this society, the forerunner of the Pi Chapter of Psi Upsilon, stem from a local fraternity organized at Genesee College in 1863. Herbert Bates Johnson of the class of 1866 and David Hall Rice and Edward B. Fenner of the class of 1867 are listed as the founders of Upsilon Kappa which held its first recorded meeting on November 12, 1863. No mention, however, of Upsilon Kappa has been discovered in any of the sources pertaining to Genesee College which is not surprising in view of official hostility at Lima to any and all secret societies. And it was a secret fraternity in the strictest sense of the word. "From the start and for many years," so the Executive Council of Psi Upsilon Fraternity wrote in December, 1949, "each member was known only by a number. . . . Secrecy remained paramount. At each adjournment the Order was wholly dissolved, so that each person could truthfully state he was *not* a member." Meanwhile and during the year 1864 a room was hired for meetings, a constitution and ritual were adopted, and contacts were established with the Psi Upsilon chapter at Middletown. The next few years witnessed increased development at Lima and on several occasions serious attempts were made to gain admission into Psi Upsilon. In the spring of 1870 Upsilon Kappa rented rooms in the Stanley Block and shortly thereafter initiated William H. Shuart, '74, "the first of the Pi Founders to enter Upsilon Kappa Society."

By this time it was evident that Genesee College had all but completed its life's mission. It was in appreciation of this fact plus the added knowledge of the founding of Syracuse University that Upsilon Kappa determined to translate itself from Lima to Syracuse. Accordingly, Chester A. Congdon and Nathaniel M. Wheeler of the Genesee Seminary were duly initiated into Upsilon Kappa, both having signified their intention of matriculating at Syracuse University. Joining these men in the exodus to a new Alma Mater were George H. Baker, Richard W. Copeland, John M. Dolph, William H. Shuart, and William W. Smallwood, seniors at Genesee College. Accordingly in September, 1871, Upsilon Kappa made its appearance at Syracuse University. The charter members, as listed in the *University Herald*, included George H. Baker, Richard W. Copeland, John M. Dolph, William H. Shuart, and William W. Smallwood of the class of 1872, George W. Elliott and Charles W. Wilbor of the class of 1873, William H. Shuart and Baxter T. Smelzer of the class of 1874, and Milton D. Buck, Chester A. Congdon, James M. Gilbert, and Nathaniel M. Wheeler of the class of 1875. In reference to these events, William H. Shuart wrote in 1941 as follows:

> The primal locale of Upsilon Kappa in Syracuse was the room of Brother Charles W. Wilbor and myself at the home of a pious family on West Genesee Street. It was the scene of the initiation of the first four pledges. Later two rooms were secured in the Granger Block, at East Genesee and Washington Streets. A convenient restaurant was in the basement with bar and pool tables. The paraphernalia previously shipped from Lima, was later carried up three flights of stairs one dark night—a friendly policeman supervising the job after being satisfied that the performance was all in the interest of higher learning. The rooms were cosily furnished. . . They were the scenes of subsequent initiations and daily gatherings of members for playing games and furtherance of genuine comradeship.

During the spring of 1872, George W. Elliott, Xi, '73, affiliated with Upsilon Kappa, so we are informed, for the sole purpose of directing the group into the fold of Psi Upsilon. He assumed the task of introducing Upsilon Kappa to the chapters of Psi Upsilon and was responsible for the visit of Daniel G. Thompson, a member of the Executive Council of Psi Upsilon, to Syracuse. Aided by Dr. Charles W. Bennett, Xi, '52, and a member of the faculty at Syracuse, the issue was brought before the National Convention of Psi Upsilon which in May, 1875, endorsed the founding of a chapter at Syracuse. Early the following month the Pi Chapter was formally installed. The charter members included Chester A. Congdon, James M. Gilbert, Milton D. Buck, Nathaniel M. Wheeler, and William H. Shuart of the class of 1875, and Alfred C. Haven, '77, a former member of Psi Upsilon at New York University. Additional members added at the time were Charles D. Holden, Joseph W. Taylor, Alfred S. Durston, Fred C. Esmond, Charles M. Moss and Charles N. Cobb of the class of 1877, and John E. Mowatt, Curtis E. Mogg and Rhoderick E. Hollett of the class of 1878.

At the time the society had its rooms in the Goot Block on South Clinton Street; four years later it is supposed to have had quarters in the Hendricks Block on East Fayette. Meanwhile, it conducted an eating club at various places, notably at 112 University Avenue and 763 Irving Street. During the late 1870's the chapter ran into difficulty from which it was able to extract itself by the early 1880's. In December, 1892, the fraternity maintained its chapter house at the latter address. Psi Upsilon, Delta Kappa Epsilon, and Delta Upsilon were all active in the promotion of the *University Herald*. As related elsewhere in this volume, Psi Upsilon directed the *University News*, a campus paper which made its appearance in November, 1877.

Another society whose genesis stems from the rich traditions of Genesee College is the Syracuse Chapter of Delta Upsilon fraternity. The relation of this chapter to student life at Lima cannot be stated with any degree of certainty. It is, however, of interest to note that among the records of the General Fraternity preserved at the New York Public Library there is a fragment of the Journal of the 1866 Convention of Delta Upsilon. According to this source the delegates to the 1866 Convention, held at Rochester, listened to a representative of a society at Genesee College which was seeking admission into Delta Upsilon. In all probability the petitioner was Mr. LaFayette Congdon, formerly a member of the Rochester Chapter of Delta Upsilon, but enrolled during his senior year, 1866-1867, as a student at Genesee. The convention seems to have been pleased with the stature of the petitioning society and after some discussion voted to grant it a charter. For some unknown reason, possibly because of faculty opposition to fraternities, though Delta Upsilon was a non-secret organization, formal installation of a Genesee Chapter did not take place. No general convention of the fraternity was held in 1867 and the records of the gathering in 1868 are silent as to a Genesee Chapter. It would appear, therefore, that Delta Upsilon was never planted at Lima.

It is known, however, that among the literary societies existing at Genesee was one known as the Atticaeum and it was from a society bearing the same name at Syracuse that the Syracuse branch of Delta Upsilon was conceived. Sponsors of the Syracuse Atticaeum were Frank Smalley, '74, and Edwin Nottingham, '76. These gentlemen were convinced that secret fraternities, by reason of their closed organization, were not advancing the cultural side of college life. Gaining the support of several other students, Smalley and Nottingham posted a notice, early in October, 1872, on the doors of the Myers Block, stating that an open literary society was in process of being founded. The editors of the *University Herald* immediately realized that Smalley's efforts constituted in part an attack upon the secret societies of which they were members. Accordingly, the editorial section of the paper carried an article in which the idea of an open society was discussed at some length. Although the tone of the article was moderate it is evident that the object in the mind of the author was to prove the futility of founding a new society at Syracuse. In spite of this mild opposition an open society was established. Indeed the same issue of the *Herald* which voiced sentiments against the plan carried a notice that the Atticaeum had been founded.

Although the Atticaeum was devoted primarily to literary pursuits some of its members desired to give attention to fraternal objects as well. The latter, however, were not entirely in agreement as to a method whereby the object might be achieved. A few were for the establishment of a secret society while others led by Smalley believed that the forming of such an organization would be contrary to the ideas that had given rise to the Atticaeum. In order to prevent a dissolution, Smalley turned the attention of the group toward Delta Upsilon though in so doing it was certain the projected society would lose two or three members of the Atticaeum who belonged to a secret society. That Syracuse was a splendid field for fraternity expansion was recognized by Delta Upsilon in 1871. The actual initiative, however, came from Syracuse with the result that the planting of a chapter at the new university was discussed at its 1873 Convention. Later in the same year Abraham Miller of the Madison (Colgate) Chapter visited Syracuse and at a meeting held in the Hall of Languages received the pledges of seventeen students. Miller's action, moreover, was accepted by the Convention of 1874.

Among those whose identity with Delta Upsilon can clearly be established as being charter members the following should be mentioned: Frank Smalley, '74, and Edwin Nottingham, Herbert Huntington, Bartholomew Keeler, Frank D. Barker, George A. Place, John T. Roberts, Richard L. Robinson, and Marvin L. Spooner, all of the class of 1876. Of these Smalley and Nottingham seem to have been the leaders. Subsequent meetings of the society were held in the Hall of Languages and still later at the rooms of the members. In the spring of 1874 quarters were rented in the Pike Block on South Salina. For over two years this was the home of Delta Upsilon. During this period the chapter records show that the members took considerable interest in debate and literary exercises. Greater growth would have taken place but for a certain amount of internal discord. Evidently some of the chapter still cherished a kindly attitude toward the secret societies. A few actually broke their pledges which resulted in their immediate expulsion from the chapter; while others asked for and obtained dismissals. On top of this came the destruction of the chapter's rooms by a group of secret fraternity men during the Christmas recess of 1876-77. In spite of these difficulties and setbacks, the society maintained its existence and in the spring of 1877 moved into the Rice Block, also on South Salina; later the society seems to have returned to the Pike Block. These various movements plus the trials of maintaining an eating club at several different addresses led the members in January, 1887 to seek permission from the Trustees of the University to erect a chapter house on the campus. Nothing came of this effort and in the spring of the same year the society purchased the home of Dr. Wellesley P. Coddington on the corner of Ostrom and Marshall Streets where the chapter remains to this day.

Fourth among the fraternities to be planted at Syracuse was Gamma of Zeta Psi. Interest in this national society demonstrated itself sometime in 1874 when Frank Z. Wilcox and four other students at Syracuse submitted a petition for a charter to the Zeta Psi Fraternity at its Twenty-eighth Convention held at Brunswick, Maine. Impressed by the evident seriousness and quality of the petitioning group, a committee consisting of the Psi Chapter at Cornell was appointed to investigate conditions at Syracuse. Shortly thereafter several of the national officers journeyed to Ithaca where they met and discussed the matter with Wilcox. Encouraged by these overtures of good-will Wilcox and his friends—Vincent A. Crandall, '76, Orville A. Merchant and Jason Parker of the class of 1877 and Giles H. Dunning, Julian H. Myers, and Frank A. Woodward of the class of 1878— organized themselves into a local secret society known as Theta Chi. The badge of the local group was in the form of a monogram, the Theta standing in front and being set with five pearls on each side. "Its members," so the *University Herald* reported in early December of the same year, "are extremely reticent as to the objects of the society. As far as we can learn they are literary." In order to promote the purposes of the society, rooms were obtained at 89 South Salina which, according to the numbering then used in Syracuse, would place Theta Chi's headquarters somewhere on the east side of the street in the general vicinity of East Jefferson.

All of these efforts brought reward and in early June, 1875, Frank Z. Wilcox, '76; Alpha R. Beal, '75; Charles A. Wall, '76; Jason Parker, '77; Roswell S. Price, '76; Vincent A. Crandall, '76; Wilbur F. Smallwood, '78; and John C. Nichols, '75, were initiated into the Zeta Psi

Fraternity at Ithaca by the Psi Chapter. A few days later, Gamma was officially installed at the "commodious and finely furnished" rooms of the old Theta Chi. Aided by several brothers in the city, notably G. W. Edwards of the *Syracuse Standard*, and overcoming a certain amount of hostility on the part of "rival societies," Gamma forged forward, recruited new members and won for itself a place on the editorial board of the *University Herald*.

During the years that immediately followed Gamma maintained quarters in the Larned Block fronting on East Genesee, the Everson Block, and in 1884 in the Durston Block. By this time the chapter was encountering considerable internal difficulty which, according to information furnished the author by the society in 1946, resulted "in a severe slump." Unable to weather the storm Gamma in early 1887 returned its charter to the National Fraternity and ceased to function at Syracuse until 1905. In commenting upon the surrender of the charter the *Syracusan* stated that Gamma's policy of limiting its members to three from each class threw too heavy a financial burden upon so small a brotherhood. The significance, the editor added, increased when one stopped to remember that "the class of students who come to Syracuse University cannot afford to join Zeta Psi."

Shortly before the unhappy break in the life of Gamma of Zeta Psi, the ancestor of the Phi Kappa Psi Fraternity at Syracuse, made its appearance. Founded as a debating club in 1881 and meeting once a week in the Hall of Languages, the excellent work of this society, which seems to have had no distinctive title and whose members are unknown, soon attracted attention and in a short time "their number was comparatively large and their men active."[1] Success prompted dreams for the future and near the close of the following year its members decided to organize as a secret society to be known as the Delta Kappa Fraternity. Campus recognition ensued, the *Herald* commenting on the society in these terms: "They are quite active. The question is not yet settled whether they shall retain their present name and become the first chapter of a new fraternity, or unite themselves with some old fraternity which it is reported they have the privilege of doing." Frank D. Tubbs, '84 and Ezra G. Eldredge, '87 are listed as the first pledges.

---

1. The receipt of a letter at the Registrar's Office addressed to the Phi Kappa Psi Society at Syracuse is mentioned in the *University Herald*, June 8, 1874.

Meanwhile contact had been made with the National officers of Phi Kappa Psi which by the spring of 1884 voted to accept the petitioning body. Installation of the New York Beta Chapter of Phi Kappa Psi took place April 18th, the charter members being Arthur E. Brigden, George B. Deuel, and Augustine W. Broadway of the class of 1884, Harley D. Wadsworth, George E. Ellis, George G. Jones, and Eugene Wiseman of the class of 1884, Joseph G. Cleveland, Clarence A. Lonergan, and Arthur C. Howe of the class of 1886, and Ezra G. Eldredge, '87. In addition, the following names appear in the *Alumni Record*, 1872-1899, as being members of the chapter: Charles D. Bean, '85, one time student at Hobart College, Alson D. Bartholmew, and Wm. LaFayette Harris, both of the class of 1886. In all probability those listed as charter members had been associated with Kappa Delta.

At the time of its establishment, the New York Beta of Phi Kappa Psi occupied rooms in the Joy Block on the corner of Market and East Washington streets. Evidently the society found these quarters to its liking as it was still being used as late as June, 1891. Meanwhile, an eating club had been started at 629 Irving Street. Phi Kappa Psi, it will be recalled, had been quite active in the management of the *Syracusan*. In the spring of 1888, however, the chapter transferred its association to the *University News*. The occasion for this action was a disagreement that had arisen between it and the Delta Kappa Epsilon Fraternity over the publication of a certain editorial. In announcing its appearance on the board of the *University News*, the society stated it had severed its relations with the *Syracusan* because the latter did not come up to its ideal of what a college paper should be. Two years later difficulties arose in the *University News* the upshot of which was the withdrawal of Phi Kappa Psi.

Approximately about the same time Phi Kappa Psi appeared at Syracuse as a debating society another group, later to be known as Sigma Psi, was founded. Its sponsors included Klen K. Shurtleff, '82, James Devine and Edward A. Hill of the class of 1883, and Silas G. Comfort, '84. Although the organization was launched in the spring of 1881 it was not until November that formal announcement of its existence was made. Rooms were secured and in the months that followed Sigma Psi became an active member of the Greek letter world on the Syracuse campus. For a time Sigma Psi was content to remain a local society but during the winter of 1886-1887 overtures for a charter were made to the national fraternity, Phi Delta Theta. The response was most cordial and in February, 1887 Sigma Psi became the Epsilon Chapter of Phi Delta Theta. The charter members included Ambrose C. Driscoll and William A. Mehan of the class of 1887, George I. Abbott, Newell E. Hulbert, John A. Murray, William S. Murray, Morgan R. Sanford, Frank L. Boothby, and T. S. Devitt of the class of 1882, and Edwin M. Sanford and Edwin M. Hasbrouch of the class of 1889, and Orator F. Cook, '89.

At the beginning of its founding the Syracuse chapter of Phi Delta Theta shared rooms with a neutral organization known either as the Volunteer or Mayflower Club. The arrangement came to an end in May of the same year when the Phi Delta Theta men moved to 150 Harrison Street. How long they remained at this latter location is not known though in January, 1891, the society seems to have acquired a home of its own at 613 University Avenue. In commenting upon this event the *University News* stated that Phi Delta Theta was the fourth Greek letter society to have a home of their own.

Last among the fraternities to be placed at Syracuse prior to the administration of Chancellor Day was Beta Epsilon of Beta Theta Pi. Established in the spring of 1889—nothing being known as to earlier antecedents—the charter members included George W. Church, '89, Frank M. Rooney and Hiram L. Church of the class of 1890, Albert D. Barnhart and Walter B. Hancock of the class of 1891, and Harry J. Hamlin, Edmund L. Dow, Marcus L. Glazer, George F. Cole, and Francis F. Brewer of the class of 1892. Other early members as listed in the *University Herald* for May, 1889, were Helcias de Oliviers, '90, Robert W. Wilde, '91, and William V. Flaherty, '94. Additional strength resulted from the action taken at the National Convention of Beta Theta Pi when in 1890 the fraternity accepted as members all those who had belonged to the Mystic Seven society. Genesee College Mystics thus became eligible for membership. However, as some of the Genesee Mystics were instrumental in the founding of Delta Kappa Epsilon at Syracuse it is uncertain how many actually affiliated with Beta Epsilon. Among those known to have joined were Charles H. Fowler, '59, George Van Alstyne, '62, William H. Webster, '60, and Oscar F. Williams, '69. During the college year 1890-1891 the society occupied rooms in the Grand Opera House Building on East Genesee. Here they remained for at least two years though the August, 1895, issue of *Beta Theta Pi* reports the chapter house as being at 905 Walnut Avenue. Meanwhile a boarding club had been maintained on Madison Street.

Meanwhile sororities had come to the campus the first being Alpha of Alpha Phi. Although founded in September, 1872, the society was not noticed by the editors of the *University Herald* prior to the November issue of that paper. Here there appears the following brittle announcement: "Alpha Phi.—The ladies of the lower classes have formed a secret society with the above name. The pin worn is a skeleton monogram, the Phi being placed horizontally and at right angles to the Alpha. A setting of pearls also adorns the ring of the Phi on some of the badges." According to the *Herald* the following were listed as members: Rena Michaels, '74, J. Louise Gage and Kate E. Hogoboom, of the class of 1875, and Clara Bradley, Hattie F. Chidester, Mattie E. Foote, Ida A. Gilbert, Jennie L. Higham, L. Grace Hubbell, Louise V. Shephard, and Clara E. Sittser all of 1876. On January 3, 1873 Alpha Phi was incorporated under the laws of the State of New York.

At first chapter meetings were held in the rooms or homes of the members though by the winter of 1873 the members began to gather on Friday nights at the offices of Miss Chidester's father on South Salina Street. Later the society occupied space on the fifth floor of the Washington Block where it remained until the fall of 1870 when rooms were acquired on the fourth floor of the Onondaga County Savings Bank Building. Four years later the sorority moved to 613 Irving Street. By this time the society had firmly established itself on the campus and its friends spoke glowingly of Alpha Phi's future particularly since the founding of the Beta Chapter at Northwestern in 1881. It was therefore quite appropriate and altogether fitting that the Mother Chapter should have a home of its own and on June 22, 1886 the corner stone was laid at 17 University Avenue. For a long time this home was the only sorority house in the country. Formal dedication took place in January of the year following. Alpha Phi's prominence at Syracuse is evidenced by the space devoted to it in the student papers. One of these, the *University News* for April, 1888, contains reference to a contract entered into with Gamma Phi Beta and Kappa Kappa Gamma not to pledge freshmen until a month after the formal opening of classes in the fall.

When college opened in the autumn of 1874 a total of 227 students appear to have registered in the University's three colleges. Of these, according to the *Annual* of that year there were fifty-four girls, thirty-four of whom were in Liberal Arts, thirteen in Fine Arts, and seven in the College of Medicine. Some of these students most certainly were not interested in sororities though this decidedly was not true of Helen Dodge, Frances E. Haven, Mary A. Bingham and Eunice A. Curtis who during the fall of 1874 determined to establish another sorority. Encouraged by Chancellor Haven and aided by Dr. John J. Brown of the Chemistry Department these young women in November founded the Gamma Phi Beta sorority. Three years later the society was formally incorporated. In 1882 the Beta Chapter was planted at the University of Michigan.

In commenting upon the appearance of the new sorority the *Herald* stated: "There is ample material for these new societies and both are needed. It is, indeed, too bad that Alpha Phi should have the field all to herself without a single rival. . . ." Convinced of its birthright, Gamma Phi Beta took to the field and in a short time added Barbara F. Crane and Adelphia M. Quivey of the class of 1877 and Kate M. Foster, '78 to their number. Later rooms were acquired in the Hendricks and Durston Blocks, and in the spring of 1895 the sorority had its chapter house on Irving Avenue. During these years Gamma Phi Beta earned well deserved praise for outstanding interest in singing. The society's select "Quartette" presented several concerts and in 1887 a song book was published which included the waltz of Gamma Phi Beta composed for them by Dr. William Schultze of the College of Fine Arts.

Third among the sororities to be established at Syracuse was the Tau Chapter of Kappa Kappa Gamma. The inception of this society stems from the efforts of seven young women who in 1885 applied for a charter from this nationally known sorority. After a short delay the petition was granted and on October 19th of the same year Miss Florence Lee of the Beta Chapter located at St. Lawrence College formally installed Tau at Syracuse. The original members included Ida Ginsberg, '85, Ellen A. Ford, '85, Ida Steengrebe, '85, Ruth E. Guibault, '84, Ella S. Blakeslee, '84, Harriet Wallace, '84, and Carrie R. Fisher, '84. During the first year meetings were held at the homes of the members though in the following year quarters were obtained in the Durston Block. Later rooms were maintained in the Wesleyan Block on East Onondaga Street but after a brief interlude the society seems to have returned to the Durston Block. In June, 1893, Tau according to the *University News* was situated at 761 Irving Street.

Meanwhile a local group known as Kappa Delta Phi petitioned and obtained a charter from Kappa Alpha Theta. Formal installation took place on October 1, 1889, the original members being Marion A. Carpenter, Anna L. Brown, and Katherine Van Benschoten of the class of 1890, Lulu P. Graff, Ada B. Parker, and Elsa L. Ames of the class of 1891, Jessica B. Marshall and Lulu Kern of the class of 1892, Mattie A. Beecher, '94, and Florence A. Larrabee, '89. During the years that immediately followed the establishment of Chi of Kappa Alpha Theta the society maintained rooms first at 209 University Avenue and later at the corner of Adams and Crouse Streets. A chapter house was not acquired until the fall of 1894.

The relations between the various sororities appears to have been most pleasant while that between them and the fraternities became increasingly more friendly and agreeable. Suppers, sleigh-rides, tobogganing, formal parties, and a score of other social activities did much to knit the Greek letter world at Syracuse into a happy family. And it is more than clear why these contacts led in many cases to engagements and marriages. In respect to campus politics the sororities played a minor role; evidently they preferred to leave such weighty matters to the men. The latter, as has been mentioned, demonstrated keen interest in all campus activities. Every class election, every contest for membership on the governing boards of student organizations, and every competition for athletic and academic honor evoked considerable rivalry among the fraternities. One has only to scan the files of the student papers and fraternity magazines to find evidence of these activities. Reference, moreover, has been made to the feuds that existed among the men's societies over the control and conduct of the *University Herald,* the *Syracusan,* and the *University News* as well as to an occasional "raid" by one group upon the rooms of another. More spirited were the activities of Tau Nu Epsilon and Sigma Delta Nu—sometimes called the "black sheep" of the fraternity system. Fortunately for the reputation of the University the life of these societies was abruptly terminated at Syracuse before the close of the century. In general, therefore, it may be concluded that except for the escapades of youth the fraternity world at Syracuse maintained an even keel and contributed in many ways to the advancement and promotion of Alma Mater.

Syracuse—A Christian Institution

17 Syracuse University stemmed from the thought and action of a determined band of Christian men and women. The Centenary Year of the American Methodist Church was to be gloriously crowned by the establishment of a great institution devoted in its purpose to God's word and work in Central New York. The decision once made was never lost sight of although on more than one occasion hearts and minds almost broke under the heavy weight of trouble and disappointment. But yet in the face of unhappy conditions and, at times, of opposition, the banners of Syracuse were raised and Methodism has always acclaimed the wisdom of the effort. More than that, the name and reputation of Syracuse University were spread far beyond the confines of Central New York. Syracuse became a national university with deserved distinction and eminence before it had spanned a quarter of a century.

Were one to search, as indeed an historian should, for an explanation as to the driving force that impelled the University onward, especially during its pioneer days, one most certainly will discover that force in the undying love and faith its founders had in Christ and the Methodist Church. Convincing testimony in this respect may be gleaned from the role played by the Genesee, East Genesee, Oneida,

and Black River Conferences when, in 1866, they hastened to implement the crusader's call, sounded by Dr. D. D. Lore, editor of the
Northern Christian Advocate, of transplanting Genesee College to a
more centrally located place where its Christian educational destiny
might be amply fulfilled. A year later, strengthened by the Wyoming
Conference, these units of Methodism centered their activities around
Syracuse as the seat of the projected university and pressed their case
to a successful conclusion with the Trustees of Genesee College. Denied what they considered their just rights by legal action imposed
upon them by the citizens of Lima, leaders like Dr. D. D. Lore, Rev.
J. B. Foote, Rev. George Lansing Taylor, and Rev. Jesse T. Peck reorganized their ranks and at the Syracuse Convention of February,
1870, won from those present sacred promises and pledges for the
founding of the University.

"Glory be to God," so wrote Dr. Taylor, "A great Methodist University for the Empire State is now a certainty." Others exclaimed
that the University was to be "a perpetual honor to the Church we
represent and an imperishable monument to the praise and glory of
the great Head of the Church." Meanwhile Dr. Peck eloquently proclaimed his views in a soul-moving address entitled "Our Rights and
Duties as Christian Soldiers." Education in general and at Syracuse
University in particular was to be conceived as a hand-maid of God.
Evidence in support of this attitude echoes throughout most every
primary and secondary source relating to the annals of the University.
The letters, diaries, and papers of the first chancellor, Dr. Alexander
Winchell, as well as the editorials and news items appearing in the
secular and religious press of that day are replete with endorsing testimony. "Brains and hearts," so Dr. Peck declared at the inaugural
ceremonies in August, 1871, were to have a "fair chance, and we propose no narrow-minded sectarianism on the one hand, nor infidelity
on the other. We are, in the words of our fundamental law, devoted
to the promotion of Christian learning." And on that eventful occasion,
Dr. Steele announced the position taken by himself and the faculty:
"We are most profoundly convinced that there is a God-ward side to
every human soul and that any process of education which ignores
this great fact, whatever excellencies it may combine, must be radically defective in its results."

These utterances, and many others might be cited, were not intended for public consumption, nor did they spring from the spirit and enthusiasm of the moment. Rather did they stand as the honest and heart-felt expression of men who believed in God and sought to do His will. And those who listened to these sentiments and who were entrusted with the management of the young institution practiced what they heard. Witness, for example, the repeated journeys and visitations of stalwarts like Chancellors Winchell, Haven, and Sims throughout the patronizing conferences pleading for funds and prayers so that the success of the great Christian venture might be assured. Or follow in the wake of an unsung band of lesser lights and observe their unceasing labor for an ideal dear to their hearts. And finally join with the first students as they climbed to their College on the Hill and with them pause and harken to the daily chapel services in the Hall of Languages.

Chapel became a fixed feature at Syracuse from the day the University opened its doors in the Myers Block. The attitude of the Administration and faculty toward religious life on the campus, as might be expected, was positive and clear. Prospective students and their parents held in their hands the *Annual* of 1872 and here they read: "The exercises of each day are opened with the reading of the Scriptures and Prayers, which all students are expected to attend. The students are also required to attend the morning service on the Sabbath at such church as they or their guardians may select." Chapel, in other words, was to be an important feature of student life. Syracuse was a Christian institution and through what better medium could that fact be demonstrated than by daily attendance at Chapel and Sunday worship at a neighboring church? Although the greater share of the student body probably frequented the University Avenue Church, which had been erected by the Central New York Conference to serve the religious life of the University and adjacent community, no student was compelled to go to the Methodist Church. True to its ideals, Methodism advocated and practiced religious toleration. Any other predication would have violated the Christian and democratic faith of that creed. Meanness and smallness of mental stature did not characterize Christian leaders like Bishop Peck, Chancellors Winchell, Haven, and Sims, and Trustees like George Comstock, the latter an

Anglican. And when a local Roman Catholic girl petitioned to be excused from daily chapel on religious grounds the request was granted without the slightest hesitation.[1]

Compulsory attendance at Chapel, as a policy established in 1872 evidently bogged down since the *Annual* of the year following carried the statement: "Attendance, for the present is not compulsory, but the propriety of it is earnestly urged, both for the devotional purpose and from the obvious necessity of a daily assembling of the students to receive communications. No student, consequently, is excused for any delinquency arising through non-attendance at Chapel." But the faculty, possibly in time-honored ivory towers, sadly misunderstood the resourcefulness of the students who were quick to see that absences from chapel did not prevent them from hearing all necessary announcements. Soon there were more empty seats than the Chancellor could tolerate and he immediately sounded a note of warning that attendance would be made compulsory unless more were present. For a time conditions improved but before long the students drifted back into their old habits. Persuasion having failed, semi-compulsory methods were introduced. At the sound of the chapel bell, which generally was sounded twice before the opening of services, the faculty would emerge from office and class room and proceed to direct the wayward to the Chapel; and when it appeared as though some were going to wander from the beaten path a firm hand descended upon the arrant's shoulder and he was gently led to the chapel door.

Student reaction to this strategy was sharp and to the point; better far to have compulsory chapel than to resort to methods that smacked of the drill ground. Quick to sense the impropriety of such policing

1. During the course of the 1880's the Faculty at odd times took a religious census of the students. One of these was made by Dr. Smalley in the spring of 1881. According to his report, to be found in the Minutes of the Faculty of the College of Liberal Arts, 132 students were interviewed out of a total enrollment of 156; see *Annual*, 1881. Of these 132, sixty-one were members of the Methodist Church, the Presbyterians were next with eight students, and were followed by the Congregationalists, Baptists, Episcopalians, Seventh Day, and Lutherans with eight, six, five, five, and two respectively. The Universalists, Unitarians, Hebrew, Roman Catholic, and Evangelical Lutheran had one each. One hundred and four students were listed as attending Sunday School and one hundred and eleven attended other services on Sunday. There were twelve students who were ministers and thirty-five taught Sunday School; nineteen had the ministry in view. Law was favored by twenty-two, teaching by seventeen, medicine by eight, business by four and civil engineering by three.

the faculty reversed itself and announced in September, 1875, that attendance was compulsory. Moreover, in order to ascertain the offenders, all students were seated alphabetically and certain members of the faculty were to note and report all absences. Later, a roll call was introduced. These devices, however, failed to gain desired conformity since it was speedily discovered that there were empty seats in spite of a perfect roll call. Those who preferred to sleep on Sunday or to absent themselves from Chapel found accomplices who answered for them. In desperation the faculty enlisted the support of the janitor who was asked to inform the Dean of all students found loitering in the building during Chapel. How effective this procedure was is not known though it probably brought no better results than did a personal appeal on the part of the faculty for more regular attendance. And so matters drifted on for several years.

During the fall of 1889 the faculty touched by increased indifference on the part of the students, reviewed the entire situation. After considerable discussion it was decided to abandon the roll call except at certain stated times during each term and then only for the purposes of notifying each student of his seat and class standing in the college. Moreover, each student was to register with Dr. Coddington as to the church he intended to worship at each Sunday, and in order to provide a check on such attendance a system was devised whereby every student handed in a card once every two weeks stating that he had been to church. But once again well laid plans failed and in January, 1890, it was voted to alter the reading in the *Annual* from "Students are also required to regularly attend the Sabbath morning church service" to "Students are also expected to attend regularly the Sabbath morning Service." Continued debate about chapel attendance punctuated faculty meetings during 1892 and in September, 1893, it was voted to make Chapel compulsory and a monitorial system was introduced.

Fair words reinforced by an appeal to one's better or religious nature could not bring all students to realize the benefits of daily Chapel. To some, it was a chore and not a privilege. Moreover, those who did go regularly often became listless participants in prayer and song. The arrangement of allocating the rear seats to the freshmen and sophomores only added trouble since many of them, so the *Herald* reported with its tongue in its cheek, "are so constitutionally tired as to be unable to stand during the singing of a hymn." Indeed one could almost gauge the success of a service by the warmth and enthusiasm of the singing. At first it was presupposed that all knew and could sing from memory the familiar songs of the Methodist Church but as those of other faiths matriculated at Syracuse the fallacy of the assumption became apparent. As a result the singing became spotty and frequently all but died after the singing of the first verse because even the faithful were not sure what followed. Clearly what was needed was a song book though not until the fall of 1879 were copies placed in the Chapel through the kindness of the College Association. Finally, there was one other factor that worked against chapel attendance and that was the absence of the Medical and Fine Arts students. In the case of the former it should be remembered that their life centered in a down town college building and that the Medical Faculty was much a law unto itself; such excuses, however, could not be presented in respect to the College of Fine Arts.

The religious life of the University did not begin and end within the Chapel walls. Each and every member of the teaching staff from the Chancellor to the lowest instructor sought by precept and example to advance the spiritual development of the University. All, with but one or two exceptions, were active members of some Protestant Church while those who were licensed ministers rendered valuable and inspiring pastoral work throughout the city and neighboring areas. Comment already has been made of the religious work of Drs. Steele, Coddington, and others. Nor were the Trustees unmindful of spiritual attitudes when they were called upon to fill the important office of chancellor. Equally careful were they in respect to faculty personnel. It was, therefore, with evident satisfaction that the Board of Trustees endorsed the appearance of Dr. Winchell who, in the spring of 1888, addressed the student body and public on the nature and existence of God. The former Chancellor—an outstanding scientist in America and well known for his repeated services to the Methodist Church—delivered a series of talks which were described as "magnificent efforts." Dr. Winchell's addresses attracted considerable attention and were, according to one source, particularly conceived as an introduction to the establishment of a Professorship of Theistic Science at Syracuse. Endowed through the generosity of Mrs. J. Dorman Steele this chair was to signify that science at Syracuse was to be taught by those who believed in God.

General applause greeted the announcement of this splendid gift which did much to stimulate interest and activity in religious life on the campus. Some of this centered around the special chapel services which had been held from time to time since the opening of the Hall of Languages. In 1885, for example, Canon Frederic W. Farrar, noted Anglican divine and author, spoke before a large and enthusiastic audience. On another occasion when the Central New York Conference was in session at Syracuse, several of the visiting clergy addressed the students and faculty in the work of the Methodist Church. Although most of these gentlemen visited the campus during the day time it is significant to note that evening sessions were quite common. Bishop Vincent of Buffalo and the Rev. Dr. John Hall of New York City, to illustrate, graced the Chapel services held at night during the spring of 1893.

Anxious to quicken the moral tone of every student the faculty encouraged and participated in what was known as the Annual Day of Prayer. On this occasion special services were held throughout a designated day and it must be concluded from references in the campus papers that the students found considerable merit in these undertakings. Equally impressive is the record relative to an "international week of prayer" held immediately before the Christmas vacation of 1887. Again, the faculty stimulated student attendance at the weekly evening prayer meetings of the University Methodist Church. In this respect it is refreshing to note that Chancellor Sims conducted a special series of religious gatherings at this church during the winter of 1888. In commenting upon these talks the *Syracusan* stated that they constituted a "good sign" of religious life and vitality. "Loyalty to our church increases religious fervor, gives a closer bond of brotherhood with individual members and above all gives a greater influence for good." So impressed was Dr. Sims with the importance of religion at Syracuse that the post of University Pastor was established, a position which he and Dr. Brown appear to have held at different times. Another illustration of the Chancellor's interest in such matters was shown in 1891 when Rev. J. T. Gracey, D. D., delivered a course of seven lectures before the students upon "The Religions of the World." All of these efforts were not unnoticed in the city and it was with evident pleasure Dr. Sims announced at the winter meeting of the Trustees in 1892 the gift by Hon. Nathan F.

Graves of Syracuse of ten thousand dollars for founding a permanent lectureship on Missions.

Meanwhile the students had not been idle. In addition to promoting religious life on the campus and at the University Methodist Church, many identified themselves with the local Young Men's Christian Association. The latter's extensive social program reenforced with religious services and annual lecture series enlisted the support of many on the Hill. The benefits derived from this Christian fellowship strongly argued for the establishment of a University branch of the Association. Agitation in this direction was heard during 1878 and 1879 but there never was sufficient interest to warrant any positive action. Early in 1880, Edgar M. Buell, F.A. '80, unofficially represented Syracuse at a state gathering of the Association at Rochester. On his return renewed interest was shown but Commencement came and went without anything being accomplished. When college opened in the fall the issue was raised again and this time thanks to the timely encouragement given by the secretary of the local city association, a committee composed of Whiting S. Worden, E. H. Moore, George E. Hutchings, Joseph D. White, George Coe—all of the Class of 1881— and L. D. Taylor, '82, was appointed to organize a campus Young Men's Christian Association.

The initial meeting took place in early November, 1880, following which most of those present hurried down town to hear Robert Ingersoll who was lecturing that season in Syracuse. Thirty-five students appear to have paid the membership fee which had been set at thirty cents. So impressed was the faculty with the demonstration of interest on the part of the students that a half-hour immediately following Friday's Chapel was taken from the existing class schedule and set aside for a general college prayer meeting. At these gatherings informal talks were often given by members of the teaching staff. The enthusiasm shown was gratifying and under the leadership of Montgomery S. Goodwin, '81, the society looked forward to a better year in 1881-1882. The opposite, unfortunately, took place and during the second term "not a single religious meeting was held" and in September, 1882, the faculty rescinded its action. New life was shown the following year and the year thereafter. And as greater vitality was evidenced the faculty, with the patent endorsement of the students eased themselves out of the association though they continued to cooperate with the society in the Annual Day of Prayer. Membership mounted each term, there being over a hundred by 1885, and the Association felt strong enough to send delegates to the state meetings of the college branches of the Young Men's Christian Association. Lectures, religious services, Bible classes, and social activities characterized the local campus meetings which by the fall of 1889 were held in a specially designated room on the first floor of the Hall of Languages; this room, it is of interest to add, had been redecorated partly through the personal kindness of Dr. Sims for the Association.

Meanwhile the society began publication of the *Young Men's Christian Association Annual of Syracuse University* and secured considerable publicity through the campus newspapers. The *Syracusan* and the *University News* gave considerable space to the society's activities, the latter paper featuring a special article each issue during most of 1892. Receptions and parties were also held from time to time, particularly important being those staged in honor of the freshmen. The Association, moreover, was an active and interested supporter of the proposed new gymnasium. It stimulated the undertaking by promoting the raising of funds, an undertaking that fitted quite nicely into the traditional policy of the Association to advance the physical well-being of American youth. There was, however, a more pertinent reason for this splendid display of enthusiasm, a reason that was pressed with telling effect upon an administration that believed whole-heartedly in the religious purposes of the Association. Thus it came about that when plans were finally launched for the construction of the gymnasium it was announced that the building would house the offices and rooms of the Young Men's Christian Association. Among those who remembered with pride and satisfaction their work in the Association were Joseph A. Wright, '92, Edward D. White, '85, Ezra S. Tipple, '84, Frederick S. Price, '87, Horace A. Crane,'85, and Frank E. Arthur, '81.

The establishment of the Men's Association prompted the formation of a Young Women's Christian Association in the spring of 1884. The initial officers included Miss Ella Parry, '86, President, Miss Ellen Blakeslee, '86, Vice-President, Miss Cora Harrington, '88, Corresponding Secretary, Miss Hattie Smith, '86, Recording Secretary, and Miss Kate Gardner, '86, Treasurer. Meetings appear to have been held at various times either at the University Avenue Methodist Church or in the Parlors of the Hall of Languages. In general the Women's Association conducted its life in the same manner as did the men's society.

Probably one of its most interesting activities was the sponsoring of a Hawley Street Mission in the city. Joint gatherings, moreover, were held with the men's organization either for religious or social purposes —activities that did much to promote love and loyalty to Alma Mater. Writing in the spring of 1946 Mrs. Hattie (Smith) Cobb commented most enthusiastically upon her past contacts with the two Christian societies, mentioned the "Liberal Arts Building" as "*the* one of those happy days," and rejoiced in the "memory of those last days at College." In her wake came other devoted members like Miss Ella Eva Seaman, '87 and Miss Lena Hammond, '90 who helped in guiding the fortunes of the Young Women's Christian Association.

In appraising the work of the Men's and Women's Associations one is impressed by the impetus these societies effected in urging young men and women to enlist in religious and missionary work. Dr. Smalley, in his *Alumni Record* for 1872-1899, lists a total of 778 graduates of the University between 1872 and 1893. Of this eighty counted themselves as being fortunate in that their lives were pledged to the service of God and man. One of these was William O. Kitchin, '82, who for a decade labored in Japan as a missionary and teacher for the Methodist Church. Mr. Kitchin at one time was Principal of Cobleigh Seminary, Nagasaki, and a Professor at the Tokyo Anglo-Japanese University. One of his closest friends, Rev. Charles F. Sitterly, '83, spent most of his entire life as Professor of Exegesis and Biblical Literature at Drew Theological Seminary. Rev. Horace A. Crane, '85, served as a pastor in Nebraska and New York and for a time was a missionary in the Methodist work in Bombay, India. Joseph G. Cleveland, '86, spent many years in Japan as a Methodist Minister, and Milton N. Frantz, '86, did the same. Finally, mention should be made of Herbert G. Coddington, '86, son of Dr. W. P. Coddington, whose services to the University are legion; Mr. Coddington entered the Protestant Episcopal Church and for forty years was priest and pastor of Grace Episcopal Church, Syracuse. Rev. Coddington is still living and those who know him can well understand the significance of the days spent in a Christian atmosphere at Syracuse University.

Years have passed since these and many others carried Christian banners on the campus and there is a vast difference between the Association's "parlors" in the Hall of Languages and the spaciousness of beautiful Hendricks Chapel. But the spirit and enthusiasm that prompted religious life at the University then and today is much the same. Chaplains and religious leaders of various faiths marshall student life into patterns of Christian service and fellowship and the lighted dome of the Chapel beckons hundreds nightly to the Heart of the Campus. And yet it should always be remembered that the light burns brightly largely because of the past efforts of Syracusans who in founding the University on the Hill—close to the stars—proclaimed that this institution was and always should be a Christian University dedicated to God and Man.

Index